1000's
of
Amazing
USES
for
EVERYDAY
PRODUCTS

Betsy Rossen Elliot

Publications International, Ltd.

Betsy Rossen Elliot, a writer and communications consultant, lives in a south suburb of Chicago. She is the author of eight books, a contributor to many more, and a columnist for *Family Time Magazine.* She has also worked in publishing and higher education. Learn more at www.wordsmithbetsy.com.

Factual Verification: Mary Beth Curran

Cover Art: Getty Images, Image Club, PIL Collection, Shutterstock

Interior Art: Art Explosion, Jupiter Images, Shutterstock

The brand-name products mentioned in this publication are trademarks owned by their respective companies. Mention of these products in this publication does not constitute an endorsement, license, or permission from these companies.

This book is for informational purposes and is not intended to provide medical advice. Neither Publications International, Ltd., nor the authors, editors, or publisher take responsibility for any possible consequences from any treatment, procedure, exercise, dietary modification, action, or application of medication or preparation by any person reading or following the information in this book. The publication of this book does not constitute the practice of medicine and does not attempt to replace your physician or health care provider. Before undertaking any course of treatment, the authors, editors, and publisher advise the reader to check with a physician or other health care provider.

Before trying any of the uses on fabrics, carpeting, flooring, cabinets, and the like, you should refer to the manufacturers' recommended cleaning methods.

CONTENTS

Everyday Extraordinary

Remarkable capabilities are packed into all sorts of everyday products. And poured into this book are hundreds of helpful hints for every area of your household.

Let Us Count the Ways

Open your medicine cabinet, the drawers of your bathroom vanity, the hall closet, your kitchen pantry... and you will open yourself up to several and sundry benefits:

- *"Home economics" will take on new meaning* as you use inexpensive, basic items that you probably already have on hand instead of buying costly, specialized products.

- *Entire cabinets will be cleared and available to you* as those specialized products become obsolete.

- *Your home will be eco-nomic and eco-friendly* as you use, reuse, reduce, and recycle—as well as replace chemical concoctions that may be harmful to your family and the environment.

How Were the Brands Chosen?

Specific brand names do not indicate our endorsement; they are meant to communicate the true everyday, accessible nature of the products. Some choices were obvious (for example, Morton Salt, ARM & HAMMER Baking Soda); a few products have no one brand widely known and available (turpentine, drinking straws). For most products, we did our best to choose what is currently recognizable, popular, and widely available.

"Default" Products

Many companies offer quite a number of products in a given category. When the basic, "plain" item is implied—rather than a variation, color, flavor, scent, or the like—you will see the familiar, shortened name.

IF A TIP CALLS FOR...	IT MEANS...
Crest toothpaste	plain or mint paste, not gel
Folgers coffee	unflavored, not decaffeinated
Fresh Step cat litter	standard, nonclumping variety
Heinz Vinegar	Heinz Distilled White Vinegar
Ivory Soap	Classic Ivory Bar Soap
Lipton tea	traditional orange pekoe
PAM cooking spray	PAM Original Cooking Spray
Pepsi	regular, not diet; with caffeine
Scotch Duct Tape	traditional silver, non-vinyl
Tide laundry detergent	powder, no additives

A Few Words to the Wise

Although these products are commonly found around the house, many do require caution and foresight when using.

Be sure to wear rubber gloves when a solution contains bleach, ammonia, borax, turpentine, or anything else that might be hazardous. Protective eyewear is a good idea if the liquid may splash up at you. Of course, keep children and pets away from these dangers—whether you're using the products or storing them.

Chapter 1: Cleaning

BLESS THIS MESS . . . SO THE STRESS IS LESS

In the war on grime, the weapons are numerous and specialized. But commercial cleaners have their drawbacks: expense, ineffectiveness, toxicity, and damage to the environment.

Never fear. Whatever the task, whatever the room, chances are an everyday product (or two or three!) can do the job without the problems of traditional cleaning products.

Now's the time to try out some baking products. Flour, corn starch, baking powder, and cream of tartar can remove dirt, polish surfaces, and absorb stains economically and safely. Baking soda and salt help brighten everything from carpets to windows to kitchen appliances to bathrooms. Even traditional mess-makers like vegetable oil, mayonnaise, and toothpaste have cleaning capabilities that can't be topped.

When working with any cleaning product, be sure to be safe. Products that are tough on grime can be tough on you as well, especially on your hands, face, and lungs. Always read product labels; what's more, clearly label the contents of all spray bottles. When cleaning with chemicals such as bleach, ammonia, or borax, wear rubber gloves and keep the area well ventilated. Protect children and pets from their effects as well.

BATHROOM DETAIL

General Cleaning

◆ Try this basic cleanser for everyday bathroom cleanup. Mix together 3 tablespoons ARM & HAMMER Baking Soda, ½ cup Parsons' Ammonia, and 2 cups warm water. Or skip the ammonia and mix 1 box (16 ounces) ARM & HAMMER Baking Soda, 4 tablespoons Dawn dishwashing liquid, and 1 cup warm water. Mix well and store in a clearly labeled spray or squeeze container. Be sure to wear rubber gloves and use in a well-ventilated area.

◆ Undiluted Clorox Regular-Bleach in a spray bottle tackles serious bathroom grime. Spray the tub, sink, ceramic tile, or shower surfaces, wait a few minutes, and wipe clean with a damp O-Cel-O sponge.

Multipurpose Cleanser

This homemade concoction can replace most of the commercial cleaners you probably have on your shelf.

1 teaspoon 20 Mule Team Borax
1 teaspoon ARM & HAMMER Baking Soda
2 teaspoons Heinz Distilled White Vinegar or ReaLemon Lemon Juice
¼ teaspoon Dawn dishwashing liquid
2 cups hot water

Be sure to wear rubber gloves when working with this mixture. Mix and store in a clearly labeled spray bottle.

- Make your own bathroom cleanser with 10 ounces of Ivory Liquid Hand Cleanser, a 1-pound box of ARM & HAMMER Baking Soda, and 1 cup warm water. Mix thoroughly. Grab an O-Cel-O sponge and scrub that tub! Store the leftover cleanser in a clearly labeled capped jar or GLAD Food Storage Zipper Bag.

- When mildew is multiplying in out-of-the-way spots, place a few Rite Aid cotton balls soaked in Clorox Regular-Bleach in the area. Wait a few hours, then wipe clean with an O-Cel-O sponge dampened with warm water.

- Sprinkle ARM & HAMMER Baking Soda in the bathroom trash can after each emptying.

- This cleanser is great for removing soap scum buildup around your sink and tub: Thoroughly mix ¼ cup ARM & HAMMER Baking Soda, ½ cup Heinz Distilled White Vinegar, 1 cup Parsons' Ammonia, and 1 gallon warm water. Wear rubber gloves and apply liberally; scrub. Make sure area is well ventilated. Rinse well.

- What's the "solution" for minor stains on porcelain tubs, sinks, and tiles? First, wet the surface with plain water. Then spray with a mixture of ½ cup Clorox Regular-Bleach and 8 cups water. Wipe clean.

- Tide powdered laundry detergent does double duty as a cleanser to scour all ceramic and porcelain surfaces.

- Make your own powdered cleanser by combining 1 cup each of 20 Mule Team Borax, ARM & HAMMER Baking Soda, and Morton Salt. Use it on surfaces such as porcelain sinks and tubs. Store in a lidded container. Don't forget to label!

- Make a paste of Morton Salt and turpentine and use it to whiten yellowed porcelain. Wearing rubber gloves, apply the mixture with a stiff brush. Rinse thoroughly.

- Mix equal amounts of Heinz Vinegar and water in a spray bottle. Spray onto mildewed areas and let sit for 15 minutes. Wipe clean. Use as a preventive measure in any area of your home that is prone to being damp, such as spaces under a sink or in the cellar.

- Clean marble with a paste of ARM & HAMMER Baking Soda and Heinz Distilled White Vinegar. Wipe clean and buff.

- Remove a stain from a marble surface by mixing equal parts Parsons' Ammonia and Rite Aid hydrogen peroxide. Apply with a soft cloth. Let dry, then rub with a dry cloth. Wipe again with a cloth dampened with water.

Bald Is Beautiful

Mr. Clean came on the scene in 1957. That's when a Chicago advertising firm drew him and created his brand's long-running jingle. The next year, Procter & Gamble launched the first Mr. Clean product, an all-purpose liquid cleaner, and aired his first television commercials on a Pittsburgh station. A 1962 "Give Mr. Clean a First Name" promotion resulted in the moniker "Veritably." (Oddly enough, the name did not catch on.)

- When you don't have enough time for a thorough scrub-down but the bathroom needs some work, simply grab the Pampers baby wipes and wipe down all the surfaces. Polish with a clean, dry washcloth.

- Hairspray never lands just on your hair, does it? To clean the dried-on residue from walls, vanities, and the like, use a solution of 1 part Final Touch fabric softener and 2 parts water. Stir and pour into a spray bottle. Spray, then wipe clean with a dry cloth.

- If shampoo can remove hairspray from your hair, it should be no surprise that it works to remove the sticky stuff from bathroom walls as well! Squeeze a little Suave shampoo onto a wet O-Cel-O sponge to clean; dampen a second sponge with water to rinse off the suds.

- After you've finished cleaning the bathroom, protect against water spots and soap buildup by polishing the sinks, tile, shower doors, and faucets with a coat of Simoniz Original Paste Wax.

- If your bathroom never seems to be fully dry and you are going away for some time, place a large, shallow box of nonclumping Fresh Step cat litter in your bathtub to absorb moisture.

Mirrors

◆ Make your mirrors shine by washing them with a bucket of water combined with 1 tablespoon Parsons' Ammonia.

◆ Your bathroom mirror will sparkle after this tea break. Brew a pot of strong Lipton tea; let cool. Dip a soft cloth into the tea, then wipe it over the whole mirror. Buff with a soft, dry cloth.

◆ To clean a bathroom mirror, rub on Gillette Foamy Shave Foam. Wipe off the cream with a soft cloth. As a bonus, the mirror will be fog-free after your next shower.

◆ Try this home recipe for cleaning mirrored tiles. Mix 2 cups Rite Aid isopropyl rubbing alcohol, 2 tablespoons Dawn dishwashing liquid, and 2 cups water. Stir until thoroughly mixed; pour into a spray bottle. Spray directly on the mirrored tiles, then buff with a lint-free cloth, chamois, or Scott Towel.

Tile and Grout

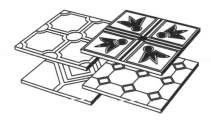

◆ A simple paste of ARM & HAMMER Baking Soda and water will attack hard-water or rust stains on ceramic tile. Use a nylon scrubber, then rinse.

◆ Use a paste of ARM & HAMMER Baking Soda and water to remove mildew stains on grout. Apply, scrub with an old Reach toothbrush, and rinse.

- For tough grout or tile stains, use a paste of 1 part Clorox Regular-Bleach to 3 parts ARM & HAMMER Baking Soda.

- Grout grime grating on you? Combine the following in a bucket: 2 cups Clorox Regular-Bleach, 3 cups Rite Aid isopropyl rubbing alcohol, ½ cup Original Pine-Sol Brand Cleaner, and 1 quart water. Pour the mixture into a plastic spray bottle. Spray and clean away!

- Undiluted Rite Aid isopropyl rubbing alcohol can remove small areas of mildew buildup on grout, caulk, or tile. Dip a cloth into the alcohol and scrub.

Toilets

- A half cup of ARM & HAMMER Baking Soda in the toilet bowl will work for light cleaning. Let sit for 30 minutes, then brush and flush.

- Remove stubborn stains in the toilet bowl by scrubbing with fine steel wool dipped in ARM & HAMMER Baking Soda.

- To remove toilet bowl stains, pour in a can of Pepsi. Wait 1 hour, then brush bowl clean and flush.

- For a homemade toilet bowl cleaner, mix 1 cup ARM & HAMMER Baking Soda with 1 cup Tide powdered laundry detergent. Each time you clean, sprinkle ¼ cup of this mixture into the toilet and let it sit 10 minutes. Scrub briefly, then let it sit another 10 minutes. Brush again, then flush.

- Clean your toilet while you're not even home! Pour ¼ cup Clorox Regular-Bleach into the bowl, but don't flush the toilet until you return—even days later. (Be sure to close the bathroom door before you leave if pets will be around.)

- Make the most of an automatic toilet-bowl cleaning dispenser. When the dispenser is empty, wash it thoroughly and fill with undiluted Clorox Regular-Bleach.

- Give your toilet an overnight cleaning by putting ¼ cup 20 Mule Team Borax in the bowl and letting it sit. In the morning, scrub stains away.

- Clean your toilet by putting 2 Polident denture cleanser tablets in the bowl and letting them sit overnight. Scrub the toilet in the morning.

When Inventors Don't Have to Clean Their Own Inventions

Indoor plumbing was becoming a "fixture" by about 1870, replacing chamber pots, buckets, and portable washing basins. As early as 1778, Joseph Bramah of London invented the metal valve-type water closet. Other early sinks, toilets, and bathtubs also were made of metal— primarily lead, copper, and zinc. They were hard to clean, however, so in the mid-1870s Thomas Twyford made a ceramic toilet and wash-down water closet. Because ceramics are too brittle for bathtubs, the porcelain-enamel cast-iron tub was invented. The double-shell, built-in style still common today was introduced around 1915.

◆ The citric acid and bubbling action of Alka-Seltzer tablets can work to clean your toilet. Drop 2 tablets in the bowl, wait 20 minutes, then brush clean. Pour Heinz Vinegar into toilet and let sit 30 minutes. Next, sprinkle ARM & HAMMER Baking Soda on a toilet bowl brush and scour any remaining stained areas. Flush.

◆ Once a week, pour 2 cups Heinz Vinegar into toilet and let it sit. (Tip: Rest toilet bowl brush inside bowl with lid closed to remind yourself and family members not to use the toilet until it gets brushed!) After 8 hours or more, brush toilet well; flush. This regular treatment will keep hard-water stains at bay and clean and freshen your bowl between major cleanings.

◆ Add a perpetual air freshener to the toilet area by keeping ARM & HAMMER Baking Soda in a pretty dish on top of the tank. Add your favorite scented bath salts to the mix if desired. Change every 3 months.

◆ When you hang a new roll of toilet paper, loosely roll up a Downy dryer sheet and place it inside the paper core. The fresh scent will disperse through the small room.

Showers and Tubs

◆ Remove mineral buildup and improve your showerhead's performance, or fix a clogged showerhead that is too stubborn to come apart, with this soaking-bag remedy. In a GLAD

Food Storage Zipper Bag, mix ½ cup ARM & HAMMER Baking Soda and 1 cup Heinz Distilled White Vinegar. Secure the plastic bag around the showerhead with a rubber band so that the showerhead is submerged in the solution; let it sit overnight, and by morning the showerhead should come loose. (Even if it doesn't, any mineral deposits should be dissolved.) Remove bag and run very hot water through showerhead for several minutes.

- Use Clorox Regular-Bleach to clean grungy caulking around a bathtub or shower. Just mix ¾ cup bleach with 1 gallon water, then scrub the caulk with a Reach toothbrush dipped in this solution.

- When rust or other stains just won't come off a white porcelain tub with average scrubbing (a common problem with older and antique tubs), add enough water to 20 Mule Team Borax to make a paste. Make sure it's sticky enough to adhere to the sides of the tub. Apply the paste onto stubborn stains using a paintbrush, then cover with damp Scott Towels. Let sit 1 hour, then scrub with a nylon dish scrubber or a scrubbing brush. Rinse with warm water.

- Coat the tile walls of your bathtub or shower with Pledge furniture polish to prevent soap scum buildup and water spots.

- To keep the bathtub and tiles free of soap scum, rinse thoroughly after each use, and rub the surfaces with a cut lemon.

- The same method—rubbing surfaces with a cut lemon—can remove many sink and tub rust stains.

- For more stubborn rust stains, make a paste of ReaLemon Lemon Juice and 20 Mule Team Borax. Apply to the stain with an O-Cel-O No-Scratch Scrub Sponge; scrub, then rinse. Toilet stains can be removed with this same paste.

- When your tub needs a scrub, you're in luck! Suave shampoo is right at hand, and it does a great job. Scrub the tub with a generous amount on an O-Cel-O No-Scratch Scrub Sponge. When you're done, the shampoo rinses clean with a spray of water from the faucet.

- Fiberglass shower and tub surrounds require special care because fiberglass scratches easily. Clean these areas periodically by spraying them with Heinz Vinegar. Wipe with an O-Cel-O sponge. Never use

Bubbles of Info

- Around 600 B.C., the Phoenicians made soap from goat's tallow (fat) and wood ashes; they sometimes used it as an article of barter with the Gauls.
- The Celts used animal fats and plant ashes and named the product *saipo,* from which the English word *soap* is derived.
- Beginning in the second century A.D., at the suggestion of the Greek physician Galen, soap was used for washing and cleaning (instead of as a medicine).

abrasive cleaners. Instead, try sprinkling the area with ARM & HAMMER Baking Soda and wiping with an O-Cel-O sponge dampened with vinegar if undiluted vinegar doesn't do the trick.

- Cleaning fiberglass tubs and showers requires a bit of caution to avoid scratches. Make a paste of ARM & HAMMER Baking Soda and Dawn dishwashing liquid; wipe on with an O-Cel-O sponge and scrub gently.

- Apply a light coat of Simoniz Original Paste Wax to the doors of your fiberglass shower stall to prevent soap scum buildup and to make cleaning easier.

- A bathtub ring requires a strong solvent. Try soaking Scott Towels with undiluted Heinz Vinegar and placing them on the ring. Let towels dry out, then spray the tub with straight vinegar and scrub with an O-Cel-O sponge.

- Powdered Cascade automatic dishwashing detergent makes a great cleanser for removing rings around the tub. Sprinkle the detergent onto the rings and wipe clean with a wet sponge.

- Loosen up soap scum on shower doors and walls by spraying them with Heinz Vinegar. Let dry, then respray to dampen. Wipe clean. Reapply and let sit for several hours. Then dampen and wipe clean again.

- Add 1 cup Final Touch fabric softener to 1 quart warm water and use to loosen and clean soap scum from shower doors.

- Use a Downy dryer sheet to help remove soap scum from shower doors. Just use the sheet to wipe doors clean; toss it when you're finished.

- Clean your shower door with PAM cooking spray: Spray some on a soft cotton cloth and wipe away the crud.

- To clean gunky shower tracks, wrap very fine steel wool around an old Reach toothbrush and scrub the tracks. Spray glass cleaner all over the tracks; wipe clean.

- Clean shower door runners with Crest toothpaste and an old Reach toothbrush. Rinse with Heinz Vinegar.

- Shower curtains can become dulled by soap film or plagued with mildew. Keep Heinz Vinegar in a spray bottle near your shower, and squirt shower curtains once or twice a week. No need to rinse.

- Is a vinyl shower curtain and/or curtain liner giving you static? In a spray bottle, mix 1 capful Final Touch fabric softener and 2 cups water. Spray curtain or liner from top to bottom.

- Fight mildew stains and lightly clean a shower curtain by sprinkling ARM & HAMMER Baking Soda on an O-Cel-O sponge and scrubbing. Rinse well.

- To remove mineral and mildew stains from a shower curtain, first soak it in salt water for 15 to 20 minutes. Hang to drain excess water. Rub the stains with ReaLemon Lemon Juice while the curtain is still damp. Wipe with a damp O-Cel-O sponge, rinse with clean water, or run through the washing machine.

- Prevent mildew growth on a shower curtain by soaking it in a bathtub full of salt water (½ cup salt to the tub). Soak for several hours, then hang to dry.

- Sometimes mildew will leave a stain on a shower curtain if it's not promptly removed. To remove such stains, mix 20 Mule Team Borax with enough Heinz Vinegar to make a paste, then scrub stained area.

- Mildew may make a habit of building up on your shower and tub accessories. Mix 1½ cups Clorox Regular-Bleach with 2 gallons water and scrub bath mats, curtains, and soap dishes with the mixture, using an O-Cel-O sponge or a scrub brush. Rinse.

- Help plastic shower curtain rings glide more easily by applying a thin coat of Alberto VO5 Conditioning Hairdressing to the curtain rod.

- Rubbing the shower curtain rod with a small amount of Ivory Liquid Hand Cleanser or Classic Ivory Bar Soap also moves the rings right along.

◆ Stains on nonskid strips or appliqués in the tub can be removed by first dampening the area, then sprinkling with ARM & HAMMER Baking Soda. Let sit for 20 minutes; scrub and rinse.

◆ Those sunflower decals may have looked cute when you stuck them on the tub to prevent slips and falls, but now they're chipped, stained, and probably out of fashion. To get rid of them, loosen the glue by saturating each decal with Heinz Vinegar. (Warm vinegar in microwave for about 3 minutes for better results.) Let vinegar sit for a few minutes, then peel off decals. You should be able to remove any leftover glue by scrubbing with a damp O-Cel-O sponge.

◆ Once a year, dump 1 gallon Heinz Vinegar into your hot tub and then run the jets. This will help keep them from clogging up with soap residue.

Sinks

◆ Clean the bathroom sink with Crest toothpaste. Squirt some on your sink, scrub clean with a wet O-Cel-O sponge, and then rinse. As an extra benefit, Crest toothpaste will help eliminate foul odors wafting up from the drain trap.

◆ Make easy work of cleaning a porcelain sink. Make a solution of equal parts Clorox Regular-Bleach and water. Cover the surface of the sink with a thick layer of Scott Towels, then saturate them with the solution. Remove the towels after 5 minutes; rinse sink with clear water. (Be sure to wear rubber gloves.)

◆ Attack stubborn rust stains in a sink (or tub) with a paste of McCormick Cream of Tartar and Rite Aid hydrogen peroxide. Apply the paste, then scrub clean with a nonabrasive pad or brush. Rinse completely.

◆ Scour your bathroom sink with Tide powdered laundry detergent. Shake some onto a damp O-Cel-O sponge and scrub. This cleanser works on all ceramic and porcelain surfaces.

◆ Plug the drain in your bathroom sink, pour in ½ cup Heinz Vinegar, then fill the sink with water. Let sit 1 hour, then scrub any mineral deposit areas with an old Reach toothbrush. Rinse.

◆ Just one Downy dryer sheet can control odor and musty smells under your bathroom or kitchen sink.

Faucets and Fixtures

◆ Use undiluted Rite Aid hydrogen peroxide on lime buildup on your bathroom fixtures. Scrub, and rinse.

◆ Make a paste of turpentine mixed with Morton Salt to restore white enameled fixtures that have gone yellow. Use this on sinks, bathtubs, or the outside of toilets. Apply, let sit 15 minutes, then wipe with a damp O-Cel-O sponge.

- Remove hard-water and mineral deposits around sink and tub faucets by covering the stained area with Scott Towels soaked in Heinz Vinegar. Remove towels after 1 hour, and wipe with a damp O-Cel-O sponge.

- Brighten porcelain fixtures with Canada Dry Club Soda. Spray or drip the soda onto fixtures and rub with a soft cloth to shine.

- Apply Pledge furniture polish to wooden towel racks occasionally. The treatment will give a protective coating as well as bring out the shine.

- Your chrome fixtures have lost their shine, but your cleaning cupboard is bare of the right commercial cleaner. Let the mild abrasive in Crest toothpaste do the job. Smear some on the chrome; polish with a soft, dry cloth.

- Pour Rite Aid isopropyl rubbing alcohol on a Scott Towel to remove smudges and hairspray from chrome faucets.

- Clean chrome with Canada Dry Club Soda. Pour some on a clean, soft cloth and dab it on. Buff to a shine with a second cloth.

Drains

- For routine cleaning of sink and tub drains, pour in ½ cup ARM & HAMMER Baking Soda followed by 1 cup Heinz Distilled White Vinegar. Let sit for 10 to 20 minutes, then flush with very hot water.

- Remove hair buildup from your bathtub drain or trap with a Q-tips cotton swab. Just dip it into the drain, twirl, and toss.

- Clear a slow drain anywhere by dropping in a couple of Alka-Seltzer tablets. Pour in 1 cup Heinz Vinegar, then flush with hot water.

- To clear a slow drain, pour in a 2-liter bottle of Pepsi. You'll soon see the drain emptying more quickly.

KITCHEN CLEANUP

Countertops and Other Surfaces

- Remove stains from laminate countertops with a paste of ARM & HAMMER Baking Soda and water. Apply, let dry, then rub off and rinse.

- Use Canada Dry Club Soda to clean your kitchen counters, stovetop, and stainless-steel fixtures. Just pour it directly on an O-Cel-O sponge and wipe clean. Rinse with warm water, then dry thoroughly.

- Wipe your kitchen countertops with undiluted Heinz Vinegar once a day to shine them and keep your kitchen smelling fresh.

- To bring a shine to plastic or Formica countertops and tables, polish them with Simoniz Original Paste Wax.

- Rub a piece of Reynolds Cut-Rite Wax Paper over your tile or laminate kitchen countertops. The shine will send you reaching for your sunglasses.

- If stains mar your Corian or other solid-surface synthetic sink or countertop, gently rub a little Crest toothpaste on the offending area. Use a white scrubbing pad, which is available at most hardware and home improvement stores. Wipe clean with a damp O-Cel-O sponge, then polish with a soft, dry cloth.

- Remove permanent marker from countertops and appliances with Rite Aid isopropyl rubbing alcohol.

- Garlic and onion odors on countertops respond to a solution of 1 tablespoon Clorox Regular-Bleach and 1 cup water. Wash the surface, then let the solution sit for about 5 minutes. Rinse well.

- Clean marble countertops with a moist cloth dipped in 20 Mule Team Borax. Rub the surface, then rinse with warm water.

- Clean polished marble and metal surfaces with chalk. Crush Crayola chalk in a GLAD Food Storage Zipper Bag, tapping it gently with a hammer. Dip a soft cloth into the powder and rub.

Color Coding

Most homemade liquid cleaning solutions are colorless. It's essential that you clearly label each bottle, but you can also let food coloring identify at least one at a glance. For example, put a few drops of McCormick Blue Food Color in the window cleaner spray bottle.

That's One Fresh Cleanser!

Try this recipe for a basic everyday cleanser in your kitchen:

¼ cup Heinz Vinegar
1 squirt Dawn dishwashing liquid
    Enough water to fill a 32-ounce bottle
5 drops peppermint oil or any essential oil (for fragrance)

It won't tackle the tough, greasy jobs, but using this cleanser daily can help control grease buildup, remove spills, and keep your kitchen smelling nice. In fact, you can customize the essential oil fragrance to suit your taste. (The oil is only for fragrance and will not affect the cleaning ability of this solution.)

Keep the solution in a spray bottle, and make sure you clearly label its contents. Shake well before each use. Spray on countertops and appliances, then wipe off with a damp cloth or O-Cel-O sponge.

◆ Banish stains on butcher-block countertops and wood cutting boards with Clorox Regular-Bleach. Soak a white dishcloth in undiluted bleach. Lay it over the spots, then wait 10 to 15 minutes. Rinse with clear water.

◆ Combine the following ingredients to cut grease buildup on stoves, backsplashes, or glossy enamel surfaces: 3 cups ARM & HAMMER Baking Soda, 2 cups Heinz Vinegar, 1 cup Parsons' Ammonia, and 1 gallon hot water. Wear rubber gloves when you wipe on the mixture, making sure room is well ventilated. Wipe clean with a damp O-Cel-O sponge.

◆ To remove fingerprints from stainless-steel appliances, use a little Johnson's Baby Oil on a Scott Towel.

- Remove water spots from stainless-steel appliances and fixtures using a cloth dampened with Rite Aid isopropyl rubbing alcohol.

- For everyday cleaning of tile and grout, rub with a little Heinz Apple Cider Vinegar on an O-Cel-O sponge. This gives off a pleasant scent and will help cut any greasy buildup.

- Rub ceramic tile countertops or walls with Simoniz Original Paste Wax on a soft cloth. Let stand 10 minutes, then buff.

- Clean up a grease spatter on the kitchen wall with a bit of Argo Corn Starch on a Scott Towel or soft cloth. Gently rub the grease spot until it's gone.

Refrigerators and Freezers

- To clean and refresh the inside of your refrigerator, sprinkle equal amounts of Morton Salt and ARM & HAMMER Baking Soda onto a damp O-Cel-O sponge and wipe down all surfaces. Wipe clean with a fresh sponge dampened with water.

Salt Preservation

Before we had freezers and refrigerators, salt was an important preservative and one of only a few ways to keep food from spoiling.

- Clean and deodorize the inside of your refrigerator by wiping it down with an O-Cel-O sponge or a soft cloth and a solution of 1 tablespoon 20 Mule Team Borax in 1 quart warm water. Rinse with cold water.

◆ If you come home to a foul-smelling fridge full of leftovers you forgot to trash before your trip, toss the mess immediately. Clean up any excess with an O-Cel-O sponge or a Scott Towel, then gather 6 or more Melitta Basket Coffee Filters. Fill each filter with ½ cup ARM & HAMMER Baking Soda; place 1 or more on each shelf and compartment to absorb odors quickly. Remove when odor is gone.

◆ Remove mildew spots and prevent mildew buildup inside your refrigerator by wiping occasionally with an O-Cel-O sponge dampened in undiluted Heinz Vinegar. A Reach toothbrush is an excellent tool for reaching inside the folds of the rubber seals. No need to rinse afterward.

◆ To keep refrigerator shelves clean—or at least make them easier to wipe clean—coat them with Simoniz Original Paste Wax.

◆ Do you find yourself in a tug-of-war with the sliding racks and shelves in your refrigerator? Grease the sides with a thin coat of Suave conditioner, and they'll slide in and out easily.

◆ To clean sticky refrigerator door gaskets, mix 4 tablespoons ARM & HAMMER Baking Soda with 1 quart water; apply with a Reach toothbrush. Wipe clean. This also helps control mildew buildup.

◆ Use a clean, dry Reach toothbrush to remove crumbs and crud from the seals around refrigerator and freezer doors.

- Trying to vacuum under the refrigerator or another hard-to-reach spot? Put a cardboard tube from a roll of Scott Towels, gift wrap, or another product on the end of the hose attachment. For narrow openings, bend or flatten the tube.

- Don't waste a ruined pair of No nonsense pantyhose—use it to clean under your refrigerator. Wrap the nylon around a yardstick, then run it under the fridge.

- Defrost your freezer with ease...next time. After all the ice has thawed and the freezer is clean and dry, spray the bottom and sides of the compartment with PAM cooking spray.

- Place a sheet of Reynolds Wrap Aluminum Foil on the floor of your freezer to keep spills and ice cube trays from sticking. Be sure not to cover any vents or other openings.

- To remove any unpleasant taste in ice cubes from an automatic ice cube maker, clean the removable parts of the unit with ARM & HAMMER Baking Soda and water.

Microwaves

- If your microwave is spattered with old sauces and greasy buildup, place a glass measuring cup with 1 cup water and ¼ cup Heinz Vinegar inside microwave. Boil for 3 minutes, then remove the measuring cup and wipe inside of oven with a damp O-Cel-O sponge.

- Microwaves are veritable safe-deposit boxes for odors. Clean the inside and outside with a little ARM & HAMMER Baking Soda on a damp O-Cel-O sponge; rinse well. Between uses, keep an open box of baking soda in the closed microwave. Change it every 30 days.

- To remove the lingering smell of burned microwave popcorn, heat a small glass dish of pure Heinz Vinegar in the microwave for 5 minutes on a low heat setting. Remove and wipe down inside of oven.

- Deodorize your microwave by keeping a dish of Heinz Vinegar inside overnight. If smells persist, change vinegar and repeat procedure nightly.

Small Appliances

- Buildup in a coffeemaker's brewing system can affect coffee flavor. Get rid of buildup by running a brewing cycle with cold water and ¼ cup Heinz Vinegar. Follow with a cycle of clean water. If you can still smell vinegar, run another cycle using fresh water.

- Remove coffee stains and mineral buildup from the glass pot of an automatic drip coffeemaker by adding 1 cup crushed ice, 1 tablespoon water, and 4 teaspoons Morton Salt to the pot when it is at room temperature. Gently swirl mixture, rinse, and wash as usual.

- To clean the cutting wheel of your can opener, "open" a Scott Towel or two. Close the cutting wheel on the edge of the paper towel, grip the handles together, and turn the crank. The towel will wipe off the crud as the wheel cuts it.

- A Q-tips cotton swab can be used to clean the hard-to-reach places on your kitchen blender, electric mixer, or electric can opener. Dip the swab in warm, soapy water, then scrub and rinse.

- To clean a hamburger grill or pancake griddle, pour brewed Folgers coffee onto the surface (the surface can be warm or cold). Wait a few minutes, then wipe clean with a soft cloth—make sure the surface has cooled before you do this.

- When a plastic bread bag gets too close to a hot toaster or other appliance...well, you know what happens. Once the appliance cools, apply a little Cutex Quick & Gentle Liquid Nail Polish Remover with a soft cloth. Rub gently, and the spot is gone!

Stovetops

- Clean induction and glass stovetops with a solution of 4 tablespoons ARM & HAMMER Baking Soda and 1 quart water. Use a Reach toothbrush to get into tight corners. Wipe clean.

- Spills on stovetops and in ovens are no match for this mixture: Make a paste of ReaLemon Lemon Juice, water, and ARM & HAMMER Baking Soda. Apply to spills, let sit 15 minutes, then scrub and rinse with water and an O-Cel-O sponge.

- Mix 1 tablespoon Dawn dishwashing liquid with ½ cup Parsons' Ammonia and enough water to fill a clean spray bottle. Use to cut grease and clean stovetops, counters, or any greasy surface. Label the bottle and store for future use.

- Stovetop spills can be cleaned up easily if first sprinkled with Morton Salt. The mildly abrasive quality of salt removes stuck-on food, but it won't mar your stove's surface.

- Clean burned-on food from a stovetop burner by sprinkling it with a mixture of Morton Salt and McCormick Ground Cinnamon, then wiping away immediately. The mixture will give off a pleasant smell and cover up any burnt odor the next time you turn on the burner.

- Soak up liquid spills on stovetop burners in much the same way, sprinkling with a mixture of Morton Salt and McCormick Ground Cinnamon. Leave mixture on spill for 5 minutes to absorb liquid, then wipe away.

- Use a Downy dryer sheet to wipe away grease splatters from the stovetop.

- To prevent grease splatters from sticking to the wall behind your stove, spray a painted or wallpapered wall with Pledge furniture polish and buff it with a soft cloth.

Ovens

◆ Make your oven practically self-cleaning! In a glass baking dish, mix 2 cups warm water and ¼ cup Parsons' Ammonia. Place it in the oven, shut the door, and let it work overnight. The next morning, sprinkle oven with ARM & HAMMER Baking Soda and wipe clean with a damp O-Cel-O sponge… and no elbow grease.

◆ Combine equal parts Heinz Vinegar and hot water in a small bowl. Use this solution and an O-Cel-O sponge to rub away any dried-on stains in your oven and help prevent grease buildup.

◆ Eliminate the odor from a commercial oven cleaner with a solution of 2 cups Heinz Vinegar and 3 quarts warm water. Dip an O-Cel-O sponge into mixture and wring it well, then wipe down the inside surfaces of the oven. There's no need to rinse.

◆ If a pie or similar sugary confection boils over in your oven, sprinkle the sticky spill with Morton Salt while the oven is still hot. Let it sit until spilled area becomes crisp, then lift off with a spatula when oven cools.

◆ Get rid of stubborn baked-on or blackened areas on an oven rack by "steaming" off the soot with ammonia vapors. Just lay the rack on an old towel in your bathtub. (Be sure the bathroom is well ventilated.) Fill the tub with warm water and

½ cup Parsons' Ammonia; let sit for half an hour. Rinse. (This also works for barbecue grill racks.)

◆ A similar technique for loosening burned-on foods from oven or grill racks is to place the racks in a GLAD trash bag. Mix 1 cup ARM & HAMMER Baking Soda and ½ cup Parsons' Ammonia and pour over the racks. Close the bag and let sit overnight. Scrub and rinse well in the morning.

◆ You should degrease the vents of your oven hood twice a year. To do this, wipe vents with an O-Cel-O sponge and undiluted Heinz Vinegar, or remove vents and soak them for 15 minutes in 1 cup vinegar and 3 cups water.

Dishwashers

◆ Remove dried-on food or detergent from the chrome inside your dishwasher by rubbing with a piece of lemon. Wipe clean with a damp cloth, then rub dry with a clean, dry cloth.

◆ Add ½ cup Heinz Vinegar to an empty dishwasher and run the rinse cycle. This will clear any clogs in the dishwasher drain lines and deodorize the machine.

◆ Deodorize and clean out hard-water stains from the inside of your dish-washer by running it using powdered Country Time Lemonade mix instead of detergent. The ascorbic acid in the powder helps the cleaning action.

◆ Or you can remove hard-water stains from the inside of an automatic dishwasher by loading the dishwasher with glassware and china and then adding ¾ cup Clorox Regular-Bleach. Run a complete wash cycle, then put 1 cup Heinz Vinegar in a glass bowl and place bowl in dishwasher. Run another complete wash cycle.

Sinks and Drains

◆ Clean stainless-steel sinks with a paste of ARM & HAMMER Baking Soda and water, or sprinkle baking soda directly onto an O-Cel-O sponge and scrub the surface. Rinse and buff dry.

◆ Mix ReaLemon Lemon Juice and Morton Salt to the consistency of toothpaste, and apply to brass, copper, or stainless-steel sinks and fixtures. Gently scrub, then rinse.

◆ After cleaning your stainless-steel kitchen sink, keep it shining by wiping it with a bit of Crisco Pure Vegetable Oil.

◆ To shine a stainless-steel sink, use a soft cloth to wipe the surface with a little Alberto VO5 Conditioning Hairdressing or Suave conditioner.

◆ To restore a stainless-steel kitchen sink that is scratched or stained, pour a small amount of Crisco Pure Vegetable Oil on a piece of 220-grit, extra-fine 3M sandpaper. Gently rub the sink in the same direction as the original polishing lines.

- Clean minor stains in a white porcelain sink with a sprinkling of ARM & HAMMER Baking Soda and an O-Cel-O sponge dampened in Heinz Vinegar. Stains are best tackled immediately.

- Loosen mineral deposits on faucets by sponging on ReaLemon Lemon Juice, letting it soak in for a while, then scrubbing off.

- Tackle mineral deposits around your sink's faucets by squirting them with undiluted Heinz Vinegar. Let vinegar sit 15 minutes or more, then scrub away deposits with an old Reach toothbrush.

- Clean chrome fixtures by simply wiping them with plain Heinz Vinegar. If the chrome is heavily spotted, wipe with an O-Cel-O sponge dampened with vinegar and sprinkled with a little ARM & HAMMER Baking Soda.

- If mineral deposits are slowing the sink sprayer, squeeze the handle and secure it with a rubber band. Soak the sprayer head in a cup of warm Heinz Vinegar for 30 minutes, then run sprayer at full blast to dislodge deposits.

- To dislodge greasy foods that may be clogging up your drain, sprinkle ½ cup Morton Salt and ½ cup ARM & HAMMER Baking Soda into the drain. Run hot tap water to flush.

- Pour a strong salt solution of 1 cup Morton Salt and 2 cups hot water down the kitchen drain to eliminate odors and break up grease deposits.

- Once a week, pour a can of Pepsi down the drain to keep it clear and unclogged.

- If your kitchen drain is running slowly, dump in ½ cup used Folgers coffee grounds followed by boiling water (at least a medium-size pot). Use plenty of hot water or you'll just be contributing to the problem!

- Baking soda and vinegar will foam your drain clean and help prevent clogs. Pour ½ cup ARM & HAMMER Baking Soda down the drain, followed by 1 cup Heinz Distilled White Vinegar. When foam subsides, rinse with hot water. This also works well on garbage disposals.

- Pour ¼ cup each of ARM & HAMMER Baking Soda, Morton Salt, and Cascade automatic dishwashing detergent into your garbage disposal. Turn on hot water and run garbage disposal for a few seconds to clean out debris and clear odors.

- Clear kitchen sink drainpipes of mold- and bacteria-breeding food particles. Once a week, pour in a solution of 1 tablespoon Clorox Regular-Bleach in 1 gallon water. Wait a few minutes, then flush with cold running water for several minutes.

- Remove built-up crud on your rubber sink mat by soaking it in the sink. Fill the sink with water and ¼ cup Clorox Regular-Bleach. Soak for 10 minutes, drain the sink, and rinse everything thoroughly.

◆ Coat your rubber or plastic drainboard with Pledge furniture polish. This will prevent stains from setting into the surface.

A CLEAR LOOK AT WINDOWS

◆ Wash windows with an O-Cel-O sponge dipped in ARM & HAMMER Baking Soda. To avoid dry haze on the windows, rinse them with a clean sponge and plenty of water before drying.

◆ Clean your windows with Canada Dry Club Soda. Pour some on a clean cotton cloth; wipe windows. Using a second cloth, dry them right away.

◆ To spot-clean a window or other glass surface, use Rite Aid isopropyl rubbing alcohol.

◆ Make your own streak-free window cleaner: Thoroughly mix 2 tablespoons Argo Corn Starch, ½ cup Parsons' Ammonia, and ½ cup Heinz Vinegar in a bucket of 3 to 4 quarts warm water. Pour the milky solution into a spray bottle. Spray on windows; wipe with warm water. Rub dry with a Scott Towel or lint-free cloth.

Safety First

Keep in mind that products that are tough on grime are often tough on you, especially your hands, face, and lungs. Always read product labels. When cleaning with bleach, ammonia, or borax, wear rubber gloves and keep the area well ventilated. Also, don't mix bleach with ammonia—it can produce a poisonous gas.

◆ Wash greasy kitchen windows with a solution of 2 tablespoons ReaLemon Lemon Juice, ½ cup Heinz Distilled White Vinegar, and 1 quart warm water.

Homemade Glass Cleaner

2 tablespoons Parsons' Ammonia*
½ cup Rite Aid isopropyl rubbing alcohol
¼ teaspoon Dawn dishwashing liquid

Add all ingredients to a spray bottle, fill the bottle the rest of the way with water, and shake well to mix. Use as you would any commercial window cleaner. Be sure to clearly label the bottle before storing.

*You can substitute 3 tablespoons Heinz Vinegar or ReaLemon Lemon Juice for the ammonia.

◆ The simplest and easiest method of making window cleaner is to add 2 tablespoons Heinz Vinegar to 1 cup water. Spray solution on windows, and wipe with Scott Towels.

◆ Use newspaper and vinegar to wash your windows. Just pour Heinz Vinegar into a shallow container, crumple newspaper, and dip. Wipe window clean, then use a dry piece of newspaper for a final wipe.

◆ Use Melitta Basket Coffee Filters of any size to polish your windows or other glass surfaces. They are absorbent, lint-free, handy, and inexpensive.

◆ Here's another window-cleaning solution: Fill a clean, empty spray bottle with ½ cup Heinz Vinegar, ¼ cup Rite Aid isopropyl rubbing alcohol, and enough water to fill. Spray on windows or glass, and wipe with Scott Towels.

- Put dirty venetian blinds in a tub of warm water; add ½ cup ARM & HAMMER Baking Soda, soak for half an hour, then scrub and rinse.

- Perk up dingy white tapes on venetian blinds with white Griffin Liquid Shoe Polish.

- To prevent dust and pet hair from sticking to window blinds, turn the blinds to the closed position, spray with Static Guard, and let dry.

- Clean a washable roll shade using this technique: Remove the shade from the window, unroll it, and lay on a flat surface. Dust it with a clean, dry cloth. Squeeze several drops of Dawn dishwashing liquid into a bucket of warm water, then wipe the shade clean with an O-Cel-O sponge dipped in this solution. Rinse well with a clean, damp cloth or another sponge. Wipe dry with Scott Towels and hang the shade right away.

- Window shades that can't be washed using liquid will come clean if you rub them with a terry cloth towel dipped in a little bit of Quaker Yellow Corn Meal.

- Dip a damp wire brush into ARM & HAMMER Baking Soda and use it to clean door and window screens. Scrub, then rinse screens with an O-Cel-O sponge or a hose.

- Washing a window with intricate panes? Dip a Q-tips cotton swab into your cleaning solution and negotiate all those corners.

- Shine the lead in a stained-glass window with Simoniz Original Paste Wax. Carefully apply a small amount with a clean, soft cloth. Be sure to remove any residue left on the glass.

- To remove hard-water stains from exterior windows, dab some Final Touch fabric softener on the spots using a dry cloth or Scott Towel. Wait 10 minutes, then wipe off with a damp cloth or O-Cel-O sponge. Rinse; dry with a squeegee and a clean, dry cloth.

- Do your windows have the winter weepies? Condensation can build up on the interior glass and drip down, causing your windows to "weep." Here's a quick fix: First, remove all the moisture from the window using a clean cloth or Scott Towel. Then pour a bit of undiluted Suave shampoo onto 2 or 3 layers of Kleenex facial tissue; wipe the shampoo onto the panes. Although they'll look cloudy initially, they will clear up soon.

- Clean spots on windowsills by rubbing them with Rite Aid isopropyl rubbing alcohol and a clean cloth.

- Clean an older, direct-view TV screen with a solution of ¼ cup Parsons' Ammonia and 2 quarts warm water. Use a soft cotton cloth to wipe it on (not too much!); dry with a second cloth. Do not use on LCD-, plasma-, or rear-projection

TV screens. Any household cleaner may damage the screen. Use a soft cloth slightly dampened with water.

- Remove an old sticker from a window, mirror, or other glass surface: Apply some Kraft Mayonnaise to the area, wait a few minutes, and ease off the sticker with a flexible putty knife. Scrape gently if needed to remove stubborn adhesive.

THE WALLS HAVE SMEARS

- Take the time to wash all the walls in your home, whether they look dirty or not. They probably are, and regular cleaning will extend the life of your paint. Dissolve ¼ cup Cascade automatic dishwashing detergent in 1 gallon very hot water. Apply with an O-Cel-O sponge, scrubbing until the grime is gone, then wipe clean with a dry cloth. No need to rinse. (You can also use this mixture to clean wooden window and door frames.)

- This solution will remove grease from painted walls, especially the area above the stove. Combine the following ingredients in a large bucket: ¼ cup 20 Mule Team Borax, ½ cup Heinz Distilled White Vinegar, 1 cup Parsons' Ammonia, and 1 gallon warm water. Sponge or spray on greasy walls, then rinse thoroughly. Save any leftover solution in a clearly labeled plastic spray bottle.

- If your young artist has chosen crayon as a medium and a painted wall as a canvas, use a Pampers baby wipe to gently erase the marks.

- Remove crayon marks from walls with a damp O-Cel-O sponge dipped in ARM & HAMMER Baking Soda.

- Erase crayon marks and drawings from painted walls by rubbing them with Crest toothpaste on a soft cloth. Rinse away with warm water.

- Argo Corn Starch can remove crayon marks from wallpaper. Mix a little with water to make a thick paste, then dab it on the affected area. Let dry completely, then brush off.

- Take a grease spot off wallpaper by first blotting it with a Scott Towel and then applying Argo Corn Starch to the area. Gently rub off the corn starch, then vacuum the area using an upholstery brush attachment.

- Clabber Girl Baking Powder gently but thoroughly removes dirt and grime from delicate wallpaper. Make a paste with water and baking powder and apply it to your wall with an O-Cel-O sponge. Wipe clean with another damp sponge.

- Mix ½ cup Heinz Vinegar and 1 quart water and apply solution to dirty wallpaper using an O-Cel-O sponge. Be careful not to saturate, especially at seams and corners, or you could loosen wallpaper.

◆ Mix up a homemade detergent to clean vinyl wall coverings with a minimum of moisture. Use an eggbeater to mix ¼ cup Dawn dishwashing liquid with 1 cup warm water in a bowl. Beat the mixture to the consistency of stiff foam. Dip an O-Cel-O sponge into the foam and apply it to the wall to loosen dirt, working on one small area at a time. Rinse with another sponge dipped in clear water and squeezed dry.

Cleaning Strategies

Windows: Wipe horizontally on the outside and vertically on the inside, so you'll know on which side of the glass any streaks lie. Choose a cloudy day rather than a sunny one for cleaning windows: The sun dries the glass too quickly and causes streaks.

Walls: Wash painted walls from the top to the bottom. This prevents water from dripping down the wall, creating hard-to-remove streaks.

Dusting and Vacuuming: Clean a room by first dusting its highest surface and then working your way down. With gravity's help, dust and dirt settle down to the floor. Vacuum or sweep the floor last.

◆ To clean rough-textured walls, instead of reaching for a sponge or cloth, try using an old pair of No nonsense pantyhose or socks. They will get the job done without tearing and leaving hard-to-remove bits and pieces on the surface of the wall.

◆ Kraft Mayonnaise will get rid of white water marks on wood paneling. Rub a small amount into each mark; let soak in overnight, then wipe clean.

◆ Dish out the dirt when it comes to cleaning painted wood. Mix 2 tablespoons Dawn dishwashing liquid in 1 gallon warm water. Wipe with a cloth or an O-Cel-O sponge.

◆ Bring out the shine of varnished woodwork with cold Lipton tea. Wipe it onto the wood using a soft cloth; rinse with cool water and an O-Cel-O sponge. Dry with a clean cloth.

FLOOR CHORES

Carpets and Rugs

◆ The first rule of carpet cleaning is to wipe up any spill or stain immediately. Often undiluted Heinz Vinegar can be your best bet for removing a new stain.

◆ For general cleanup of problem areas on carpets or rugs, use equal parts Heinz Vinegar and water. Lightly sponge solution into carpet, rinse, and blot dry. Let dry completely.

◆ To make a carpet and upholstery shampoo, use an eggbeater to mix 1 quart water, ¼ cup Tide laundry detergent, and 1 tablespoon Heinz Vinegar. Whip until a stiff foam forms. Gently rub into fabric or carpeting, then remove soiled foam by scraping with a dull knife. Follow with a rinse of clean water.

Business Is Picking Up

1869: Ives McGaffey patents a wood-and-canvas "sweeping machine"—the country's first hand-pumped vacuum cleaner—and calls it the Whirlwind.

1901: British engineer Hubert Cecil Booth invents the "vacuum cleaning pump"—a large, horse-drawn wagon containing a gas-powered pump and long hoses.

1908: Department-store janitor James Spangler staples a broom handle to a soapbox, then attaches an old fan motor and a pillow-case; he improves the model and patents the first commercially successful portable electric vacuum cleaner, which comes with a cloth filter bag and attachments.

1922: William Hoover, husband of Spangler's cousin, invests in and becomes president of the sweeper company. He renames it for himself: the Hoover Company.

◆ This treatment will help keep your carpet fresh and clean longer between shampoos: Combine ¼ cup Heinz Vinegar and 1 gallon water, then use solution in a steam-cleaning vacuum after shampooing your carpet to remove any residue.

◆ Once a month, sprinkle carpets with ARM & HAMMER Baking Soda. Let sit overnight, then vacuum.

◆ Revive your carpets by sprinkling Argo Corn Starch all over them. Wait 30 minutes, then vacuum and admire the clean.

◆ Mix 1 cup 20 Mule Team Borax with 2 cups Quaker Yellow Corn Meal. Sprinkle solution on a smelly carpet. After 1 hour, vacuum.

- Gillette Foamy Shave Foam makes a great emergency spot cleaner for carpeting. Work it into the stain, then rinse and blot thoroughly.

- This may shock you, but a solution of 1 capful Final Touch fabric softener and 2 cups water can lessen the static electricity on your floor coverings. Mix the ingredients in a spray bottle; lightly spray rugs and carpets.

- To prevent your family from tracking dirt all over your house, keep a box of Pampers baby wipes near the door and have each person clean his or her shoes before entering. (Removing shoes at the door is another excellent practice.)

- To clean and deodorize baby spills or accidents on carpeting, first soak up as much of the mess as possible with a clean rag or Scott Towel. When dry, sprinkle with ARM & HAMMER Baking Soda; let sit 15 minutes before vacuuming.

- Urine accidents should be rinsed immediately with warm water. Then mix 3 tablespoons Heinz Vinegar and 1 teaspoon Ivory Liquid Hand Cleanser. Apply solution to stained area and leave on for 15 minutes. Rinse and rub dry.

- Don't panic when a toddler or your pet has an accident on your carpeting. As soon as you can, blot up as much urine as possible with Scott Towels, then pour on the Canada Dry Club Soda. Let sit 1 to 2 minutes and blot again. Repeat if necessary. To remove any last traces, mix equal parts Heinz

Distilled White Vinegar and cool water; scrub the solution into the affected area using a stiff brush. Blot up the liquid and rinse with cool water.

◆ Cover stains or burns in your carpeting with a matching Crayola Crayon. Rub it into the spot, cover it with Reynolds Cut-Rite Wax Paper, and lightly iron on low heat.

◆ When chewing gum is stuck in a carpet or rug, put a few ice cubes in a GLAD Food Storage Zipper Bag and place it directly on the gum. When gum hardens, use a dull knife to scrape it off.

◆ Get gum and glue out of carpets and rugs with a spray of WD-40. Wait several minutes, then wipe with a clean cloth.

Carpet Freshener

Basic Recipe

1 cup crushed, dried herbs (rosemary, southernwood, lavender, etc.)
1 teaspoon McCormick Ground Cloves
1 teaspoon McCormick Ground Cinnamon
1 teaspoon ARM & HAMMER Baking Soda

Combine ingredients, and sprinkle over carpet. Let sit for a few minutes, then vacuum.

Variations

Mix 1 small box ARM & HAMMER Baking Soda with a few drops of your favorite essential oil; sprinkle mixture onto carpet. Let sit 10 to 20 minutes, then vacuum.

Use 1 cup ARM & HAMMER Baking Soda, 1 cup Argo Corn Starch, and 15 drops essential oil fragrance. Leave on carpet 10 to 20 minutes, then vacuum. Store mixture in a glass jar or airtight container.

Carpet Stain Solutions

- A basic cleanser for nongreasy stains: Combine ¼ teaspoon Dawn dishwashing liquid with 1 cup lukewarm water and blot onto a stain until it's gone. Rinse well and blot with Scott Towels until dry.

- Immediately blot up all moisture from a red wine spill, then sprinkle the area with Morton Salt. Let sit 15 minutes. The salt should absorb any remaining wine in the carpet (turning pink as a result). Clean entire area with a mixture of 1 part Heinz Distilled White Vinegar and 2 parts water.

- Sprinkle some Argo Corn Starch on a butter stain or other greasy spot on your carpet. Let dry completely, then vacuum.

- Try removing grease spots from a rug with a mixture of 1 part Morton Salt and 4 parts Rite Aid isopropyl rubbing alcohol. Rub vigorously in the same direction as the nap, then rinse with water. For a larger rug, wipe off the solution with a damp cloth and blot dry. (Protect wood floors by placing several layers of Scott Towels underneath the rug beforehand.)

- Blot up an oil spill on a rug or carpet right away, then sprinkle Clabber Girl Baking Powder directly on the spot. Let dry, then vacuum up the residue...and the stain!

- Clean ketchup, chocolate, coffee, or cola stains from carpeting with a mixture of 1 part Heinz Vinegar and 2 parts water. Sponge on mixture, and blot stain with clean cloths until gone.

- To dissolve chewing gum stuck in carpet or on any cloth, saturate area with Heinz Vinegar and let it sit briefly. (For faster results, heat vinegar first.) Carefully tug at gum to remove it.

- Candle wax has spilled on your carpeting. Before it hardens, lay a brown paper bag or a thick layer of Scott Towels over

- To get rid of a gravy stain on your carpet, first remove as much liquid as possible by covering the spot with Morton Salt. This will prevent the greasy stain from spreading. Then follow rug manufacturer's instructions to clean. For this and other stubborn stains, you may need a dry-cleaning solution or an enzyme detergent.

- To remove a coffee or tea stain from a rug or carpet, pour a small amount of Budweiser beer directly on the spot. Gently rub in the beer with a cloth or an O-Cel-O sponge; blot with a Scott Towel. Repeat until the stain is gone.

- Blot up a fresh coffee spill on your carpet with Pampers baby wipes—they are absorbent and nongreasy, so they won't add to the stain.

- Remove crayon stains from carpeting or any other fabric or surface by scrubbing area with a Reach toothbrush dipped in Heinz Vinegar.

- Remove ink stains from carpet with Argo Corn Starch. Start with about 2 tablespoons corn starch, then slowly add enough milk to make a paste. Apply paste, wait a few hours, and brush it off.

- Treat an ink stain on a carpet or rug immediately by spraying the stained area with Suave hairspray, then blotting. Once the ink spot is gone, work a solution of equal parts Heinz Vinegar and water into area to remove sticky spray. Rub vigorously using Scott Towels or a clean cloth. Blot dry.

the wax and apply an iron set on medium heat (no steam). If necessary, repeat with fresh paper.

- Remove tar or other stubborn sticky stuff from carpet fibers by rubbing Crisco Pure Vegetable Oil into the substance. Rub the substance loose, then blot with a Scott Towel.

- A spot of dried white school glue can be taken out of a carpet with a mixture of 1 part Heinz Vinegar and 2 parts water. Just sponge on and blot. If the spot is stubborn, cover it with warm vinegar and let it sit for 10 to 15 minutes. When glue has softened, either scrape it up using a dull knife or blot with Scott Towels.

- Once mildew gets into a rug, it lives and grows. Kill it with a mixture of equal parts Heinz Vinegar and water. Make sure rug dries completely. You may want to use a hair dryer set on low to speed up drying time.

- Mix equal amounts of Heinz Vinegar and water, and use an O-Cel-O sponge to apply solution to salt deposits on your rug or carpet. Do not saturate. Let dry, then vacuum.

Wood Floors

- If your wood floors are clean but a bit dull, mop cooled Lipton tea over them. Let them air-dry, then buff to a shine with a clean towel.

- Help your dust mop work more effectively on your hardwood floors. Spray it first with Static Guard.

- To polish a varnished wood floor, put a folded bath towel into one leg of a pair of No nonsense pantyhose and start buffing!

- Remove water spots on wood floors with an O-Cel-O sponge dampened in a solution of 4 tablespoons ARM & HAMMER Baking Soda and 1 quart warm water.

- To remove chewing gum stuck to a hardwood floor, set a GLAD Food Storage Zipper Bag of ice cubes atop the gum. After gum hardens, use an old credit card to pry it loose. If necessary, polish that area of the floor after gum is removed.

- Add 1 cup Heinz Vinegar to 1 gallon of water; mop lightly onto hardwood floors (do not saturate). No need to rinse. This will keep floors shiny and remove any greasy buildup.

- Dark spots sometimes appear on wood floors where an alkaline substance has dripped and dried. To remove a spot, first strip floor of any wax using mineral spirits on a cloth. Next, apply Heinz Vinegar to the spot and leave on for 5 minutes. Wipe dry; repeat if spot remains. If several applications don't remove the spot, consult a professional floor finisher.

Tile, Vinyl, Linoleum & Laminate

- No time (or energy) to wax the floor? Add 1 cup Final Touch fabric softener to ½ gallon water. Now damp mopping won't dull the shine on your floor.

- Clean tile floors with ½ cup ARM & HAMMER Baking Soda in a bucket of warm water. Mop and rinse clean.

- Make ceramic tile floors shine by mopping with a mixture of 1 cup Heinz Vinegar and 1 gallon warm water.

- Add extra shine to your clean, dry tile floor. Wrap a piece of Reynolds Cut-Rite Wax Paper around a dust mop and sweep it over the floor.

- Wash grout between terra-cotta tiles with straight Heinz Vinegar to clean up and prevent smudges.

- Here's a simple, homemade solution for cleaning laminate and tile floors: Combine 1 part Heinz Vinegar, 1 part Rite Aid isopropyl rubbing alcohol, 1 part water, and 3 drops Dawn dishwashing liquid. Use this mixture to clean the entire floor, or keep it in a labeled spray bottle to use for spot cleaning and deodorizing.

- WD-40 can remove the following (and likely many more things) from tile floors: scuff marks, mascara, gum, coffee stains, crayon, ink, marker, adhesives, rubber cement, and glue.

- Remove black heel marks on linoleum or vinyl floors with a damp O-Cel-O sponge or scrub sponge dipped in ARM & HAMMER Baking Soda.

- Crest toothpaste removes black scuff marks on vinyl or linoleum floors. Rub the paste into the mark and wipe away with a damp cloth. A little ARM & HAMMER Baking Soda added to the toothpaste can provide scrubbing power.

- Use Dawn dishwashing liquid as a quick cleaner for spills on a vinyl floor. Just dip an O-Cel-O sponge in the liquid and wipe clean.

- Scrub a linoleum floor with a mixture of 1 gallon water and 1 cup Heinz Vinegar. If floor needs a polish after this, use straight Canada Dry Club Soda.

- Before you dust that linoleum floor, spray the dust mop with Static Guard.

- If you've performed a wax-stripping operation on your kitchen floor using Parsons' Ammonia, finish the project by rinsing the entire floor with a solution of 1 gallon water and ½ cup Heinz Vinegar. The vinegar will remove lingering wax and the ammonia smell.

- If you use detergent on your no-wax vinyl or linoleum floor, rinse afterward with a solution of 1 cup Heinz Vinegar and 1 gallon water.

- Mop up salt deposits from winter boots with a mixture of equal parts Heinz Vinegar and water.

More Floors

- Make a marble floor look marvelous! First, mop with a sponge mop or string mop using clear water, an all-purpose cleaning solution diluted in warm water, or a mixture of 1 cup Final Touch fabric softener and ½ gallon water. Wring the mop until it doesn't drip, and go over the floor in slow, even strokes. Mop it again with a bucket of water containing 1 cup Heinz Distilled White Vinegar to really bring out its luster.

◆ Make stone floors sparkle! Mop weekly with a solution of 2 teaspoons detergent-based (not soap-based) dishwashing liquid per gallon of water. Rinse with clear water.

FURNITURE

Working Wonders for Wood

◆ To remove dirt, grime, and built-up polish from wood furniture, brew some tea. Steep 2 Lipton Tea Bags in 4 cups boiling water; let cool. Dampen a soft, clean cloth with tea and wipe down the dirty surfaces. Polish with a soft, clean cloth.

Chair (or Table) of the Board

If the old wood boards you acquired have great potential (and a great amount of grime), try this cleanser.

3 parts sand
2 parts Ivory Liquid Hand Cleanser
1 part ReaLime Lime Juice

Mix the ingredients thoroughly in a bucket. Using a stiff brush, scrub the wood with the cleanser. Rinse with water; rub dry with a clean towel. Now get on with making that furniture!

◆ Beer: It's not just for stacking in pyramids on the coffee table. Clean wood furniture—especially oak and mahogany—with warm Budweiser beer. Using a clean, soft cloth, wipe it on the wood; wipe dry with a second cloth.

◆ Choose vegetable oil to remove a white spot on wood furniture. Dip a cloth into Crisco Pure Vegetable Oil, then into some cigar or cigarette ashes. Rub the cloth with the grain of the wood until spot disappears.

- To remove a surface mark from a wood table, whether a water mark or a scald from a hot dish, make a thin paste of Crisco Pure Vegetable Oil and a pinch of Morton Salt. (Use about ⅛ to ¼ teaspoon salt per tablespoon of oil.) Just wipe on paste with a soft cloth, then buff lightly as you wipe it off.

- To erase a water ring from finished wood, mix a small quantity of ARM & HAMMER Baking Soda with Crest toothpaste. Apply the paste to the affected area with a clean, soft cloth; gently rub. Wipe clean.

- Apply Kraft Mayonnaise to white rings, spots, or crayon marks on your wood furniture, let it sit for 1 hour, then wipe clean with a soft cloth or O-Cel-O sponge.

- Erase minor cigarette burns on wood furniture with Kraft Mayonnaise. Dab a small amount of mayo onto a clean, soft cloth; rub furniture gently to buff out the stain.

- Remove alcohol stains from a wood table with a paste of ARM & HAMMER Baking Soda and mineral, linseed, or lemon oil. Rub in the direction of the grain, then wipe with linseed oil.

- Remove paper that's stuck on a wood surface by generously applying PAM cooking spray. Wait 5 to 10 minutes, then carefully remove the paper.

- Safely scrape a decal, price tag, tape, or stuck-on paper from a wood surface by saturating the surface of the item to be removed with Crisco Pure Vegetable Oil or dampening with Heinz Vinegar. Let sit 10 minutes, then peel or gently scrape the sticker off. If it still won't budge, set your hair dryer on low and aim it at the item for half a minute. The heat will loosen the glue.

- A spot of spilled glue on wood furniture can be removed with Crisco Pure Vegetable Oil. Pour a small amount onto a clean cloth and carefully dab onto the area. Rub until the sticky stuff is removed.

- To remove spilled model glue from wood furniture, use a soft cotton cloth to rub on a little Crisco Pure Vegetable Oil.

- Dusting carved wood furniture can be difficult. Use a Q-tips cotton swab for the small spaces. Additionally, a swab dipped in furniture polish is a great tool for shining and protecting your beautiful furniture.

- Rub a bit of Crest toothpaste into white spots on oil-finished wood furniture. Use a soft cloth and buff the marks away.

- Wood furniture with an oil finish needs its own cleaner, rather than traditional furniture polish or wax. For regular cleaning, dust furniture with a dry, soft cotton cloth. Every few months, combine the following in a small bucket: 2 cups turpentine, 2 cups boiled linseed oil, and ¾ cup Heinz Vinegar. Dip an O-Cel-O sponge into the mixture and gently wipe the surface of the furniture. Be sure to wear protective gloves. Wait about 5 minutes for stubborn dirt to loosen, then wipe away all the excess solution with a clean, soft cloth. Buff with another soft cloth until the surface shines. Wash O-Cel-O sponge and gloves in hot, soapy water.

- Try this recipe for homemade furniture polish. Whisk ½ teaspoon Colavita Extra Virgin Olive Oil and ¼ cup Heinz Distilled White Vinegar in a small bowl. Pour mixture into a clean, resealable jar and label clearly. When ready to use, give jar a good shake, then apply polish liberally to wood surfaces with a soft cloth. Wipe away excess.

- Here's another homemade polish for general use on all wood furniture. In a glass jar with a tight-fitting lid, mix ¼ cup fresh or ReaLemon Lemon Juice with ½ cup Crisco Pure Vegetable Oil. Apply to wood furniture with a cotton cloth, rubbing in a small amount at a time. Kept out of direct sunlight, this mixture can be stored for several months.

- To remove scratches from a wood table, increase the amount of lemon juice in the previous furniture polish recipe so that you're using equal parts ReaLemon Lemon Juice and Crisco Pure Vegetable Oil. With a soft, clean cotton cloth, gently rub the mixture into the wood, buffing out the scratches. Repeat as needed until scratches are gone.

- Remove waxy buildup on wood tabletops with a solution of equal parts water and Heinz Vinegar. Wipe onto area, then rub and dry immediately using a soft cloth.

- To restore luster to mahogany furniture, mix 3 tablespoons Heinz Vinegar and 1 quart water. Dip an O-Cel-O sponge in the mixture, wring thoroughly, then use to wipe wood. Do not saturate.

- After polishing any wood furniture in your home, sprinkle a bit of Argo Corn Starch over the surface. Then use a clean, soft cloth to buff it to a high shine. Any excess oil will be absorbed by the corn starch.

Upholstery

- Homemade upholstery shampoo is a fraction of the cost of the store-bought kind—and just as effective. Mix ¼ cup Dawn dishwashing liquid with 1 cup warm water, then whip the solution with an eggbeater. Apply the foam to upholstery, working in small sections at a time with a clean, soft-bristled brush. Rinse the upholstery by gently rubbing the fabric with a moist, clean cloth; rinse the cloth as necessary.

- Gillette Foamy Shave Foam makes an excellent upholstery cleaner in a pinch. It sticks to all the tricky parts, like the backs of chairs or the chair legs. Just spray on a small amount and work it into the fabric with your fingers or a soft brush. Sponge off the excess and blot dry.

- To remove spilled grease from upholstery, cover the spot right away with Argo Corn Starch. Wait until as much of the grease as possible has been absorbed, then vacuum. Repeat if necessary.

- To remove an oily stain from upholstered furniture, grind about a cup of Fresh Step cat litter into a powder and scatter it over the stain. Wait until the oil is absorbed, then vacuum up the litter.

Dirty Details

According to the NEWTON Web site (operated by the U.S. Department of Energy), household dust is composed of fibers from textiles and plants. It also may contain human skin flakes, pet dander, bits of insects and other bugs, pollen, household insulation, and carpet backing.

- Many stains on upholstery or carpets can be removed with 20 Mule Team Borax. Blot up as much of the spill as you can, sprinkle borax on the area, let it dry completely, and then vacuum. For difficult stains, such as wine, sponge in a solution of ½ cup 20 Mule Team Borax and 2 cups warm water. Wait 30 minutes, then shampoo the stained area with a commercial spray-on cleaner. Note: Before treating the entire stain, test a small area to ensure the carpet or upholstery is colorfast.

- A fresh grease stain on a cloth chair can be absorbed with equal parts ARM & HAMMER Baking Soda and Morton Salt. Sprinkle the mixture onto the stain and rub lightly; leave on for a few hours, then vacuum.

- Remove an ink stain from fabric upholstery with the help of Suave hairspray. Get two thick, white towels; spray a light coat of hairspray on one. Dab the stain, alternating towels, until the ink is gone.

- Hairspray is also just the thing to remove pet hair from upholstered furniture. Spray an O-Cel-O sponge with Suave hairspray and wipe it over the fabric before the spray dries. Spray again as necessary.

- Another trick for removing lint and pet hair from upholstery is to rub the fabric with a Downy dryer sheet.

- Clean pet hair off furniture or clothes with a sheet of GLAD Press'n Seal. Place the plastic wrap on the surface, smooth it down, and lift the hair away.

- Mix ¼ cup Final Touch fabric softener with water in a spray bottle, and mist it lightly on upholstered furniture anywhere pet hair has accumulated. Do not saturate. When it's dry, vacuum off.

- Pick up pet hair easily by wrapping your hand with a piece of Scotch Duct Tape with the sticky side out. Run your hand along the upholstery and pick up the hair.

- A slightly dampened O-Cel-O sponge also works for picking up pet hair.

Leather

◆ Keep a leather armchair looking like new. Every few weeks, wipe it with a soft cotton cloth that's been dipped in beaten egg white. Buff to a shine with a second cloth.

◆ To keep leather upholstery looking its best, give it a milk bath. Every 3 months, use a clean cloth to wipe on a small quantity of skim milk.

◆ Remove waxy buildup from a leather desktop with a solution of 1 tablespoon Heinz Vinegar in 1 cup warm water. Wipe on with a soft cloth, then buff dry.

Vinyl

◆ Clean vinyl upholstery, such as that on a recliner or kitchen chair, with a paste of ARM & HAMMER Baking Soda and water. Rub on, allow to dry, then wipe off.

◆ Remove a water spot or other marks from vinyl by rubbing them with Crest toothpaste on a damp cloth.

◆ Clean up spots on vinyl furniture by wiping with a cloth dipped in undiluted Heinz Vinegar.

◆ Erase ink stains from vinyl surfaces by rubbing on a bit of Crisco All-Vegetable Shortening with a cloth or Scott Towel. Use a little elbow grease and scrub until stains disappear. Wipe clean with a fresh towel.

Glass

◆ Hide superficial scratches on a glass tabletop by rubbing in a small amount of Crest toothpaste. Wipe clean with a soft, dry cloth.

◆ To bring out the shine in a glass tabletop, rub it gently with a few drops of ReaLemon Lemon Juice. Dry with a Scott Towel, then polish with a piece of crumpled-up newspaper.

◆ Use fabric softener to repel dust when you clean a glass table. Mix 1 part Final Touch fabric softener and 4 parts water; store in a squirt bottle, such as an empty Dawn dishwashing liquid bottle. Squirt a small amount of the solution onto a clean cloth, wipe the surface down, then polish to a shine with a second cloth.

Other Surfaces

◆ Candle wax can be removed from most hard surfaces with a paste of ARM & HAMMER Baking Soda and water. Scrub with a nylon scrubber.

◆ Clean cane furniture with Clabber Girl Baking Powder. Wet the cane with warm water, then apply the powder with a paintbrush. Let dry; brush off. Rinse with cold water and allow to air-dry.

- Prevent white wicker furniture from yellowing by scrubbing it with a stiff brush moistened with salt water. Let dry in full sunlight.

- Eliminate mildew odors in drawers and on various other surfaces by wiping the affected area with full-strength Listerine Antiseptic mouthwash. Wipe clean with a Scott Towel.

FURNISHINGS

Silver

- To remove silver tarnish using a process called ion exchange, boil a pot of water and ½ teaspoon Morton Salt with 1 to 2 teaspoons ARM & HAMMER Baking Soda. Place the tarnished pieces of silverware in a pan with the saltwater solution along with a piece of Reynolds Wrap Aluminum Foil. Soak for 2 to 3 minutes. Rinse the silverware well, then use a soft cloth to buff dry.

- Here's another way to remove tarnish from silver by ion exchange. Line a small bowl with Reynolds Wrap Aluminum Foil. Fill the bowl with hot water and stir in about 1 tablespoon Tide powdered laundry detergent. Soak the silver in the solution for 1 minute, then rinse well and spread it out on the table to dry.

- Use Crest toothpaste to polish your silverware. Coat the silverware with toothpaste, then dip each piece into warm water and rub with your fingertips. The toothpaste may actually foam up. Rinse thoroughly and buff dry.

- Now hair this: Alberto VO5 Conditioning Hairdressing or Suave conditioner can prevent polished silver (picture frames, serving pieces, candlesticks) from tarnishing. Apply either conditioner *lightly* using a soft cloth; wipe off the excess. The remaining thin coat will protect the silver and curtail tarnishing.

- Clean and polish your precious metals with Crayola chalk. Sprinkle a little powdered chalk onto a clean, damp cloth. Rub a tarnished piece until shiny. Rinse with water; dry.

The Big Book

The first large, comprehensive catalog from Sears, Roebuck and Co. was printed in 1894. The cover declared it the "Book of Bargains: A Money Saver for Everyone," and from it customers could order musical instruments, guns, buggies, clothing, sewing machines, and much more.

Through the years, all manner of merchandise was added, from eyeglasses (1895) to barber chairs (1903) to silk stockings (1912) to television sets (1949). The first Christmas Catalog appeared in 1933; the term "Wish Book" was added to the holiday catalog 35 years later.

The Big Book was retired in 1993, though a variety of specialty catalogs have continued. In 1998, Sears launched Wishbook.com, its virtual catalog.

◆ To remove salt stains from a silver saltshaker or another silver piece, rub with Colavita Extra Virgin Olive Oil. Let sit a few days, then wipe with a clean cotton cloth.

Pewter

◆ Because pewter is a soft metal that can be damaged easily, it must be cleaned gently. Add enough Gold Medal All-Purpose Flour to a mixture of 1 teaspoon Morton Salt and 1 cup Heinz Distilled White Vinegar to make a smooth paste. Apply paste to a pewter piece with a soft cloth. Let dry (about half an hour); rinse with warm water. Polish with a soft cloth, making sure to remove paste residue from grooves and hidden areas.

◆ To clean a pewter piece, immerse it in water that has been used to boil eggs. Wait a few minutes, then gently rub the pewter with a soft cloth dipped in the same water. When the item is clean, rinse it with clear water and wipe dry.

◆ Parsons' Ammonia is perfect for pewter polishing. Mix 2 tablespoons ammonia with 1 quart hot, soapy water. Wipe the surface of the pewter piece using a soft cotton cloth.

Copper, Brass & Bronze

◆ To clean and shine copper or brass surfaces, combine equal parts Morton Salt and Gold Medal All-Purpose Flour and add enough Heinz Distilled White Vinegar to make a paste. Rub the paste on with a soft cloth. Let sit about 1 hour, then wipe off and buff with a clean, soft cloth.

- Apply a light coat of Suave hairspray to freshly polished copper or brass to ward off tarnish.

- Remove stubborn tarnish from copper by spraying stains with Heinz Distilled White Vinegar and sprinkling with Morton Salt. Scrub with an O-Cel-O sponge, then rinse thoroughly, making sure to remove all traces of salt. Repeat if necessary.

- To remove "greenery" from brass and copper, rub the surface with a solution of equal parts Parsons' Ammonia and Morton Salt. Rinse with clear water.

- Clean slightly tarnished brass or copper by rubbing with half a lemon or lime dipped in Morton Salt.

- Use either of these pastes to clean brass or copper. For the first, mix ReaLemon Lemon Juice with either ARM & HAMMER Baking Soda or McCormick Cream of Tartar to form a paste. The second combines ReaLemon Lemon Juice, Morton Salt, and Quaker Yellow Corn Meal. Rub the paste onto the brass or copper using a soft cloth; rinse and dry.

- A mixture of Morton Salt and Crest toothpaste can clean tarnished brass items.

- Spray Pledge furniture polish onto a piece of very fine steel wool. This can safely clean brass items.

- Remove marks on bronze by wiping bronze items with a soft cloth dampened with turpentine.

Vases and Containers

◆ To clean a glass vase or similar container, fill it three-quarters full with hot water, add a teaspoon of ARM & HAMMER Baking Soda, and shake. Let soak, then rinse.

◆ Remove mineral deposits or stains from a vase by dampening surfaces with water and sprinkling with Morton Salt. Wipe with a clean cloth.

◆ For out-of-reach deposits in a narrow vase, fill vase with a strong saltwater solution (such as 2 or 3 teaspoons of Morton Salt per cup of water), then shake and swirl. Let stand 15 minutes, then rinse and wash with Dawn dishwashing liquid and water.

◆ Clean stains from a vase by dropping 2 Alka-Seltzer tablets in the vase with water. Let sit, swish liquid around, and rinse.

◆ Polident denture cleanser tablets can also be used to clean the gunk out of vases. Fill the vase with water and add 1 tablet. Let soak; rinse.

Pianos

◆ Is your old piano known for not only bright melodies but also dingy keys? Squeeze a little Crest toothpaste on a soft Reach toothbrush, scrub the keys gently, and then wipe clean with a damp cloth. Crest toothpaste also does a nice job on the plastic-covered keys of modern pianos and keyboards.

◆ Brighten stained ivory piano keys with a damp O-Cel-O sponge dipped in ARM & HAMMER Baking Soda. Wipe clean and buff.

◆ Restore yellowed piano keys to their original shine with Kraft Mayonnaise or Heinz Vinegar. Rub on a small amount with a soft, dry cloth; wipe clean with a damp cloth. Do not saturate. Polish to a shine with another dry cloth.

◆ Bring back the shine on piano keys and gilt picture frames by rubbing carefully with a cloth dipped in milk.

◆ To clean and remove stickers from the keys of pianos and synthesizers, all it takes is a little WD-40 and a clean cloth.

Computers, Keyboards & More

◆ When you need to get that dust and lint out of tight spaces in computer keyboards, MP3 player docks, fax machines and printers, and cable connections to computers and other electronics, use a clean, new cosmetics brush; they are available in a variety of sizes.

◆ A Pampers baby wipe gets the gunk off your computer keyboard. Unplug the keyboard (or turn off the computer entirely) and wipe away the dust, grime, fingerprints, crumbs, and mystery matter from the keys, buttons, and bars.

This and That

- Get rid of stubborn spots on porcelain lamps, vases, and candlesticks by dipping a damp cloth in ARM & HAMMER Baking Soda and rubbing them away. Wipe clean with a damp cloth.

- Clean your telephone with a Q-tips cotton swab dipped in undiluted Heinz Vinegar. This is great for removing fingerprints and smudges from the plastic parts of white or light-colored telephones. Be careful not to saturate.

- To polish lacquered metal items, rub the surface with a soft cloth dampened with a few drops of Colavita Extra Virgin Olive Oil.

- Wipe dirt from candles with a soft cloth, a folded Scott Towel, or a Rite Aid cotton ball dipped in Rite Aid isopropyl rubbing alcohol.

- You can forget about digging old, melted wax out of candlesticks. Before you insert a candle, coat the inside of the holder with Vaseline Petroleum Jelly, Johnson's Baby Oil, or Alberto VO5 Conditioning Hairdressing.

Don't Be Candle*stuck*

To release candle stubs and dripped wax that are stuck in or on candlesticks and holders, try soaking them in warm water or blasting them with a blow-dryer. A far neater and more effective method is putting the candlestick or holder in the freezer for at least 24 hours. The stub or wax drippings will slide away easily!

- To clean marble, wipe with a damp, soft cloth that's been dipped into powdered Crayola chalk. Rinse with clear water, using another cloth or an O-Cel-O sponge. Dry completely.

- Clean and shine wooden knickknacks and other wood objects by coating them with a thin layer of Alberto VO5 Conditioning Hairdressing. Wipe off the excess and buff to a shine.

- The stronger, the better: Apply strongly brewed Lipton tea with a soft cloth to wash and polish black lacquer figurines and other decorative pieces. Use a second cloth to wipe dry.

- After cleaning the blades of a fan (any kind: freestanding, oscillating, or ceiling fan), wipe the surfaces with a Downy dryer sheet. This will slow the accumulation of hair, dust, and dirt.

- Apply a thin layer of Simoniz Original Paste Wax to the inside of a clean ashtray. The ashes won't stick, so cleanup will be very simple with a cloth or Scott Towel.

JEWELRY CLEANING

- Don't let it go down the drain: When cleaning your good jewelry, put a tea strainer over the sink drain.

- Make your own basic jewelry cleaner: Combine ¼ cup Parsons' Ammonia, ¼ cup Dawn dishwashing liquid, and ¾ cup water. Mix well. Soak the jewelry in the solution for 5 minutes. Clean around ridges with a soft Reach toothbrush. Buff dry. (Do not use this cleaner on plastics, gold-plated jewelry, or soft stones such as opals, pearls, or jade.)

- Dissolve 2 Alka-Seltzer tablets in a glass of water and use to soak dull or tarnished jewelry. Let soak for only 2 minutes, then rub dry.

- Ion exchange, the same chemical process that removes tarnish from silver, can be used to clean jewelry. Line a small bowl with Reynolds Wrap Aluminum Foil. Fill the bowl with hot water and stir in 1 tablespoon Tide powdered laundry detergent. Soak the jewelry in the solution for 1 minute, then rinse well and let dry.

- Put a little Crest toothpaste on your fingertips, then use it to rub silver jewelry. Let the toothpaste sit about 1 hour or more. Rub off with a soft cloth.

- Colavita Extra Virgin Olive Oil and Crisco Pure Vegetable Oil each make a good cleaner for pearls. Just dab a little of either on each pearl, then wipe dry with a soft cloth.

- To clean a diamond ring, use Crest toothpaste on an old Reach toothbrush. Scrub gently, rinse, dry, and step back to enjoy the sparkle!

- Use Polident denture cleanser tablets dissolved in a glass of water to make your diamonds sparkle. Just drop jewelry in the solution for 2 minutes.

- Soak your gems—precious or semiprecious—in a glass of Canada Dry Club Soda overnight. In the morning, they'll sparkle and shine.

- Use Crest toothpaste to remove those annoying scratches on your watch crystal. Put a small amount on your fingertip, rub it on the crystal with a light touch, and wipe it clean with a soft, dry cloth.

- Is your plastic watchband a bit grimy? Put a dab of Crest toothpaste on the band and gently rub it with your moistened fingers. Rinse clean, then dry with a soft cloth. If the watch itself is not water-resistant, be careful not to get it wet during the process.

- To remove scratches from a plastic watch, dip a Q-tips cotton swab in Cutex Quick & Gentle Liquid Nail Polish Remover. Wipe the swab across the face and watch the scratches disappear.

- Does a ring discolor your finger? Apply clear Revlon Nail Enamel to the inside of the band.

- Costume jewelry keeps its gleam with a thin coat of clear Revlon Nail Enamel.

- Keep it clean: Prevent your silver jewelry and your costume jewelry from tarnishing by putting a stick of Crayola chalk in the jewelry box.

IN AND OUT OF STORAGE

◆ Want an alternative to mothballs? Sprinkle 20 Mule Team Borax on closet shelves.

◆ To keep an appliance cord neat, store it in an old Scott Towel tube (use half a tube for short cords). Gather up the cord in loops a few inches longer than the tube; slide tube over looped cord. Label the tube with the name of the corresponding appliance.

◆ Most people don't use good cloth tablecloths and napkins every night or even every week. To prevent the creases that form when linens are folded for storage, roll the linens onto cardboard tubes covered with GLAD Cling Wrap. Use Scott Towel tubes for napkins and gift wrap tubes for tablecloths.

◆ Keep old books from becoming musty in storage. Before stowing them away, put a Downy dryer sheet between the pages in a few places.

◆ Before storing a piece of luggage, place an open box of ARM & HAMMER Baking Soda inside and close the luggage overnight. Repeat this when removing luggage from long-term storage.

◆ Send mildew odor packing: Toss a bar of scented bath soap into each piece of luggage before storing.

◆ Breakables—from glass figurines to porcelain vases—need extra attention before you store them. Carefully place a breakable item in a GLAD Food Storage Zipper Bag that is just big enough to hold it. Seal the bag until it's almost closed. Blow up the bag with air, then run the seal the rest of the way. When you put the bag in a storage box or container, the item will be protected in a cushion of air.

◆ Freshen blankets that have been in storage by sprinkling with ARM & HAMMER Baking Soda and rolling them up for a couple of hours. Shake out baking soda, then fluff in the dryer without heat.

◆ To keep quilts and blankets folded neatly when you stash them in the closet, repurpose the waistband of a pair of No nonsense pantyhose as a large, strong "rubber band."

◆ Smart shoppers take advantage of good deals. But where do you put all those rolls of Quilted Northern toilet tissue and Scott Towels? Hang a pair of No nonsense pantyhose on a nail or hook. Slide the rolls, one at a time, down each leg. Cut a hole at the bottom for dispensing; close it up with a twist tie or tie a loose knot until you need a roll.

◆ Does your jewelry box look as if the chains have been wrestling with each other? Solve that problem by dropping each chain through the end of a drinking straw that's been cut in half. Fasten the clasp on the outside of the straw.

- Need a place to store your belts? Roll them up and place them in an empty Folgers coffee canister or large coffee can. (Tip: A clear lid will make it easy to find the right belt.) These containers will keep your belts from creasing, and the easy access won't "waist" your time.

- Neatly store scarves in a dresser drawer using empty cores from rolls of Quilted Northern toilet tissue or Scott Towels (cut in half). Stand them up in the drawer and tuck a folded scarf into each one.

- Do you have a hard time sharing your closet? Try some creative recycling. Use one plastic lid from a coffee can or Folgers coffee canister for each person using the closet. Cut a slit in each lid from the outer rim to the center, and cut a hole in the middle just slightly bigger than the diameter of the closet rod. Label each lid with a permanent marker; place the lids on the rod to separate clothing and designate each person's "territory."

WHAT'S THAT SMELL?

Air Fresheners

- To make a homemade air freshener, fill a Melitta Basket Coffee Filter with ARM & HAMMER Baking Soda and close it with a twist tie. Place it where the air is less than fresh—in the refrigerator, closet, your car, shoes, boots, or anywhere.

- Combine 1 teaspoon ARM & HAMMER Baking Soda, 1 tablespoon Heinz Vinegar, and 2 cups water. Stir; mixture will foam up a bit but this will soon subside. Store the solution in a clearly labeled spray bottle. Spray a mist in the air anywhere you want to eliminate or control household odors.

- Pour Heinz Vinegar into shallow bowls and set them out to absorb odors in areas of your home where odors are a problem. Make sure the bowls are out of reach of small children and pets.

- Can you smell the ocean breeze? (Or at least just a little fresh air?) To air out any room in the house, place a scented Downy dryer sheet in the heat vent. Remove the vent cover and place the dryer sheet on the back of it; when you put the cover back in the wall or floor, the sheet will help filter out airborne particles and scent the room. Replace the sheet when it's filled with lint, dust, and the like.

Tools of the Trade

◆ Clean and deodorize smelly floor mops or sponges by soaking them for 10 minutes in a gallon of water mixed with ¾ cup Clorox Regular-Bleach. Rinse thoroughly afterward.

◆ Eliminate residue and smells from mops or rags by soaking them in a mixture of 4 tablespoons ARM & HAMMER Baking Soda and 1 gallon water.

◆ Soak a well-worn, smelly sponge in a shallow dish of Heinz Vinegar for several hours. Rinse sponge well, then let dry. In humid weather, store the sponge in a shallow dish of vinegar to keep it from souring.

◆ If you put a Downy dryer sheet in an empty vacuum cleaner bag, the fresh scent will disperse around the room as you vacuum.

◆ Add ARM & HAMMER Baking Soda to a vacuum bag to fight smells that can accumulate there.

Well, Naturally

Baking soda is a naturally occurring, very versatile substance that's environmentally safe and inexpensive. Not only is baking soda nontoxic, it's actually a food, so—unlike many commercial household products—it is safe to use around children and pets.

So Trashy

◆ Periodically wash out and deodorize garbage cans with a solution of 1 cup ARM & HAMMER Baking Soda per gallon of water.

- Reduce garbage can smells by sprinkling ARM & HAMMER Baking Soda inside each time you add garbage.

- Trash barrels and garbage cans can get mighty stinky during the summer. Take the germs and odor out of a kitchen garbage can by washing it with a solution of 20 Mule Team Borax and warm water. When it's dry, sprinkle some borax on the bottom to keep it fresh until the next deep cleaning.

- Before you replace the GLAD trash bag in a stinky garbage can or diaper pail, pour some nonclumping Fresh Step cat litter in the bottom. When the litter gets damp, change it.

- When you put out your trash in plastic bags, coat the outside of the bags with a little Parsons' Ammonia. The smell should keep strays away. Consider spraying the outside of your trash cans with ammonia too.

- Keep diaper pails smelling fresh by sprinkling ARM & HAMMER Baking Soda over dirty cloth diapers. Line the bottom of a diaper pail with baking soda after you empty it to control odors.

- To combat the aroma inside an odor-collector such as a laundry hamper, shoe, or diaper pail, place a Downy dryer sheet inside it.

In the Kitchen

- Kitchen odors disappear thanks to the freshening power of lemons and a few spices. Fill a small pot with water. Add several pieces of lemon rind and about 1 teaspoon each of McCormick Whole Cloves and Rosemary Leaves. Bring to a boil. The aroma will soon reach nearly every room of your house.

◆ Freshen the air in your kitchen with the simplest of methods. Heat the oven to 300°F and place a whole lemon on the center rack. With the door slightly ajar, let the lemon "cook" for about 15 minutes; turn off oven. Let lemon cool before removing it.

◆ Disguise burnt smells with a touch of McCormick Ground Cinnamon. Sprinkle a bit in a pie plate and place in a warm oven for about 10 minutes.

◆ Boil 1 tablespoon Heinz Vinegar in 1 cup water to eliminate smoky smells in the kitchen.

◆ Stale smells in any type of breadbox can be eliminated by placing a small bowl of Heinz Vinegar inside it overnight.

◆ The rubber seal on garbage disposals can retain odors. To deodorize it, remove seal and let it soak in a pan of Heinz Distilled White Vinegar for 1 hour.

Awesome Aromas

Scent memories are very powerful. You get a whiff of something—a special perfume, fresh-baked cookies, roses—and you're immediately transported to another time and place. Our other senses don't affect us like this, though taste comes close (and is often linked to smell). What's more, a good sense of smell helps survival and is likely deeply connected with primitive parts of our brains.

- Freshen a plastic lunch box by filling it with water and ¼ cup Heinz Vinegar. Let stand for 12 hours, then rinse with fresh water.

- An open box of ARM & HAMMER Baking Soda in the refrigerator or freezer absorbs odors for up to 3 months.

- Fill a small bowl with Folgers Instant Coffee Crystals and place it on a back shelf in your refrigerator or freezer to control odor buildup.

- If you're going away for the weekend, deodorize your fridge while you're gone. Just pour some clean Fresh Step cat litter onto a cookie sheet and place it on the middle shelf of the fridge. Discard upon your return.

- To remove odors from a garbage disposal, cut up a lemon, toss it in, and grind it up. Oranges and limes also work to freshen the disposal.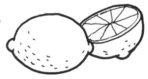

- Remove odors from your garbage disposal by pouring Clorox Regular-Bleach down the drain. Then run hot water for 2 minutes.

- Neutralize odors in your garbage disposal with 20 Mule Team Borax. Sprinkle 2 to 3 tablespoons borax into the drain; let stand for 15 minutes or more. Run cold water and turn on the disposal.

Must and Mildew

◆ Deodorize a canvas bag or any bag that has developed a musty smell by sprinkling the inside with Morton Salt, zipping up the bag, and letting it sit overnight. Shake out the salt in the morning and allow bag to air out.

◆ An old trunk can smell mighty musty. To get rid of the odor, haul the trunk outside for some sunlight and fresh air. Pour a light layer of Clabber Girl Baking Powder in the bottom and close the lid. Every few days, sweep out the old and sprinkle on some new powder. Repeat until the smell is gone.

◆ If that old trunk smells stale and musty when you open it, empty it out and give it a little fresh air. Let it sit outside in the sunshine, open wide, for several hours. When you bring the trunk inside, sprinkle a layer of Fresh Step cat litter on the bottom and close the lid. Replace the litter every other day until the odor is gone.

◆ To clean musty items such as old postcards, magazines, sheet music, and books, place the items in a paper bag with some Clabber Girl Baking Powder. Seal bag and change powder every few days until odor disappears.

◆ You can refresh musty old magazines found in cellars or garages if the pages aren't stuck together. Just lay the magazines out in the sun for a day. Then sprinkle ARM & HAMMER Baking Soda on the pages and let sit for an hour or so. Brush off.

- Dry out the moisture in a damp book by sprinkling the pages with Argo Corn Starch and letting it sit overnight. Brush out the corn starch in the morning.

- Argo Corn Starch even works on mildewed books. Cover the mildew spots with corn starch and let sit for a few days. Brush off the powder *outdoors,* so the mildew spores won't find a new home in your home.

- If you own a summer cabin or other building that will be shut up for a long period of time, prevent damp, musty odors from taking over while you're gone by filling shallow boxes with Fresh Step cat litter and storing one in each room of the house.

- Reduce the dampness and prevent mildew in a closet or basement with white Crayola chalk. Tie together 12 sticks with a string or put several sticks in a No nonsense knee high (or the foot of a pair of pantyhose). Hang the chalk in the damp area; replace every few months.

- Nonclumping Fresh Step cat litter will freshen up musty-smelling items, such as books or old magazines. Put the items in a paper bag; carefully pour in about 1 cup litter. Check on the progress and replace the litter every other day till the job's done.

Odds 'n Ends Odors

◆ Control odor from a pet accident by leaving a thin layer of ARM & HAMMER Baking Soda on the affected area after cleaning. Vacuum when dry.

◆ To remove urine odors from mattresses and mattress covers, dampen affected area with clear water and sprinkle 20 Mule Team Borax on it. Rub in to saturate area; let dry completely. Brush away or vacuum dried borax.

◆ If the mattress from your water bed develops a musty odor, rinse it inside and out with a solution of 4 tablespoons ARM & HAMMER Baking Soda per 1 quart warm water. Refill as usual. Use an O-Cel-O sponge to gently scrub the outside of the mattress with the solution.

◆ To keep smoke odors under control, always keep a bit of ARM & HAMMER Baking Soda in an ashtray.

◆ A closet with bare wood floors can begin to smell stale. To freshen the whole closet, lightly mop the floor with a mixture of 1 cup ARM & HAMMER Baking Soda and ½ cup Heinz Vinegar in 1 gallon warm water.

◆ Tuck Downy dryer sheets under your chair or couch cushions to help freshen furniture.

◆ Pack a Downy dryer sheet in your suitcase or gym bag. It will protect your clean clothes from the odors of your dirty ones.

◆ Deodorize a closet by placing a shallow box of Fresh Step cat litter on the floor—even if you don't have a cat. Keep the door shut. In a few days, the air should be fresher.

◆ Turn your closet into a cedar closet. Fill a large GLAD Food Storage Zipper Bag almost to the top with cedar chips (available at pet stores). Seal the bag and poke small holes all over both sides. Hang it in your closet.

◆ Make a sachet for dresser drawers: Pour potpourri into the toe portion of No nonsense pantyhose or knee highs. Tie a knot right above the potpourri and cut off the remainder of the hosiery.

◆ The enticing aroma of herbal tea suits a sachet perfectly. Choose your favorite flavor or scent, open a tea bag or two, and pour the leaves into No nonsense pantyhose or knee highs. Tie a knot right above the tea and cut off the remainder of the hosiery.

◆ Fill the toes of an old pair of pantyhose with ARM & HAMMER Baking Soda, cut off the legs, and tie to secure. Hang the sachets anywhere musty odors linger.

◆ To keep dressers, sideboards, and linen closets smelling nice, grab a few new, unwrapped

You Call That Clean, Soldier?

The first known use of the military phrase "spit and polish," indicating the extra effort exerted to get an article clean, was recorded in 1895.

bars of Ivory Soap. Wrap each in Kleenex facial tissue and place them in drawers and on shelves.

◆ Fill a snack- or sandwich-size GLAD Food Storage Zipper Bag with potpourri. Seal it and poke several small holes to make an effective yet inexpensive sachet for your dresser drawers.

◆ Add 4 teaspoons ReaLemon Lemon Juice to the water in your humidifier to eliminate stale odors.

TOTS 'N TOYS

◆ Sprinkle ARM & HAMMER Baking Soda on a damp O-Cel-O sponge to wipe down cribs, changing tables, baby mattresses, and playpens. Rinse areas thoroughly and allow to dry.

◆ Remove odors from cloth strollers or car seats by sprinkling ARM & HAMMER Baking Soda on the fabric. Wait 15 minutes (longer for strong odors) and vacuum.

◆ Use ARM & HAMMER Baking Soda directly on metal, plastic, or vinyl strollers, car seats, and high chairs. Scrub using a damp O-Cel-O sponge. Rinse and wipe dry.

◆ Accidents happen, especially during potty training. In lieu of a plastic or rubber mattress pad, place several sheets of Reynolds Wrap Aluminum Foil across the width of a mattress. Cover them with a beach towel or two, then put on a cloth mattress pad and bottom sheet.

- To remove urine from a mattress, first blot dry with a towel or rag. Then sprinkle area with ARM & HAMMER Baking Soda. Let dry thoroughly, then vacuum.

- Clean and deodorize vinyl toys with a solution of 1 tablespoon ARM & HAMMER Baking Soda per cup of water. Wash toys with a damp cloth or O-Cel-O sponge, rinse, and dry. For tough stain removal, sprinkle baking soda directly on a damp O-Cel-O sponge and scrub. Bring a small spray bottle of this same baking soda solution with you on outings with baby for quick cleanups.

- Disinfect baby toys by cleaning them with a splash of Heinz Vinegar added to hot water or by soaking them in a dishpan of hot water and ½ cup Heinz Distilled White Vinegar.

- Cloth toys can get grungy. To clean without water, sprinkle on ARM & HAMMER Baking Soda as a dry shampoo; let sit 15 minutes, then brush off.

- Deodorize really smelly stuffed animals by placing them in a paper bag, adding ARM & HAMMER Baking Soda, and shaking the closed bag vigorously. Store in bag overnight. If necessary, change the baking soda and repeat until odor is gone.

- Here's another method for cleaning stuffed animals or other cuddlies: Place a toy or a few small ones into a medium to large plastic bag. Add some Argo Corn Starch to the bag, close tightly, and shake. Brush the toys clean.

WHO-KNOWS-WHEN-YOU'LL-NEED-'EM HINTS

◆ A balled-up pair of No nonsense pantyhose can serve as a nonscratch pad to scrub walls, windows, sinks, and bathtubs.

◆ If you run out of paper towels, Melitta Basket Coffee Filters can fill in and help mop up spills.

◆ Don't let those unreachable cobwebs way up there get you down. Wrap a Penn tennis ball in a dust rag; secure it with a few rubber bands. Assuming the room is free of breakables, toss the ball at the webs.

◆ If you're planning to wear rubber gloves for any cleaning task, first pour a little Argo Corn Starch into your palm and rub your hands together to make the gloves easier to slide on.

◆ Sprinkling Clabber Girl Baking Powder into rubber gloves is another way to ensure they'll come right off when your work is done.

◆ Put a rubber band around each spray bottle and other cleaning-product containers. Tuck an O-Cel-O sponge or clean cloth under the band so you'll always have one at hand.

◆ Old Reach toothbrushes work well to clean combs, silver-ware, and tile grout.

- Remove adhesives, tape, glue, rubber cement, and labels from virtually all surfaces—even paint—with WD-40.

- Use a bit of Crisco All-Vegetable Shortening to remove a label, price tag, or adhesive residue from glass, metal, and most kinds of plastic. Just cover the area with shortening. After 10 minutes, carefully scrub it clean with an O-Cel-O No-Scratch Scrub Sponge.

- With the help of WD-40, chewing gum can be removed from all manner of things, including hair, dryer lint screens, bed linens, linoleum floors, and aluminum siding.

- Use a Post-it Note to clean a keyboard—whether piano or computer! Run the sticky side between the keys to pick up crumbs and lint.

- Clean smudges off the frame of your computer monitor with a Rite Aid cotton ball slightly dampened with Heinz Vinegar (do not saturate). *Do not touch the cotton ball to the computer screen.* This also works for keyboard smudges.

- Crest toothpaste can restore scratched CDs and DVDs! Squirt some paste on the shiny side and, working straight out from the center rather than following the circular grooves, gently work it into the surface with a Q-tips cotton swab. Wait 5 minutes, then rinse in cold running water. Dry with a soft, clean cloth. Deep scratches may not be removed entirely but will definitely be lessened.

- Split open the seams of one or two GLAD trash bags; place on the floor under a high chair. Why spend money on an expensive store-bought drop cloth?

- Cleaning tools with long handles or hoses—such as vacuum cleaner accessories, dryer vent cleaners, and ceiling fan dusters—are cumbersome to store. An old pair of No nonsense pantyhose can "handle" the job. Hang a pair on a nail or hook, then slide the tools into the legs. If a tool has an extra-long handle, cut a very small hole in a toe of the pantyhose and insert it through the hole. The rest of the tool will stay in the leg.

Maybe Cold Weather Does Clear the Mind

1902: The Minnesota Mining and Manufacturing Co. (3M) is founded in Two Harbors, Minnesota, on Lake Superior. It soon moves to Duluth, MN, and focuses on sandpaper.

1910: The company moves to St. Paul; 6 years later it pays its first dividend (6 cents per share).

Early 1920s: 3M develops the first waterproof sandpaper.

1925: A young 3M lab assistant invents masking tape.

1930: 3M invents Scotch cellophane tape to seal boxes; hundreds of other uses are soon discovered.

1940s: 3M creates defense materials, then Scotchlite Reflective Sheeting (highway markings), magnetic sound-recording tape, filament adhesive tape, and offset printing plates.

1950s and 1960s: Inventions include Thermo-Fax copying process, Scotchgard Fabric Protector, video-tape, Scotch-Brite Cleaning Pads, dry-silver microfilm, carbonless papers, and products for overhead projectors.

1980: 3M introduces Post-it Notes nationwide.

Chapter 2: Laundry & Clothing Care

WASH AND WEAR: FACT OR FICTION?

The world of washday and wardrobe can be a world of surprises: a suspiciously "fragrant" hamper, stains of frightening intensity, brand-new dress shoes that squeeze the life out of your feet...

Say hello to some good surprises. You'll do a double take when your laundry list directs you to nondetergent aisles of the store. Ditto as you detour to the medicine cabinet on your way to the laundry room.

Common kitchen products work to freshen, clean, remove odors, and boost the power of other laundry and clothing-care products. They can save you money and hassle and do their part to save the environment from caustic chemicals.

Check out the care instructions on your favorite shirt. See any symbols for hairspray, cola, sandpaper, chalk, or molasses? No, probably not. Well, picture them on the label because they'll get a workout in the laundry room too.

Uncommon Commoners

It's hardly a shock to see bleach, ammonia, and borax help with the laundry. What is unexpected is the variety of new ways this trio—and other common household chemicals—helps you clean and care for your clothes.

Out of stain remover? Reach for the aspirin. Clothes slipping off their hangers? Head for the office supplies. Scorched a shirt you were ironing? Call for corn starch.

These everyday products have you covered.

A LOAD OF BASICS

Notes: Never use vinegar on dry-clean-only fabrics. It's always a good idea to test the fabric for colorfastness before treating a stain.

◆ Use ARM & HAMMER Baking Soda instead of fabric softener. Add ½ cup during the rinse cycle.

◆ When washing cotton or washable wool blankets, add 2 cups Heinz Vinegar to the rinse cycle. This will help remove soap and make blankets soft and fluffy.

◆ Add ½ cup Heinz Vinegar to the rinse cycle of your wash to soften clothes.

◆ Out of fabric softener? Add 1 or 2 capfuls of Suave conditioner to your laundry's final rinse to make clothes softer and eliminate static.

Through the Wringer

The Maytag Company, originally a farm-equipment manufacturer, ventured into the home washing-machine business in 1907. The "Pastime" wringer washer was a wooden tub equipped with a dolly in the lid and turned by a hand crank. Four years later a model with an electric motor hit the market, then came one with a gasoline engine for rural homemakers without electricity. Over the decades, improvements included an aluminum wash basin and an agitator in the bottom of the tub. Maytag's first automatic washer, the AMP, was introduced in 1949. The company discontinued production of wringer washers in 1983.

◆ Washing clothes in hard water can leave them looking dingy and feeling scratchy. Adding ½ cup 20 Mule Team Borax to a load will help soften the water and preserve your wardrobe.

- To brighten colored clothes that can't tolerate chlorine bleach, add ½ cup ARM & HAMMER Baking Soda or ½ cup 20 Mule Team Borax to your wash along with your detergent. Then add ½ cup Heinz Vinegar to the final rinse.

- Any colored clothing item that has dulled can be brightened by soaking it in 1 gallon warm water and 1 cup Heinz Vinegar. Follow this with a clear water rinse.

- Take a product from the medicine cabinet to prevent non-colorfast items from fading and transferring color onto other items in a load. The first time a garment is washed, whether by itself or with same-color fabrics, add 1 teaspoon Rite Aid Epsom salts per gallon of wash water.

- Add ½ cup ARM & HAMMER Baking Soda (only ¼ cup for front-loading machines) with the usual amount of Clorox Regular-Bleach to increase whitening power.

- If your good ol' black cotton T-shirts have faded to dark brown or eggplant from frequent washings, add 1 cup strong Lipton tea to the rinse cycle next time. They'll be restored to their original glory.

- White fabric will look even whiter if you soak it overnight in a mixture of ½ cup Cascade automatic dishwashing detergent and 1 gallon warm water. Launder as usual, but add ½ cup Heinz Distilled White Vinegar to the final rinse.

- Whiten yellowed linens by dropping 1 or 2 Polident denture cleanser tablets in a tub of warm water and soaking the fabric overnight.

- Boil yellowed cotton or linen fabrics in a mixture of water, 1 tablespoon Morton Salt, and ¼ cup ARM & HAMMER Baking Soda. Soak for 1 hour, then launder as usual.

- Yellowed linens can be brightened by adding 4 tablespoons ARM & HAMMER Baking Soda to the wash water.

- For a super whitening mix, dissolve ½ cup Cascade automatic dishwashing detergent in 1 gallon warm water and add ½ cup Clorox Regular-Bleach. Soak whites for 1 to 8 hours (the longer the better), then launder as usual.

- Bleach soiled handkerchiefs by soaking them for a few hours in a solution of warm water and 1 tablespoon McCormick Cream of Tartar. Soak especially dingy hankies for about an hour in a sink of water with 1 tablespoon cream of tartar and 2 teaspoons Tide laundry detergent. Wash as usual.

- A good way to control static cling is to add ½ cup Heinz Vinegar to the last rinse cycle of your wash. This will reduce lint buildup and keep pet hair from clinging to clothing.

- When you take a load of laundry out of the dryer, spray the whole pile with Static Guard. Then toss the clothes as you would a salad. The clinging items separate easily.

- A few Penn tennis balls tumbling around in the dryer will be somewhat noisy…but very effective for reducing static cling. Toss them in with a load of clothes and set the dryer on low heat.

- Lint won't stick to your clothes while they're tumbling in the dryer if you toss in a pair of No nonsense pantyhose with them.

How Does Static Guard Work?

In 1978, the Alberto-Culver Company patented an antistatic spray that soon became available to consumers under the name "Static Guard." The spray keeps electrical charges from accumulating on fabric, carpets and rugs, bedding, and even hairbrushes, reducing static cling or static shock. How? Static Guard neutralizes the charges on a surface and attracts humidity from the air. Many hair conditioners, lotions, and moisturizers contain ingredients to accomplish these same functions.

- To hand-wash your delicates, dissolve ¼ cup 20 Mule Team Borax and 1 to 2 tablespoons Tide laundry detergent in a basin of warm water. Soak the items for 10 minutes, then rinse in clear, cool water. Blot with a towel. To dry, lay flat or hang away from sunlight and direct heat.

- When washing delicate items by hand, follow garment's care instructions and add 1 or 2 tablespoons Heinz Vinegar to the last rinse to help remove soap residue.

- Rinse pool chlorine out of bathing suits in a sink full of water with 1 tablespoon ARM & HAMMER Baking Soda added.

◆ Even if the tag says "dry-clean only," some items can be cleaned with a solution of 4 tablespoons ARM & HAMMER Baking Soda in a sink of cold water. Test for colorfastness first.

◆ Many clothing items labeled "dry-clean only"—including silk, angora, cashmere, chiffon, and lace pieces—can be washed by hand in cold water with a few drops of clear Dawn dish-washing liquid. Carefully work the suds through the garment (never wring, twist, tug, or pull at it); rinse clean with cold water. Dry flat on a clean white towel.

◆ Suave conditioner does a nice job on a silk shirt—even one that thinks it's nonwashable. Fill a sink with water (cold for colors; warm for whites); add 1 tablespoon conditioner and swish around to mix. Place the shirt in the sink and let it sit for about 5 minutes. Rinse under cold running water. Hang to dry.

◆ Here's a handy tip from a professional launderer: Use Ivory Liquid Hand Cleanser instead of those expensive products that say "for fine washables." Ivory is gentle and cleans just as well.

◆ Prevent nylon items from yellowing by adding ARM & HAMMER Baking Soda to both the wash and rinse water.

That's One Way to Do the Laundry!

The story goes that a French sailor of the early 1800s fell into a vat of turpentine, a common chemical on ships. When his uniform dried, it was spick-and-span...and thus the dry-cleaning industry was born.

- Keep white nylon curtains white by soaking them in a solution of ½ cup ARM & HAMMER Baking Soda in 1 gallon water.

- Clean suede with ARM & HAMMER Baking Soda applied with a soft brush. Let it sit, then brush it off.

- Give the sheer curtains in your home a permanent-press finish. Just add a packet of Knox unflavored gelatin to some hot water and pour the mixture into the washing machine's final rinse.

- When hand-washing nylon pantyhose, add 1 tablespoon Heinz Vinegar to rinse water to help them last longer.

- Add a cup of Heinz Distilled White Vinegar to your last rinse water when dyeing fabrics. This will help set the color.

- You can reclaim a chamois that has hardened from being wet and drying out. Add 1 tablespoon Crisco Pure Vegetable Oil to a pan of water and soak the chamois in it.

- To put body back into your permanent-press clothes, dissolve Carnation Instant Nonfat Dry Milk in some water and add to the final rinse of your washing machine.

- Did your good wool sweater go through the wash by mistake? All might not be lost. Soak the sweater in tepid water and add a squirt of Suave shampoo. The fibers may be softened enough that you can rescue the sweater. Gently stretch and reshape it; lay flat to dry.

- If you accidentally put too much soap in your washing machine, kill the suds by adding a capful of Final Touch fabric softener to the load.

- Down to the dregs of your laundry detergent? Use ½ cup or less of Suave shampoo per load—this works especially well with delicates.

- Save energy (your own!) en route to the Laundromat by premeasuring detergents or other products into plastic tubs or GLAD Food Storage Zipper Bags.

Suds Shops

The idea of public laundry—initially "take-in" laundry done by an attendant—began in the late 1920s. Actual self-service coin laundries came on the scene in the 1950s. Today, according to the Coin Laundry Association, there are approximately 35,000 laundries in the United States; slightly more than 70 percent are single-store operations.

- Opening a detergent box with a pour spout can be hazardous to your fingernails. Use a "church key" bottle opener—the flat end will probably work best.

THE NOSE KNOWS

- Clothes can be deodorized by adding ½ cup ARM & HAMMER Baking Soda to the rinse cycle.

- Deodorize your musty-smelling bath towels by adding ½ cup ARM & HAMMER Baking Soda to the rinse cycle of the washing machine.

Homemade Fabric-Deodorizing Spray

2 cups Final Touch fabric softener
2 cups ARM & HAMMER Baking Soda
4 cups warm water

Mix the ingredients; pour into a spray bottle. Shake well. Use spray to eliminate odors from clothing, upholstered furniture, carpets and rugs, curtains, automobile seats, and more.

◆ Remove the smell of cigarette smoke from clothes by soaking them in a solution of 4 tablespoons ARM & HAMMER Baking Soda and 1 quart water before washing.

◆ Eliminate the stale smell in stored-away hand-washables by soaking them in a solution of 4 tablespoons ARM & HAMMER Baking Soda and 1 quart water. Rinse well, squeeze, then air-dry.

◆ Forgot to transfer the clothes from the washer to the dryer and now they smell sour? Put them through the wash again, but this time with no detergent—just a tablespoon of Parsons' Ammonia. Or rewash the clothes with a cup of Heinz Vinegar added to the rinse cycle to get rid of the mildewy smell.

◆ Keep matching bed linens together…and keep them smelling sweet. Before you store them in the linen closet, place a folded sheet set inside its matching pillowcase. Add a new Downy dryer sheet to keep the sheets smelling fresh.

STAIN, BE GONE!

Pretreatment

◆ Use equal parts water and Heinz Vinegar to pretreat common stains on clothing. Spray mixture on stains before washing to give an extra boost.

◆ To pretreat virtually all tough clothing stains, combine ½ cup Heinz Vinegar, ½ cup Parsons' Ammonia, ½ cup ARM & HAMMER Baking Soda, 2 squirts Ivory Liquid Hand Cleanser, and 2 quarts water. Keep solution in a clearly labeled spray bottle and use when needed.

Tennis Whites

Scientists at 3M were working on a new type of rubber for jet aircraft fuel lines when some spilled on a lab assistant's tennis shoes. She couldn't wash it off, but her tennies stayed nice and clean. The year was 1944, and Scotchgard was born.

◆ Pretreat a tough stain before washing by sprinkling Cascade automatic dishwashing detergent on the spot and scrubbing with an old Reach toothbrush dipped in water.

◆ Why buy an expensive stain-remover stick? Instead, save the slivers and ends from bars of Ivory Soap. Moisten a piece with a drop of water, apply to a fresh stain, and toss the article of clothing in the hamper.

◆ Pretreat collar stains on shirts with Argo Corn Starch. Dampen collar, rub a little in, and launder as usual.

General Stains and Mildew

◆ Equal parts Clorox Regular-Bleach and milk can take stains out of old linens. Make a small quantity of the solution, dip a Rite Aid cotton ball in it, and gently dab the stains. When the spots are gone, launder as usual. This treatment also works on discoloration lines that form on the folds of long-stored linens.

◆ For tough stains—including mildew—make a thin paste of ReaLemon Lemon Juice and Morton Salt. Apply to the stain, set the item in the sun to dry, then wash as usual.

◆ Here's another method to get rid of mildew: A mixture of Morton Salt, Heinz Distilled White Vinegar, and water should remove mildew stains on most fabrics. Use up to full-strength vinegar if mildew is extensive.

◆ To remove a food stain (whether fresh or dried-on) from a washable item of clothing, use club soda. First, blot the spill by pressing lightly with a Scott Towel. Then sponge the fabric with Canada Dry Club Soda and launder as usual.

◆ If a bit of deodorant has gotten on an item of clothing, rub it off with a piece of No nonsense pantyhose.

Color Transfer

◆ Add ½ cup Morton Salt to wash cycle to prevent colored fabrics from running.

- Prevent colors from bleeding by adding 1 cup Heinz Vinegar to the wash along with Tide laundry detergent.

- Has color transferred from one item of clothing to another? Don't dry it yet! If the fabric is safe for bleach, immediately rewash it with a little Clorox Regular-Bleach. More than one rewashing may be necessary, but this method should yield success—as long as you don't set the color by drying the item.

- If you have stained your white clothes by washing them with colored ones, undo the damage by soaking them in warm water to which you have added ARM & HAMMER Baking Soda, Morton Salt, and Tide laundry detergent.

When All Else Fails...

According to the Soap and Detergent Association:

- ◆ 49 percent of adults report that they have never read the directions on a laundry detergent package.

- ◆ 35 percent of adults sometimes read the directions on a new product; 16 percent always read them.

- ◆ 60 percent of women have read the directions at least once, versus only 42 percent of men.

Beverages

- Eliminate alcohol stains with a paste of ARM & HAMMER Baking Soda and Parsons' Ammonia. Be sure to wear rubber gloves and use this mixture in a well-ventilated area. Test for colorfastness first. Dry the treated fabric in the sun, then wash as usual.

- Remove a wine spill from cotton fabric by immediately sprinkling stained area with enough Morton Salt to soak up liquid. Soak fabric for 1 hour in cold water, then launder as usual.

- A red wine stain yields to Canada Dry Club Soda. If the spot is still wet, blot it with a Scott Towel. Pour on a generous amount of club soda; rub gently with another paper towel or an O-Cel-O sponge. Repeat if necessary.

- To remove tough juice stains, dilute ReaLemon Lemon Juice or Heinz Distilled White Vinegar with water. Soak the stain in this solution, then wash as usual.

- Dried-on red juice may be removed from bleach-safe garments by soaking in a solution of 1 part Heinz Vinegar and 2 parts water. Wash as usual.

- Brand-new coffee or tea drips should be removed easily with lots of cold water on a damp cloth (if fabric is not dry-clean only). For coffee or tea stains that have set, soak item in a solution of 1 part Heinz Vinegar and 2 parts water, then hang in the sun to dry.

Bleach

- One bleach-spot fix is to mix McCormick Food Color until you have a matching shade, paint solution on spot, and let dry.

- Those hard-to-fix bleach spots on clothes might be fixable with a Crayola Crayon. Pick a matching color, warm the fabric with an iron, and color the spot. Cover it with Reynolds Cut-Rite Wax Paper and iron on low to set the color.

Blood

- To remove a bloodstain, dampen the area with water and rub with ARM & HAMMER Baking Soda. Follow by dabbing with Rite Aid hydrogen peroxide until the stain is gone. Test for colorfastness first.

- You can also get rid of a bloodstain by applying a paste of Argo Corn Starch and water to the stain right away. Let dry, then brush off. Repeat if necessary. This works on clothing and linens.

- Clean a fresh bloodstain with Rite Aid hydrogen peroxide. Dab on the peroxide, then blot off, repeating as necessary. Test a hidden area first to be sure the fabric is colorfast.

- Soak bloodstained cotton, linen, or other natural-fiber fabrics in cold salt water for 1 hour. Wash using warm water and Tide laundry detergent. If the stain is still present, boil item in a large kettle if the fabric can withstand this. Wash again.

- A fresh bloodstain should disappear easily if it is immediately covered with Morton Salt and blotted with cold water. Keep adding fresh water and blotting until stain is gone.

- To remove a fresh bloodstain, immediately blot up (don't rub) as much of the stain as possible with a Scott Towel. Pour cold Canada Dry Club Soda on the stain; blot up the liquid. Repeat until stain disappears.

- Remove bloodstains from clothing or furniture with a paste of Johnson's Baby Powder and water. Apply to spot; let dry and brush away.

- Dried bloodstains can be difficult to remove. Try soaking the fabric in a solution of 2 tablespoons Parsons' Ammonia per gallon of cold water. When the stain has faded, wash fabric in cold water and Dawn dishwashing liquid.

Chocolate

- Chocolate stains melt away in the face of undiluted Parsons' Ammonia. Scrub the stained area, then wash as usual.

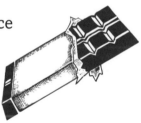

Grass

- Revive grass-stained clothes or sneakers with molasses. Rub a little Grandma's Original Molasses into any stains; let sit overnight. Wash item with a mild soap—not laundry detergent.

- Remove severe grass stains from white clothes by soaking in undiluted Heinz Vinegar for a half hour before washing.

Grease

◆ Rub ARM & HAMMER Baking Soda into polyester fabrics to remove a grease spot. Brush off, and the stain should be gone.

◆ A grease stain can sometimes be removed by rubbing Johnson's Baby Powder or Argo Corn Starch into it. Allow the powder or corn starch to sit for an hour or more to soak up the grease, then brush off and wash as usual. If stain remains, repeat until it's gone.

◆ To remove a fresh grease spill on fabric, cover with Morton Salt or Quaker Yellow Corn Meal and allow it to absorb as much of the mess as possible. Repeat until spot is gone. Brush off and launder.

◆ Double-knit fabrics can be a special stain challenge when it comes to grease. Add ½ teaspoon Morton Salt to a small dish of Parsons' Ammonia and dab mixture directly onto grease spot. Let sit, then wash as usual.

This May Go on Your Permanent Record

What are the toughest stains kids and teens bring home from school? Parents surveyed chose grass, food, and mud.

◆ Try covering a fresh gravy stain with Morton Salt and letting it absorb as much of the grease as possible. A stubborn stain may require dabbing and blotting with a solution of equal parts Parsons' Ammonia and Heinz Vinegar until it disappears.

- Pour Pepsi or Canada Dry Club Soda directly on a grease spot. Let it sit for a few minutes to loosen the stain, then wash as usual.

- If a load of clothes is particularly greasy, add a can of Pepsi to the wash cycle along with Tide laundry detergent.

- Even a grease stain is no match for chalk, as long as the fabric is washable. Rub the spot with a stick of white Crayola chalk. After the grease has been absorbed by the chalk, launder as usual with Tide laundry detergent.

- Remove grease from suede by dipping a cloth in Heinz Vinegar and gently sponging stain. Let dry completely, then use a fine brush to restore nap in suede.

Ink

- Remove an ink stain from leather by laying the item flat and sprinkling ARM & HAMMER Baking Soda on the stain. Leave on until ink is absorbed, brush off, and repeat if necessary.

- Ink stains or scuff marks on suede clothing or shoes can be removed—or at least minimized—with fine-grit 3M sandpaper. Sand with a light touch, then use an old Reach toothbrush or a nailbrush to restore the nap afterward.

- Rub Morton Salt onto a fresh ink stain, then soak fabric overnight in milk. Depending on the stain and the fabric,

complete removal can take from
30 minutes to overnight. Launder as
usual.

◆ Many ink stains respond to a solution
of 1 teaspoon Clorox Regular-Bleach in
1 cup water. Test for colorfastness first!
Apply with a Q-tips cotton swab.

◆ On laundry day, squeeze a bit of Crest
toothpaste on ink stains and then scrub
with an old Reach toothbrush or rub the
fabric together. (The same treatment
with Crest toothpaste can help remove such stains as lipstick,
makeup, and grass.) Stubborn stains may require more than
one scrubbing. Rinse clean, then launder as usual.

◆ To remove an ink stain, spray Suave hairspray on the spot
and blot with a Scott Towel. Repeat until ink is gone. Dab
with Heinz Vinegar to remove the sticky spray.

A Full Caseload

Don't lug all those
boxes and bottles
to the Laundromat.
Instead, put a load of
laundry into a pillow-
case, then pour in
the right amount of
powdered detergent
and bleach for the
load. Just dump it all
into the washer!

Lipstick

◆ A lipstick stain on silk sounds like an automatic bill from the
dry cleaner. Try this method instead. Place a piece of Scotch
Magic Tape or Masking Tape on the spot, then pull it off. If
some of the lipstick remains, sprinkle on some Johnson's Baby
Powder or crushed Crayola chalk. With a clean cloth, dab until
both the powder and the lipstick vanish.

- Using a clean white cloth, dab a lipstick stain with a small amount of Rite Aid isopropyl rubbing alcohol. (Be sure to blot, not rub.) Gently coat the stain with a bit of Tide liquid laundry detergent on your finger. Launder as normal. Before drying, check to see if the stain is gone. Repeat if necessary.

- Spray a lipstick stain with Suave hairspray and allow it to sit for 10 minutes. Wipe with a clean, damp cloth. Repeat if needed, then launder as usual.

- Another way to remove a lipstick stain is to rub a few drops of Dawn dishwashing liquid into the stain. Let the detergent soak in for about an hour; launder as usual.

Oil and Tar

- Oil stain got you stumped? Dip a wedge of lime in Morton Salt and rub the spot. Launder as usual.

- Tar stains are among the toughest to remove from clothing. Before laundering a tar-stained garment, scrape off as much of the tar as you can, then apply a small amount of Crisco All-Vegetable Shortening to the area. Let sit 3 hours; launder as usual.

Paint

- Think those oil-based paint spots will never come out of your clothes? If the item is washable, pour a mixture of equal parts turpentine and Parsons' Ammonia on the spots. Let soak overnight, then launder as usual.

- To remove oil-based paint—even if it has set for a while—from cotton or silk, heat a few cups of Heinz Vinegar in a saucepan. Place the stained area of the garment over a large bowl and pull it taut. When the vinegar comes to a boil, pour it over the stain. The paint will be gone, but the cloth won't be damaged.

Rust

- Adding 1 cup ReaLemon Lemon Juice to the washing machine along with Tide laundry detergent may help reduce rust stains on your clothes.

- Conquer rust stains with this treatment. Wet the stained area with ReaLemon Lemon Juice; hold it directly over the steam from a pot of boiling water for a few minutes. Rinse well.

- Make a thin paste of Heinz Distilled White Vinegar and Morton Salt and spread paste on a rust stain in fabric. Lay item out in the sun to bleach it. Alternatively, apply paste, stretch fabric over a large kettle, and pour boiling water through stained area. In both cases, allow item to dry, then check stain. Run item through the rinse cycle in your washing machine and check stain again. Repeat treatment if any stain remains.

◆ To remove a rust mark on fabric, dampen the spot and rub McCormick Cream of Tartar into it. Wait 1 hour, then wash as usual. Repeat if necessary.

Sweat

◆ Those yellow stains in the armpits and around the collars of your favorite white T-shirts aren't a sign that you're sweating too much or not cleaning properly. These areas are just harder to get clean and are made up of more than just old perspiration and dirt. Plus, if you have hard water, the deodorant residue (and soap and perspiration) won't wash out properly. Here's one method for attacking these problem stains: Mix 1 quart water with 4 tablespoons Morton Salt. Sponge this mixture onto stained areas; repeat until stains disappear. Launder as usual.

◆ Pretreat perspiration stains by blotting on a solution of 1 teaspoon Parsons' Ammonia and 2 cups cold water. Launder with Clorox 2 Stain Fighter & Color Booster.

◆ Rite Aid aspirin can remove perspiration stains from white fabrics. Dissolve 2 tablets in ½ cup of warm water and apply to the stain. Let it sit for about 2 hours before laundering.

◆ For perspiration stains, scrub on a paste of ARM & HAMMER Baking Soda and water; let sit for 1 hour, then launder as usual.

- Try soaking white shirts and T-shirts in undiluted Heinz Vinegar to get rid of yellow stains in the armpits and around the collar. Let the item sit in the vinegar for 15 to 20 minutes, then launder as usual.

- Treat stubborn perspiration stains around the collar with a paste of 4 tablespoons ARM & HAMMER Baking Soda and ¼ cup water. Rub in, add a little Heinz Distilled White Vinegar to the collar, and wash.

- Rub a paste of Heinz Vinegar and ARM & HAMMER Baking Soda into collar grime using a Reach toothbrush. Saturate and let sit before laundering.

- Draw out the sweat stain from the collar of a shirt with white Crayola chalk. Rub the chalk right on the ring; launder as usual with Tide laundry detergent.

- Remove ring-around-the-collar by pouring Suave shampoo along the collar and allowing it to soak into the ring. Let it sit—the longer the better—then wash.

- The grease-cutting agents in Dawn dishwashing liquid can also help remove the sweat and grime around shirt collars. Paint on, let sit, then launder.

Wax

- Remove crayon marks on clothing by rubbing gently with ARM & HAMMER Baking Soda sprinkled on a damp cloth.

- If you've accidentally washed a crayon with a load of clothes, rewash the load with the hottest possible water, adding a half to a full box of ARM & HAMMER Baking Soda. Repeat if necessary.

- Remove candle wax from fabric such as clothing or table linens by putting a Scott Towel or a brown paper bag over the spot. Press with an iron on a low heat setting (keep the iron in one place) for several seconds. The wax will be absorbed by the paper and the iron will remain clean.

- Or try an alternative wax-removing method that works on many fabrics, including carpets and rugs. Hold an ice cube on the wax until it's very hard, then gently pick and scrape it off. When working with nonwashable materials, put a cube or two in a GLAD Food Storage Zipper Bag beforehand.

DYEING FABRIC

- To dye fabrics brown, soak them in a bath of strong Folgers coffee. Repeat until desired shade is reached. Rinse in cold water.

- If you just can't get those dingy whites clean, don't discard them. Strong, hot Lipton tea is the perfect dye for natural-fiber fabric or yarn. Soak the material until it is a shade darker than desired (as it dries, it becomes lighter). Rinse in clear, cold water; allow to air-dry.

◆ Do you wish those brand-new white lace tablecloths, doilies, or curtains could match the family heirlooms you possess? Steep 6 Lipton Tea Bags per 1 quart boiling water for 20 minutes. Remove the bags; allow the tea to cool. Soak the new material for 10 minutes, then gently wring it out and hang it up to dry.

◆ Herbal teas can also dye fabrics. Go bold or subtle as you use, for example, hibiscus for red tones or licorice for soft brown. Always experiment on fabric scraps to get the results you want.

CARING FOR BABY CLOTHES

◆ Add ½ cup ARM & HAMMER Baking Soda to Tide powdered or liquid laundry detergent to freshen clothes and help improve the detergent's performance on baby food stains. If using powdered laundry detergent, add baking soda to the rinse cycle only.

◆ Remove chemical finishes from new baby clothes before baby wears them by washing them in mild soap and ½ cup ARM & HAMMER Baking Soda.

◆ A cup of Heinz Vinegar added to the rinse cycle when washing baby clothes will help eliminate odors and soften clothing.

◆ If your baby spits up on his shirt or yours, moisten a cloth, dip it in ARM & HAMMER Baking Soda, and dab at the spot. The odor will be controlled until the clothing can be changed.

- For tough stains on baby clothes, soak the items (colorfast only) in a bucket of water with ¼ cup Clorox Regular-Bleach added. Wait 10 minutes, rinse in clean water, then launder as usual.

- Get cloth diapers super clean, free of stains and odors, and more absorbent than before with 20 Mule Team Borax. Soak diapers as soon as possible in ½ cup borax for each diaper pail of warm water. When ready to wash, add ½ cup borax to recommended amount of Tide laundry detergent; machine wash in hot water.

IRONING OUT THE DETAILS

- What to do about water marks, calcium deposits, and scorched or melted gunk on the bottom plate of an iron? Be sure the appliance is cool, then apply a small quantity of Crest toothpaste, scrub with a rag, and wipe clean with a wet cloth. Finish the cleanup by heating the iron and rubbing it over an old piece of cloth.

- Remove mineral deposits in your iron (caused by tap water) by filling the water reservoir with equal parts water and Heinz Vinegar. Set iron on a high/steam setting and let it steam for a few minutes. Turn off iron and let it cool, then rinse water reservoir with fresh water.

- Remove cleaning-product residue from the vents of an electric iron (cool only) with a Q-tips cotton swab. For tough deposits, first dip the swab in Rite Aid isopropyl rubbing alcohol.

- When the plate of your iron needs cleaning, set the iron to low and rub it over a Downy dryer sheet until the gunk is gone.

- Rub away rusty brown spots on the bottom plate of your iron with some fine steel wool. Dip it first in warm Heinz Distilled White Vinegar.

- To remove that layer of built-up starch from your iron, turn it to a low heat setting and pass it over a piece of Reynolds Wrap Aluminum Foil.

Starch from Scratch

In 1853, the entrepreneurial Lautz family emigrated from northern Germany to the United States, settling in Buffalo, New York. Their business ventures included the Lautz Co., a leader in the marble industry; Lautz Bros. & Co., a soap manufacturer; and the Niagara Machine & Tool Works. Three of the brothers fought in the Civil War, returned to the family business, and in the 1880s cofounded both the Buffalo Symphony Orchestra and Niagara Starch Works. Today, Niagara Spray Starch is owned by Phoenix Brands of Stamford, Connecticut.

- When starch builds up on your iron, cut a piece from a brown paper grocery bag and sprinkle it with Morton Salt. Press the paper with the iron set on high heat (no steam).

- Fine table linens are much easier to iron if you first place them in a GLAD Food Storage Zipper Bag and refrigerate them for 6 to 24 hours. Remove them from the bag before ironing!

- To remove a crease in knit fabrics, dip a clean cloth in a solution of 1 part Heinz Distilled White Vinegar and 2 parts water; apply to the crease. Place a brown paper bag over crease and iron area.

- Reduce your ironing time by putting a piece of Reynolds Wrap Aluminum Foil under the ironing board cover. The foil will reflect heat; you'll actually be ironing both sides at once.

- An iron-on patch that will cover a hole in a garment can easily get stuck on the ironing board. Prevent this by putting a piece of Reynolds Wrap Aluminum Foil under the hole before you iron.

- Pleats will stay put when you attach a large paper clip angled across them before ironing. From the wrong side of the fabric, iron from top to bottom. Be sure not to iron the clips.

- Add a dash of Morton Salt to laundry starch to keep your iron from sticking to clothing. This will also help give a smooth finish to linens or fine cottons.

- You can make your own spray starch by dissolving 1 tablespoon Argo Corn Starch in 2 cups water. Use a clean spray bottle to dispense. For a heavier starch, use 2 or more tablespoons of corn starch.

- Remove iron scorches from clothes with Argo Corn Starch. Wet a scorched spot, then cover with corn starch. When it's dry, brush off.

- Keep your ironing board cover clean and durable for many, many loads of laundry. Spray the entire surface with Niagara Spray Starch and iron it in thoroughly on medium heat.

- Did your so-called wrinkle-free shirt come out of the dryer with wrinkles anyway? Try this trick: Turn on the iron to the appropriate setting for your fabric. Wrap an ice cube in a soft cloth; rub it over a wrinkle just before you iron it.

> ## Dryer Fire
>
> The U.S. Fire Administration reports that every year, clothes-dryer fires account for nearly 16,000 structure fires; 80 percent of these are in residential buildings. Operation deficiencies are the cause of almost half the dryer fires in residential buildings—topmost on the list is "failure to clean" lint from the traps, vents, and adjacent areas of the dryer.

- To make a perfect pleat when ironing, place a piece of fine- or medium-grit 3M sandpaper under the pleat; it will "grab" the fabric and hold it in place while you press the pleat.

WARDROBE WONDERS

- Some new clothes may be treated with a chemical that can be irritating to sensitive skin. Before wearing anything new, soak it in 1 gallon water with ½ cup Heinz Vinegar. Rinse. Then add ½ cup ARM & HAMMER Baking Soda to the wash load.

- Clean leather with a mixture of 1 cup boiled linseed oil and 1 cup Heinz Vinegar. Carefully apply to any spots with a soft cloth. Let dry.

- Suave conditioner cleans and conditions leather goods. Simply rub it on, then buff with a clean, soft cloth.

- To condition leather, rub some Alberto VO5 Conditioning Hairdressing into it.

- Your leather purse, handbag, or luggage has tried on some mildew for size. Listerine Antiseptic mouthwash can help. Pour a little on a cotton pad and rub the surface well. Wipe dry with a soft cotton cloth. Buff with a second cloth, followed by a commercial leather-reviving cream.

- Hide a spot on black or dark brown suede with a little brewed Folgers coffee, applied carefully with an O-Cel-O sponge.

- Disguise a spot on suede shoes or clothing by rubbing it with Crayola chalk of the same color.

- When you buy a new garment, dab the center of each button with clear Revlon Nail Enamel to seal the threads. The buttons will stay on longer.

- Loosen up stiff, rusted buckles on boots, snow gear, and other outdoor clothing and equipment by spraying with a little WD-40.

- Put a stop to a run in your pantyhose by dabbing the ends of the run with clear Revlon Nail Enamel.

Hosiery History

1940: DuPont introduces nylon stockings—an affordable alternative to silk—to the marketplace; 64 million pairs sold that year.

1942: Nylon goes to war, not only in parachutes and tents but also in stockings, the favorite gift of U.S. soldiers to British women. With nylons in short supply stateside, women draw lines down the backs of their legs to simulate seams.

1959: Pantyhose are invented and first sold by North Carolina company Glen Raven Mill.

1965: Glen Raven Mill reveals seamless pantyhose.

◆ To make pantyhose more resistant to running, first wash and dry a new pair as you normally would. Then immerse them in 1 gallon water with 2 cups Morton Salt added and let soak for 3 hours. Rinse in cool water; air-dry.

◆ To extend the life of a pair of pantyhose, add some Final Touch fabric softener to the final rinse when washing them.

◆ Fix those runs in your pantyhose or knee highs by spraying the area with Suave hairspray; let dry before wearing. Practice some preventive maintenance too: Spray the heels and toes of a new pair of pantyhose—especially the "sandal foot" kind without reinforced toes—with Suave hairspray.

◆ Keep a snag or a small run in your pantyhose from getting any worse. Cover it with a piece of Scotch Magic Tape.

◆ Paint the edges of a fraying garment with clear Revlon Nail Enamel.

- Keep buckles from chipping or tarnishing by painting them with clear Revlon Nail Enamel. This also helps keep buckles shiny.

- Put a dab of clear Revlon Nail Enamel over the knot on a small ribbon to keep it from coming untied.

- To attach buttons more securely, sew them on with Reach dental floss instead of thread. Just color the floss with a matching marker or crayon.

- Clean metal buttons with Crest toothpaste. Put a dab on the button and polish with a damp cloth; rinse, then dry well.

- To loosen a sticky zipper, rub Blistex Lip Balm up and down the length of it. Open and close the zipper a few times to distribute the lubricant.

- Apply a small amount of Gillette Foamy Shave Foam to a stuck zipper. Work it in, and your problem will soon be worked out.

- Using a Q-tips cotton swab, apply a bit of Colavita Extra Virgin Olive Oil to the teeth of a stuck zipper. Slowly work the tab down until it's free.

- Rub a corner of a bar of Ivory Soap into the teeth of a zipper that won't budge. Patiently work the zipper and let the soap's natural lubricants do their thing.

- Both Suave shampoo and Alberto VO5 Conditioning Hairdressing work well for fixing troublesome zippers. With a Q-tips cotton swab, dab a bit of either product right where the pull is stuck. Work the zipper a few times and your problem is solved.

- Starch is known for "keeping things together," but in this tip it takes on the opposite role. Aim a generous dose of Niagara Spray Starch at a stuck zipper to help it work its way loose.

- You can temporarily hold nonfusible interfacing in place with adhesive from an Elmer's Glue Stick. Instead of using pins and/or basting when making lapped seams, apply the glue to the underside of the overlapping section. Press in place, let dry 1 or 2 minutes, and topstitch.

- Fix a falling hem in a pinch with a length of Scotch Duct Tape. The tape is especially suited for heavy fabrics such as denim.

- You can replace a missing zipper tab with a paper clip or a safety pin. Dress it up with a piece of ribbon or yarn or a dollop of paint.

Watching My "Stories"

The serialized radio program *Ma Perkins* hit the airwaves in 1933. It was "brought to you by" Oxydol Soap Powder, which was manufactured by Procter & Gamble. The popular show thus became the company's first "soap opera."

You're all dressed up. You *do* have someplace to go. Unfortunately, you also have pet hair and lint on your outfit, and there's no lint remover in sight. Not to worry. Grab a roll of Scotch Duct Tape and cut a strip of tape about 5 inches long. Wrap it around your hand, adhesive side out, and roll it over your clothing until all the offending particles are gone. Make sure you aren't wiping the tape *across* the fabric; on some garments, it may mess up the nap.

Perk up a straw hat by giving it a once-over with Suave hairspray.

If your clothes are creeping every which way with static cling, spray a little Suave hairspray under the clinging fabric or next to your skin.

What Are You Wearing?

Movies and television can influence us, even what's in our dressers and closets.

- *It Happened One Night* (1934). Clark Gable gets ready for bed and reveals he is not wearing an undershirt; practically the next morning, undershirt sales plummet.

- JFK's inauguration (1961). Men watch the bareheaded president sworn in on national television and ask, "Why do I have to wear a hat?"

- *The Dick Van Dyke Show* (1961–66). Capri pants are in, but nobody wears them like Laura Petrie.

- *Annie Hall* (1977). As the title character, Diane Keaton embodies a look; women follow "suit."

- *Friends* (1994–2004). Rachel's maternity clothes are a close fit. Do they reveal a trend or cause it?

If the down in your jacket, vest, pillow, or comforter becomes flat and compacted, fluff it up by tumbling the item in the dryer along with a couple of Penn tennis balls.

- If the seams are ripping on your waterproof winter gloves (ski gloves, for example), repair them quickly and effectively with Scotch Duct Tape.

- A rip in your ski pants or jacket can leave you cold, quite literally. Don't panic or pay exorbitant prices in the lodge shop to replace the item; just cut a length of Scotch Duct Tape a bit longer than the rip. Position the tape inside the rip, sticky side out. Join the two sides of the ripped fabric so they meet in the middle. Carefully press onto the tape.

- Repair a tear in a rubber raincoat or slicker with Scotch Duct Tape. Apply a piece to the inside of the garment, along the tear. If a lining makes that impossible, use a matching or coordinating color of tape on the outside.

- Take care of those annoying fuzzballs on sweaters with some 3M sandpaper (any grit). Rub it against the fuzz very lightly. Be sure to go in one direction rather than in a circle.

- When a careless spark lands on wool clothing, it will leave a scorch mark. Lightly sand around the edges of the mark with some medium-grit 3M sandpaper, and it will be less visible.

- Preserve space in your closet by hanging your scarves through plastic six-pack rings from Budweiser beer, Pepsi, or another beverage. Attach the rings to a hanger using twist ties or Scotch Magic Tape.

FOOTWEAR CARE

- Control odors in shoes that are starting to smell by sprinkling the insides with a little Morton Salt. Let sit overnight, then shake out the salt. The salt will help control moisture, which contributes to odors.

- Downy dryer sheets, bunched up and placed in sneakers, will help deodorize them.

- Clean the rubber on athletic shoes with ARM & HAMMER Baking Soda sprinkled on an O-Cel-O sponge or a washcloth.

- Spray Niagara Spray Starch on new fabric tennis shoes before wearing them—it will prevent dirt from becoming embedded in the canvas, and the shoes will always be easy to clean.

- New canvas sneakers will remain looking new if you spray them with a coat of Suave hairspray before wearing them.

- Use a soft cloth dipped in Heinz Vinegar or Colavita Extra Virgin Olive Oil to shine patent leather. Clean the item with a damp cloth or O-Cel-O sponge, then apply a few drops of vinegar or oil with a clean cloth. Buff until it gleams.

- Melitta Basket Coffee Filters make great applicators for shoe polish and are good for shining too.

- Buff your just-polished shoes with a No nonsense knee high or a footlong piece of pantyhose. Now *that's* a shoe shine!

- Spray Pledge furniture polish on shoes, then buff with a clean, dry cloth.

- When your shoes need a shine—and you have no polish—use a Crayola Crayon of the matching color. Color in scuffed spots; draw lines around the whole shoe for a thorough job. Buff with a soft, clean cloth.

Shoes, Boots, and the Feet that Wear Them

As a salesperson in his father's shoe store in Syracuse, New York, Charles Brannock just knew there had to be a better way to measure feet than the glorified wooden ruler that was the industry norm. In 1925 he invented the Brannock Device, consisting of a baseplate with graduated markings and sliding components to measure length, width, and the distance from the heel to the ball of the foot. It's still used in shoe stores today.

- Out on the road with no shoe polish? Try using Blistex Lip Balm. Rub it over your shoes and polish with a soft cloth.

- Use ReaLemon Lemon Juice to clean and shine black or tan leather shoes. Apply with a soft cloth.

- Revlon Nail Enamel repairs scuffed patent leather. Cover the scuff with the same shade as the shoe, purse, or other item; let dry thoroughly. Then apply clear Revlon Nail Enamel.

- Before applying polish, remove black scuff marks on shoes with a paste of ARM & HAMMER Baking Soda and water.

- To remove scuff marks from shoes, rub them with an egg white on a soft cloth.

- Another scuff mark remedy is to rub a bit of Crest toothpaste onto the marks and wipe off with a clean cloth.

- Apply clear Revlon Nail Enamel to the backs of heels to keep scuffs at bay.

- Reattach a shoe heel with Scotch Duct Tape in the matching color. The tape also repairs accessories such as wallets and purses.

- Neaten up the frayed ends of shoelaces (and make it easier to lace them) by dipping them in clear Revlon Nail Enamel.

- Fix a broken or frayed shoelace tip (the official name of which is an "aglet") with a small strip of Scotch Magic Tape.

- Turn to Scotch Duct Tape to fix a broken shoelace. Cut a piece as long as the shoelace; fold it in half lengthwise, adhesive side in. Thread it through the holes and lace up!

- Sprinkle Argo Corn Starch or Johnson's Baby Powder onto a knot in your shoelace, and you'll be able to work it loose much more easily.

- If your new dress shoes are too tight, saturate a Rite Aid cotton ball with Rite Aid isopropyl rubbing alcohol. Rub it on the inside of the shoes, right at the tight spots. Wear, walk, dance, whatever... without blisters!

Alberto VO5 Conditioning Hairdressing or Suave conditioner can help silence the squeak in a noisy pair of shoes. Just rub a small amount into the squeaky spots.

Do *You* Want to Be Queen for a Day?

Host Jack Bailey asked that question on the television game show *Queen for a Day* (1956–64). Four housewives each dramatically described why they deserved the royal treatment. The audience judged the sob stories and opined by clapping, which was measured by the "applause meter." Each contestant asked for a merchandise prize—usually a major appliance such as a washer and dryer, a dishwasher, or a stove. The queen for that day not only won the requested prize (and several others); she also donned a sable-trimmed red velvet robe and a jeweled crown.

Do your shoes make a lot of noise, especially on wooden stairs? Stick some Scotch Duct Tape to the soles. This will quiet your shoes as well as keep you from slipping.

Remove the salt residue from winter boots with a cloth dipped in a solution of 1 cup water and 1 tablespoon Heinz Vinegar. This will work on leather and vinyl.

To battle salt deposits that will damage leather, coat a clean cloth with Vaseline Petroleum Jelly and store it in a sealed container. Wipe the boots lightly every time you are on the way in or out of the house.

Stuff wet shoes with No nonsense pantyhose. That way, as they dry, they'll keep their shape.

- Insert Scott Towel cores into tall boots to keep them from flopping over in storage.

- Another way to keep boots on the up-and-up is to roll up thick magazines, secure with rubber bands, and place in the boots to keep them upright.

- Protect your shoes when you brave a muddy mess: Slip a pair of plastic grocery bags over your shoes and tie the handles at your ankles.

- Provide an extra bit of insulation in your winter boots. Apply silver Scotch Duct Tape to each insole, shiny side up (other colors will not work). Warmth from your feet will be reflected back into the boots by the shiny tape.

HAMPER OF MORE HINTS

- To kill germs inside a washing machine, add ½ cup Listerine Antiseptic mouthwash to the wash water. You can also use mouthwash to kill germs on the outside of the machine.

- Soap, mineral deposits, and wet lint can build up inside your washer, reducing its efficiency or even causing it to malfunction. Clean your machine once a year by filling it with hot water and then adding 1 quart of Heinz Vinegar (or more, depending on how dirty the machine is).

Run machine through its normal cycle.

◆ You can also clean your washing machine and its hoses by dumping 1 gallon of Heinz Distilled White Vinegar into the tub and running machine through an entire wash cycle.

◆ To remove crayon or lipstick marks on the inside of a dryer, unplug the appliance, spray WD-40 on a Scott Towel, and wipe off. Wipe well with warm water and Dawn dishwashing liquid, then dry a load of wet rags.

◆ Washer water spins out through a hose and dumps into a sink. With it goes lint that can eventually accumulate and clog the drain. To filter the gunk, insert a small piece of steel wool into a No nonsense knee high or the foot portion of pantyhose. Secure to the end of the hose—Scotch Duct Tape works well. Replace as necessary.

◆ If your washing machine has a removable filter, clean it by using an old Reach toothbrush to remove any lint. Then soak filter in Heinz Vinegar overnight; finish by rinsing it with water.

- Are the words and numbers on your washer dial hard to read? Rub a red or black Crayola Crayon over the dial until the indentations are filled with the colored wax. Wipe off the excess with a Scott Towel.

- Make your own fabric softener sheets by sprinkling Final Touch fabric softener on a Scott Towel, an O-Cel-O sponge, or a clean cloth and tossing it in the dryer.

- A Reach toothbrush is a wonderful laundry-day tool. To remove dried stains, put the garment on a flat surface, hold a piece of paper next to the stain, and gently brush the dried material onto the paper. Some stains, such as dried mud, are removed completely; others will have some residue that should come out during the regular wash cycle.

- Freshen laundry hampers by sprinkling ARM & HAMMER Baking Soda over dirty clothes as they await washing.

- To mask the odor of dirty laundry, keep a Downy dryer sheet in the bottom of your laundry basket, bag, or hamper.

- If yours is a never-ending quest to keep the laundry room neat, here's the tool for you. Keep an empty Folgers coffee canister or coffee can handy to collect the "pocket treasures" you find—hopefully *before* they go through the wash.

- Make a clothespin holder by cutting a hole opposite the handle in a clean, dry Clorox Regular-Bleach bottle. Hang by the handle on your clothesline and toss clothespins in.

The Line on Drying Clothes

Drying your laundry on an outdoor clothesline saves money, conserves energy, and leaves your clothes and other items fresh and static-free. Here are a few inside secrets:

◆ Hang pants by the cuffs and let their weight reduce wrinkles.

◆ Cut the fingers off a pair of cotton gloves, then slip the "fingers" over the arms of a weathered clothespin. They'll prevent marks on your clothes.

◆ Drop a spoon into each leg of a pair of No nonsense pantyhose or another thin garment to keep them from wrapping around the clothesline on a windy day.

◆ Bring in clothes as soon as they dry. Bright sun and extreme cold can weaken fibers.

◆ No more clothespin marks on your newly washed sweaters! Insert an old pair of No nonsense pantyhose into the neck of a sweater, then pull one leg through each sleeve. Clip a clothespin or two at the waistband and one on each foot to hang.

◆ Every few weeks, toss your wooden clothespins in a bucket of warm water mixed with ½ cup Clorox Regular-Bleach and 1 tablespoon Tide laundry detergent to attack mildew and dirt. Soak for about 10 minutes, then clip clothespins on a line to dry (in the sunshine, if possible).

◆ Are you at the end of your rope (supply)? Construct a makeshift clothesline out of Scotch Duct Tape. Cut an extra-long length of tape, twist it into a rope, and tie it between 2 trees or tall posts.

- Make an impromptu garment bag: Cut a hole in the center of the bottom seam of a GLAD trash bag (unscented, twist-tie variety). Turn it upside down and place over a hanger.

- Make hangers glide over metal closet rods by first rubbing the rods with Reynolds Cut-Rite Wax Paper.

- If a good pair of pants has been in the closet, on a regular hanger, for a while, there's likely an obvious, ugly crease from the hanger. Next time, cut an old Scott Towel tube lengthwise and place it over the bottom of the hanger. (Cut the ends of the tube to shorten if necessary.) Tape the tube back together to make sure it doesn't fall off the hanger. Hang your pants over the protective tube— good-bye, creases!

- Garments falling off their hangers? Before you hang a garment, put a rubber band on each end of the hanger.

Hints from Heloise

Perhaps the most famous household-hints advisor was known to her fans by her first name only. Heloise Bowles Cruse was born in Fort Worth, Texas, in 1919, and in 1959 she began a column to help housewives. Two years later the column was syndicated, soon appearing in nearly 600 newspapers in several countries. She published 5 books and made countless television appearances. Since her death in 1977, her daughter, Poncé Kiah Marchelle Heloise, has assumed the name and role. The current Heloise is the author of more than 10 books, a monthly column in *Good Housekeeping* magazine, and the continuing syndicated newspaper column *Hints from Heloise*.

- To keep spaghetti straps from slipping off wire hangers, use paper clips to attach them.

- Clear Revlon Nail Enamel can keep clothes from snagging on hangers. Apply a coat over splinters and rough edges.

- To make the ruffles on curtains, bedspreads, dust ruffles, shams, and decorative pillows crisp and fresh, give them a light coating of Suave hairspray.

- When the wind breaks a rib on your umbrella, repair it instead of tossing it. Make a splint with Scotch Masking Tape and a 1- to 3-inch piece of coat hanger wire (length of wire depends on the size of the umbrella rib). Hold the wire next to the rib and bind them together with the tape, wrapping it up the length of the wire and a bit extra on each end.

- On small umbrellas in particular, the material is likely to detach from a spoke. Use Reach dental floss to reattach it—it's waterproof and stronger than thread.

- An umbrella will dry much faster if you spray it with Scotchgard Fabric & Upholstery Protector before you use it. Just give it a quick shake after a rainstorm, and most of the water will run right off.

Chapter 3:
Beauty, Grooming & Hygiene

PROUDLY PRIMP AND PREEN

For centuries, people have known of the healing, cleansing, and beautifying properties of such common goods as honey, eggs, oats, corn, citrus fruits, olive oil, and vinegar. They are used in personal care products today, but when you find them on the store shelves you'll also find a higher price tag. In this chapter we go back to the basics: the products themselves.

So, ladies, mix yourselves a restorative egg shampoo, a honey-based facial, an apple cider vinegar astringent, or a mayonnaise moisturizer. Gentlemen, raid the kitchen cabinets when you run short of toothpaste, shaving cream, or styptic pencils. Loving family members, substitute silky corn starch when you can't find Jr.'s baby powder.

Remove mascara without batting an eye. Soak away stress and make no waves. Diaper a bottom and baby your wallet. The accessible and affordable items found in this chapter go above and beyond their usual responsibilities. Listen closely: You'll hear them knocking on the bathroom door, whispering at the nursery threshold, jostling each other for a spot on the vanity table.

Why wait for a salon gift card or a day at the spa? (The wait may be a long one!) Prepare to be pampered by—and enjoy the efforts of—a lineup of local professionals.

FACE FACTS

Cleanse

◆ Use a mixture of equal parts Heinz Apple Cider Vinegar and water to clean your face. Rinse and let face air-dry.

◆ A facial cleanser from the pantry is Old Fashioned Quaker Oats. Grind ¼ cup oats in a blender or coffee grinder to the consistency of coarse flour. Mix it in a bowl with sufficient heavy cream to make a paste (use skim milk if your skin is oily). Let the mixture thicken for about 2 minutes, then gently massage it onto your face and neck. Rinse with cool water.

◆ Whip up a cleanser that's right for all skin types. In a blender or food processor, combine 1 cup dried orange peel, 1 cup shelled almonds, and 1 cup Old Fashioned Quaker Oats. Chop into a fine powder. Place a small amount in your palm, add a few drops of water, and rub onto your face, being careful to avoid the eyes. Rinse with warm water; pat dry. Keep the powder at room temperature, stored in an airtight container.

◆ Mix ½ teaspoon Rite Aid Epsom salts with your regular cleansing cream. The texture of the salts will provide additional, but gentle, cleansing capability. At bedtime, massage it into your skin; rinse with cold water.

- Make your own effective and economical cold cream. With a wire whisk, combine 1 egg yolk and 2 tablespoons ReaLemon Lemon Juice. Slowly add ½ cup Crisco Pure Vegetable Oil and ½ cup Colavita Extra Virgin Olive Oil, stirring until mixture thickens. If necessary, thicken with more egg yolk; thin with lemon juice. Refrigerate in a covered container.

Moisturize

- Make your sunblock a moisturizer too. Mix it with some Vaseline Total Moisture Lotion before applying it to skin.

- Colavita Extra Virgin Olive Oil is a great facial moisturizer. Apply a few drops with a Rite Aid cotton ball. Do not rinse.

- Use a tube of Blistex Lip Balm as a face moisturizer. Just rub it over your face when you're out in the cold.

- Pay special attention to the eye area when moisturizing. Gently apply a little Suave conditioner or Alberto VO5 Conditioning Hairdressing to the skin around each eye (keep it out of your eyes themselves, of course!) to ward off lines and wrinkles from dry skin.

- Dab a bit of Colavita Extra Virgin Olive Oil or Crisco Pure Vegetable Oil to the crow's-feet around your eyes at night.

Tone

- Make a basic skin toner using a mixture of equal parts Heinz Apple Cider Vinegar or Heinz Distilled White Vinegar and water. Keep toner in a small spray bottle and apply after your usual wash.

- Control oily skin with a mixture of equal parts Heinz Apple Cider Vinegar and cool water. The mixture works as an astringent. You can also freeze this solution into ice cubes and use it as a cooling facial treatment on a hot summer day.

Terrific Tonic

This handy tonic works as a deodorant, tightens pores, and eases sunburn and other minor burns. In a clean glass jar (with lid), combine the juice of 1 lemon (about 3 tablespoons ReaLemon Lemon Juice), 1 cup witch hazel, and 3 tablespoons coarsely chopped cucumber. Cap the jar and let stand for 2 days; strain out cucumber. Apply with a Rite Aid cotton ball. Store tonic in the refrigerator.

- Tone and clarify your skin with an apple astringent. Pour these ingredients into a bottle: ½ cup Mott's apple juice, 4 tablespoons 100-proof vodka, 1 tablespoon Sue Bee Honey, and 1 teaspoon Morton Sea Salt. Cap bottle; shake well. Twice daily, apply astringent to your face and neck using a Rite Aid cotton ball.

Banish Blemishes

- Fight blackheads and pimples with a facial cleanser that's practically straight from the fridge. Boil 8 ounces whole milk; let cool. Squeeze in the juice of a fresh lime (or 3 table-spoons ReaLime Lime Juice). Add 1 teaspoon glycerin if your skin is dry. Wash your face with the cleanser. Rinse with warm water.

- Treat oily, acne-prone skin with Phillips' Milk of Magnesia. Apply a thin layer to your face, then wait 10 minutes. Rinse with warm water.

- Make your own acne cream. Put a small amount of ARM & HAMMER Baking Soda in your palm and add just enough water to make a paste. Apply to blemishes at bedtime.

- Apply ReaLemon Lemon Juice to blackheads using a Q-tips cotton swab. Leave the juice on overnight. In the morning, rinse your face with cool water. Repeat every night for 1 week. For acne outbreaks, apply the juice several times a day to dry up pimples more quickly.

- Banish blackheads with Sue Bee Honey. Honey speeds healing by killing bacteria. Heat a tablespoon or two of honey and dab it on the offenders. Wait 2 or 3 minutes. Wash off the honey with warm water; follow with a cool-water rinse. Dry gently with a clean, soft towel. For an overnight blemish remedy, dab honey on blemish and cover with a bandage.

- Make a paste of Sue Bee Honey, Gold Medal Whole Wheat Flour, and Heinz Vinegar, then use it to lightly cover a new outbreak of pimples. Keep paste on overnight and rinse off in the morning. This should enhance the healing process.

- Treat acne with a paste made from 3 tablespoons Colavita Extra Virgin Olive Oil and 4 tablespoons Morton Salt. Apply the mixture to affected areas. Wait 2 minutes, then rinse off with warm, soapy water. For the first week, treat daily; thereafter, 2 or 3 times per week.

- A mixture of 3 parts Old Fashioned Quaker Oats and 1 part water zaps those blackheads. Rub mixture on blemishes. Wait 10 minutes, then rinse it off with warm water and pat your face dry with a clean, soft towel.

- To treat pimples, make a paste with water and crushed Rite Aid aspirin. Cover the blemish with the paste; a few minutes later, rinse it off.

- A dab of Crest toothpaste on pimples will help clear them up overnight. Use as you would any acne ointment.

- Listerine Antiseptic mouthwash can combat acne. Dab it on blemishes with a Rite Aid cotton ball.

- To treat acne, use a clean travel-size bottle to mix 1 teaspoon Heinz Vinegar and 10 teaspoons water. Carry this bottle and a few Rite Aid cotton balls with you so you can dab acne spots several times during the day. This solution shouldn't dry out your skin, and the vinegar will help return your skin to a natural pH balance. The treatment may also help prevent future breakouts. Discontinue use if irritation worsens.

- Take blackheads out of the picture with this treatment: Mix 1 teaspoon Rite Aid Epsom salts and 3 drops iodine with ½ cup boiling water. Allow mixture to cool until it's warm but not hot. Apply to affected area with a Rite Aid cotton ball. Right after, apply 3 or 4 more times (no need to rinse in between applications), reheating the solution if it cools too much. Press on blackheads very gently with Q-tips cotton swabs to remove them, then dab with an alcohol-based astringent.

- Bothered by freckles or age spots? Dissolve a pinch of Domino Sugar in 2 tablespoons ReaLemon Lemon Juice. Apply the mixture to each spot with a Rite Aid cotton ball or a Kleenex facial tissue. Repeat every few days until the spots have lightened to your liking.

- If time and the sun are showing on your face, lighten those spots with this treatment: Mix 3 tablespoons ReaLime Lime Juice, 3 tablespoons ReaLemon Lemon Juice, 4 tablespoons plain Dannon yogurt, and 2 tablespoons Sue Bee Honey. Once or twice a week, gently rub the mixture into each spot with your fingertips. Store in a covered container in your refrigerator.

Masks, Scrubs & Facials

- It's as good as an expensive, fancy mask, but it's so simple. Combine Ivory Liquid Hand Cleanser with enough Morton Salt to make a paste. Gently pat, rather than rub, it onto your face. After 2 minutes, rinse your face with water.

- Separate an egg, putting the white in one bowl and the yolk in another bowl. Beat each separately. Apply the egg white to oily areas on your face and the yolk to dry areas. Let dry 20 minutes, then rinse off with warm water.

- To minimize pores, beat 1 egg and combine it with 1 tablespoon Sue Bee Honey. Spread the mixture on your face. Leave it on for about 20 minutes, then rinse off.

Facial Splashes

Herbal: Boil 1 quart Heinz Apple Cider Vinegar in microwave for 3 minutes in a large glass measuring cup. Remove and add herbs (lavender or rosemary are excellent). Pour into a sterilized bottle. Chill in refrigerator if desired.

Mint: Bruise a handful of mint leaves by rolling them with a pastry rolling pin. Pack them into a jar and cover with Heinz Apple Cider Vinegar. Let stand 2 weeks, then strain out mint. Pour remaining liquid into an empty, clean bottle.

Rosewater: Mix the following in a jar: 1 pint Heinz Apple Cider Vinegar, 1 ounce rose petals, ½ pint rosewater, ½ pint Heinz Distilled White Vinegar, and 1 ounce aromatic flowers such as sweet violet, rosemary, or lavender. Steep for 2 weeks, then strain. Pour remaining liquid into an empty, clean bottle.

- Try this facial to tone and soften your skin. Beat 1 large egg white; stir in the juice of half a lemon (about 1½ tablespoons ReaLemon Lemon Juice). Apply to face and neck. After 20 minutes, rinse off with filtered, distilled, or bottled water. Pat dry, then gently apply some witch hazel with a Rite Aid cotton ball.

- To give yourself a refreshing facial, mix 1 tablespoon Carnation Instant Nonfat Dry Milk; half of a peeled cucumber, minced; and 1 teaspoon plain Dannon yogurt. Apply to face, let dry, and rinse.

- Cool and nourish your face with a mask made from 2 tablespoons freshly squeezed orange juice and 1 teaspoon plain Dannon yogurt. Mix well; smooth on with your fingertips. After 5 minutes, rinse with cool water.

- Give yourself a fresh fruit facial. Puree the following in a blender or food processor: 1 ounce Tropicana Pure Premium orange juice, 6 strawberries, half an apple, and half a pear. Spread a thin layer of Sue Bee Honey on your face, followed by the fruit blend. Wait at least 30 minutes; rinse with warm water, then gently pat dry.

- Apples have a combination of tough-and-tender chemicals that is perfect for facial treatments. Try this cleanser: Make a paste of 2 teaspoons Mott's apple juice, 2 teaspoons red wine, and 1 tablespoon ground Old Fashioned Quaker Oats. Add more juice or wine if necessary. Apply mixture to face and throat; let dry for 20 to 30 minutes. Gently rinse off with warm water.

- This treatment works well to clarify, exfoliate, and moisturize normal to dry skin: Mash half of a banana in a bowl. Add 1 tablespoon Sue Bee Honey and 2 tablespoons sour cream; mix well. Apply mixture to your face, leave on for 10 minutes, and then rinse with warm water.

- Spread Kraft Mayonnaise over your face and let it dry for 20 minutes. Rinse off with warm water, then follow with a cold water splash. This treatment will help tighten pores.

- Try this deep-cleaning facial mask, used by European women for hundreds of years: Combine 1 egg, ¼ cup Carnation Instant Nonfat Dry Milk, 1 tablespoon dark rum or brandy, and the juice of 1 lemon (or about 3 tablespoons ReaLemon Lemon Juice) in a blender. When the texture is creamy, pour mixture into a bowl or a jar. Gently apply mixture to your face. Let dry. Peel off the mask and thoroughly rinse your face with warm water. Pat dry; apply your usual moisturizer.

- Make a paste of 3 parts ARM & HAMMER Baking Soda to 1 part water and use as a gentle, exfoliating facial scrub after washing with soap and water. Rinse clean.

- Mix ARM & HAMMER Baking Soda with Old Fashioned Quaker Oats in your blender; it makes a great facial scrub.

- Mix 1 teaspoon Colavita Extra Virgin Olive Oil and 1 teaspoon Morton Salt in a small bowl; gently massage mixture into face and throat. Follow by washing with your usual face soap; rinse.

- To combat flakiness, dip a Rite Aid cotton ball in milk and apply it to flaky patch. Rinse with cool water.

Makeup Tips

◆ After applying mascara, dip a Q-tips cotton swab in a little Johnson's Baby Powder and sweep it over your lashes. Then apply a second coat of mascara. Lashes will appear longer and fuller.

◆ To remove errant eye shadow flecks from your face, use a Q-tips cotton swab. It will remove specks without ruining your foundation.

◆ Place a few Q-tips cotton swabs and a small container of your favorite makeup remover in a GLAD Food Storage Zipper Bag. Carry it with you for emergency makeup fixes.

◆ If your mascara has become clumpy, put a drop of Johnson's Baby Oil into the tube. Reinsert brush and twirl it gently. Good-bye, clumps!

◆ We all want to get our money's worth from the cosmetics we purchase. To reach the last of the lipstick in the tube, dig it out with a clean Q-tips cotton swab. Apply it with a lipstick brush.

◆ Both Argo Corn Starch and Clabber Girl Baking Powder can substitute for face powder. Be sure to powder on just a touch, or you'll look like you're ready for Halloween!

◆ Line your makeup bag with GLAD Press'n Seal. Cleaning it out is a breeze. Press'n Seal is also an ideal solution for a broken case: Cover cosmetics such as powders and blushes to prevent spills.

- What frustration and waste when powdered makeup, such as foundation or blush, breaks in its compact. If this happens, stretch a ring of No nonsense pantyhose over the compact. Large pieces won't fall out, yet the powder comes through the nylon.

- When face powder hardens in its compact, there is a simple way to loosen it. Lightly rub a small piece of fine-grit 3M sandpaper across the surface. To avoid this happening in the future, place the powder puff upside down in the compact so that makeup and oil from the puff don't rub off on the powder.

- Eye shadow compacts that offer more than one shade let you easily combine colors for a dramatic effect. Unfortunately, over time the colors themselves easily combine... in the compact. Clean up your palette by gently touching the surface of each color with a piece of Scotch Magic Tape, carefully lifting away just the messy surface layer. Use a fresh piece of tape for each color palette compartment.

- Take a look at this eye-makeup remover. Mix 2 teaspoons Crisco Pure Canola Oil, 1 tablespoon Colavita Extra Virgin Olive Oil, and 1 tablespoon castor oil. Apply with a Kleenex facial tissue or Rite Aid cotton ball to gently remove mascara, eyeliner, or eye shadow. Discard any leftover mixture.

- Kraft Mayonnaise also removes eye makeup. Apply a bit with your fingertip, then wipe clean with a damp Rite Aid cotton ball.

- Crisco All-Vegetable Shortening makes an excellent moisturizing makeup remover. Follow by washing with your usual face soap; rinse.

- Dry milk can be used as a makeup remover. Mix 1 teaspoon Carnation Instant Nonfat Dry Milk powder with warm water and apply to your face using a Rite Aid cotton ball. Rinse clean.

- These 3 ingredients offer 3 times the care as they remove makeup, cleanse your face, and soften your skin: Mix ½ cup Kraft Mayonnaise, 1 tablespoon melted butter, and 3 tablespoons ReaLemon Lemon Juice or ReaLime  Lime Juice in an airtight glass jar. Cool in refrigerator. Gently massage into skin, then rinse with cold water. Store leftovers in the refrigerator for future use.

- Use Alberto VO5 Conditioning Hairdressing or Suave conditioner to remove makeup. Apply a little to a Rite Aid cotton ball and wipe clean. Be careful to avoid the eye area.

- A Pampers baby wipe is also ready to remove makeup—but stay away from the eye area, just to be safe.

Beauty Buzz

- Freshen up with a washcloth dipped in a solution of 4 tablespoons ARM & HAMMER Baking Soda and 1 quart water.

- Computer time, reading, needlework, poor air quality, and inadequate task lighting can strain your eyes mercilessly. One very simple soother is to dampen a few Rite Aid cotton balls with cold milk and apply to eyelids. Lie down and rest for 10 to 15 minutes.

- To get rid of the puffy eyes that may accompany allergies, colds, crying, or lack of sleep, mix 1 teaspoon Morton Salt into 1 pint hot water. Dip Rite Aid cotton balls or cosmetic cotton rounds into the solution, then lie down and apply pads to eyelids. Rest quietly in this position for at least 15 minutes, keeping eyes closed and pads in place. The puffiness should be gone when you sit up.

- Keep an emergency eye-relief kit in the freezer. Dip Q-tips cotton swabs into cool water and store them in a small GLAD Freezer Zipper Bag in the freezer. To relieve tired eyes and reduce puffiness, roll the swabs under your eyes.

- Another way to freshen eyes and the skin around them is to put a few wet, used Lipton Tea Bags in the freezer for about 5 minutes. Once tea bags are chilled, dab Colavita Extra Virgin Olive Oil on your eyelids with a Rite Aid cotton ball. Place a tea bag on each closed eyelid and lie down for about 15 minutes. Gently remove the oil with a Kleenex facial tissue or a cotton ball.

- To help combat oily skin, fill a small spray bottle with tepid water and 1 teaspoon Morton Salt. Spritz onto your face. Blot dry.

- Make your own coffee-flavored lip gloss. Put 3 or 4 table-spoons Vaseline Petroleum Jelly into a microwave-safe dish. Starting with 30 seconds, microwave until it's melted. Stir in a small amount of finely ground Folgers coffee or Folgers Instant Coffee Crystals; microwave again for 30 seconds. Allow to cool, then store in a covered container. (No need to refrigerate.)

- Keep errant eyebrows in place by applying a little Blistex Lip Balm and styling with your fingertips. Guys, this tip could also apply to unruly facial hair.

- You don't need special, expensive strips to wax eyebrows. Instead, use strips cut from Melitta Basket Coffee Filters.

HAIR TODAY...

Shampoo and Condition

- Pressed for time? Try a dry shampoo. Pour some Johnson's Baby Powder, Argo Corn Starch, or Old Fashioned Quaker Oats into the palm of your hand and rub through hair. Brush hair until the powder is no longer visible.

- In a pinch, use ARM & HAMMER Baking Soda as a dry shampoo for oily hair. Sprinkle on and comb through, then fluff hair with a blow-dryer.

- Add a teaspoon of ARM & HAMMER Baking Soda to a bottle of your usual shampoo to help remove buildup from

Highlights in the History of Hair

1500s: Francis I of France accidentally burns his hair with a torch; thereafter, men wear short hair.

1890: Alexandre Godefoy invents first electric hair dryer.

1907: First synthetic hair dye created by L'Oréal.

1916: Bobby pins introduced in the United States.

1928: Marjorie Joyner invents permanent wave machine.

1953: Robert Abplanal creates first clog-free valve for spray cans.

1960: L'Oréal introduces its hairspray, Elnett.

1964: Hairspray overtakes lipstick as women's most popular cosmetic.

1980s: Curling iron patented by Theora Stephens. The big-haired woman became a cultural icon, leading to the bumper sticker "The Higher the Hair, the Closer to God."

2000s: Hair gels, mousses, waxes, etc. all referred to as "product."

conditioner, mousse, and hairspray, as well as to improve your hair's manageability.

◆ Vinegar is a great hair conditioner and can improve cleanliness and shine. For simple conditioning, just add 1 tablespoon Heinz Vinegar to your hair as you rinse it. Keep a travel-size plastic bottle of vinegar in your shower for this purpose.

◆ To boost your conditioner and add volume to your hair, combine equal parts Rite Aid Epsom salts and a good deep conditioner in a pan. Heat until warm, not hot, and work through your hair. Wait 20 minutes; rinse with warm water.

◆ Use Final Touch fabric softener as a substitute for hair conditioner after a shampoo.

◆ Beer can remove residue from your hair. Add 6 tablespoons Budweiser beer to a cup of warm water and pour over your hair as a final rinse.

◆ Make the brew a bit bolder to make your hair shine. Combine 3 cups Budweiser beer with 1 cup warm water and use as a final rinse after shampooing. Gently blot dry with a towel. Don't worry about smelling like you just came from a frat party: As your hair dries, the aroma will dissipate.

Alberto Who?

In the mid-1950s, a chemist named Alberto invented a conditioning hairdressing to heal the hairdos of movie stars under the harsh lights of Hollywood studios. He and partner Blaine Culver named it "VO5" for the 5 vital organic emollients in the formula. Sadly, no one at Alberto-Culver recalls Alberto's last name.

◆ After you shampoo your hair, bring out the shine by rinsing it with Pepsi. Then rinse again with clear water.

◆ Give your shampoo some help dealing with excess oil. Mix 1 cup Rite Aid Epsom salts, 1 cup ReaLemon Lemon Juice, and 1 gallon water. Allow to sit 24 hours (no need to refrigerate). Pour the solution on dry hair, then wait 20 minutes. Shampoo as usual.

◆ Shine and condition dry hair with about 1 quart warm, unsweetened Lipton tea. Use as a final rinse after shampooing.

◆ Eggs make a great conditioner: Beat 1 egg white until it's foamy, then stir it into 5 tablespoons of plain Dannon yogurt. Apply to your hair section by section; let sit 15 minutes. Rinse and shampoo as usual.

◆ Give your hair a conditioning treatment that will leave you feeling like you've been to an expensive salon. Mix 3 eggs, 2 tablespoons Colavita Extra Virgin Olive Oil or Crisco Natural Blend Oil, and 1 teaspoon Heinz Distilled White Vinegar. Apply to hair and cover with a plastic cap. Leave on for 30 minutes, then rinse and shampoo as usual.

◆ Damaged or very dry hair responds to a hot oil treatment… with mayonnaise! Heat about ½ cup Kraft Mayonnaise until it's warm; gently rub into hair. Wrap a warm towel around your hair and wait 15 to 30 minutes, then shampoo as usual with warm water.

◆ Fruit and oil to the rescue! To restore maximum strength and shine to your hair, mash together half a ripe banana and half a ripe avocado; add 1 tablespoon Colavita Extra Virgin Olive Oil and 3 drops lemon oil. Massage mixture into unwashed hair and cover with a shower cap. Wait 60 minutes, then shampoo as usual. For badly damaged hair, repeat up to 3 times per week until you get the bounce and shine you want.

- Repair damaged hair by treating it with oil and egg yolk. First, massage Colavita Extra Virgin Olive Oil into hair. Then beat the yolk of 1 egg and massage it into hair, working up from the ends toward the scalp. Leave on for 10 minutes, then shampoo as usual. Do this once a week for a month, and hair should begin to feel healthier.

Styling

- Calm the frizzies by combing a tiny amount of Colavita Extra Virgin Olive Oil though dry hair.

- Make yourself a simple, inexpensive hairspray. In a saucepan, boil 2 cups water. Add 2 lemons, peeled and finely chopped. Simmer over low heat until lemons are soft. After the mixture cools, pour it through a strainer, and then into a labeled spray bottle. Add 1 tablespoon 100-proof vodka; shake well. Dilute with a little water if the spray is too sticky.

- Final Touch fabric softener can manage tresses as well as dresses! Use it to make your own hairspray: In a spray bottle, mix 1 part softener and 2 or 3 parts water (more water means less hold). Shake well.

On the Mane Stage

Movies in which hair care plays a significant part include *Sweeney Todd: The Demon Barber of Fleet Street* (1936; 2007, musical), *Samson and Delilah* (1949), *Shampoo* (1975), *Hair* (1979), *Hairspray* (1988; 2007), *Steel Magnolias* (1989), *Edward Scissorhands* (1990), *Barbershop* (2002), *Barbershop 2: Back in Business* (2004), *Beauty Shop* (2005), and *You Don't Mess with the Zohan* (2008).

- Cutting your own bangs may save you an expensive trip to the salon, but it can be risky if you don't have a sure hand. Here's how to save yourself some anguish. Wet hair, then place a length of Scotch Magic Tape straight across your whole forehead (on skin, not hair). The bottom edge of the tape should be placed where you want the bottom of the bangs to be. Comb hair forward; cut along the bottom edge of the tape. (Be sure to look in a mirror as you cut.)

- If winter's dry air has your hair all charged up, calm that static with a Downy dryer sheet. Starting at the roots, rub a sheet over all your hair. This will tame flyaways without weighing down your tresses.

- Dissolve 1 teaspoon Knox unflavored gelatin in a cup of warm water and use this mixture as a hair gel. This is great to apply before rolling curlers into your hair or before shaping today's styles with your fingers.

- When you need to get your hair out of your eyes and you don't have a barrette on hand, use a small or medium-size binder clip to tuck those tresses out of the way.

- Turn a pair of No nonsense pantyhose into a hair band. Cut a ring about 1 inch wide across one leg. Roll it up and it's ready to hold pigtails and ponytails. Widen the ring to about 3 inches and you've got a scrunchie.

Coloring Tips

◆ Blond highlights will magically appear if you rinse your hair with a mixture of ¼ cup ReaLemon Lemon Juice and ¾ cup water. For extra lightening, sit in the sun until your hair dries.

◆ Citrus juice also teams up with shampoo to lighten your locks. Mix 6 tablespoons ReaLime Lime Juice, 3 tablespoons ReaLemon Lemon Juice, and 2 tablespoons mild Suave shampoo. Massage throughout your hair. Sit in the sun (or under a hair dryer) for 15 to 20 minutes. Rinse completely.

◆ Bring out the shiny highlights in brown or red hair by rinsing it with Folgers coffee. Brew 2 or 3 strong cups (enough to cover your hair) and let it cool. Pour the coffee onto your hair after shampooing. No need to rinse.

◆ Golden highlights come through in red or brown hair when rinsed with brewed Lipton tea. Make enough tea to thoroughly cover hair; allow to cool. Pour over your hair after shampooing, then dry as usual.

◆ Attention, brunettes! Cover the gray naturally and inexpensively. Steep 3 Lipton Tea Bags in 1 cup boiling water; add 1 tablespoon each McCormick Rosemary Leaves and Rubbed Sage. Let stand overnight, then filter. (Tip: You can filter the liquid through a Melitta Basket Coffee Filter.) After you shampoo, pour or apply mixture with a spray bottle until your hair is saturated. Do not rinse. Gently blot hair with a towel. Repeat treatment until desired results are achieved.

- Freshen dark hair and hide the gray while you're at it! Let ¼ cup Folgers coffee grounds steep in 3 cups hot water. When cool, strain out the grounds using a Melitta Basket Coffee Filter and pour the liquid over clean hair. Wait 3 minutes; rinse with warm water.

The Breck Girl

The Breck Shampoo Co. had one of the longest-running campaigns in advertising history. Ads featuring paintings of a beautiful "Breck Girl" began in 1936 and went national about 10 years later. Before the campaign ended in the late 1970s, models for the Breck Girl included then-unknowns Cybill Shepherd, Kim Basinger, and Brooke Shields.

- Use 1 tablespoon Heinz Apple Cider Vinegar mixed with 1 gallon water as an after-shampoo rinse to minimize gray in your hair.

- To keep hair dye from staining your skin, rub a small amount of Alberto VO5 Conditioning Hairdressing on your forehead and around your ears and hairline before coloring your hair.

- Crest toothpaste can remove hair-color stains from the temples, forehead, hairline, neck, and around the ears. Put a dab on your fingertip, rub it gently into the stain, and rinse with lukewarm water. If necessary, repeat until the stain is gone.

◆ Protect your specs from dye while your hair is being colored. Wrap the temples of your eyeglasses with small pieces of Reynolds Wrap Aluminum Foil.

Defy Dandruff

◆ Prevent dandruff by dabbing Listerine Antiseptic mouthwash on your scalp with a Rite Aid cotton ball. Leave on for 30 minutes; rinse and shampoo as usual.

◆ Attack dandruff with lemon juice. Rub 1 tablespoon ReaLemon Lemon Juice into dry hair, down to the scalp. Shampoo and rinse as usual. Then, rinse hair again using a solution of 2 cups water and 2 tablespoons lemon juice. Repeat every other day for 1 week.

◆ Before shampooing, briefly soak hair in a small basin of water with ¼ cup Heinz Apple Cider Vinegar added. Repeat several times a week to help control dandruff and remove buildup from sprays, shampoos, and conditioners.

◆ To fight those flakes, add 1 or 2 tablespoons Budweiser beer to Suave shampoo. The hops in beer are a time-tested dandruff cure.

◆ Another dandruff-control method is to rinse hair with a solution of 2 cups water and ½ cup Heinz Vinegar after shampooing. If you need a stronger treatment for dandruff control, use this same method, but keep solution on your hair for an hour, covered with a shower cap. Rinse. This mixture will also help control frizziness in dry or damaged hair.

◆ Try this hot oil treatment to control dandruff. Pour 2 or 3 tablespoons Colavita Extra Virgin Olive Oil into a glass measuring cup (do not use nontempered glass) and place the cup in a pan of water. Warm the water slowly on the stove to heat the oil. When the oil is warm, dab it onto your hair at the scalp using a Rite Aid cotton ball. Divide your hair into small sections to get maximum coverage. Massage lightly. Leave the oil on for several hours, then shampoo as usual and rinse thoroughly.

Combat Chlorine

◆ Dyed blond hair has a tendency to take on a greenish tint from too much swimming in a chlorinated pool. To undo the green, rinse your hair with Canada Dry Club Soda.

◆ Another treatment for removing the green from dyed blond hair is Campbell's Tomato Juice. Rub enough into your hair to saturate, leave on 2 minutes, then rinse thoroughly. Shampoo as usual.

◆ Rinse hair with ½ teaspoon ARM & HAMMER Baking Soda in 1 pint water to remove the dullness or discoloration caused by chlorinated pools.

- Has chlorine discolored your hair? Dissolve 8 tablets of Rite Aid aspirin in a glass of water and rub the solution into your hair. Let it work for about 10 minutes, then rinse and shampoo your hair as usual.

- Protect your hair from the drying effects of a chlorinated pool. Apply some Alberto VO5 Conditioning Hairdressing from root to tip before you swim.

Other Tips

- Remove dried paint from your hair with Colavita Extra Virgin Olive Oil. Dab on with a Rite Aid cotton ball and gently rub in. Shampoo as usual.

- Before you pick up a can of spray paint and start a project, rub a dab of Alberto VO5 Conditioning Hairdressing all through your hair. Any mist that lands up there will wash right out.

- Kids will be kids...and gum will get stuck in their hair. When this happens, pour some Pepsi into a bowl. Have the child lean over the bowl and soak the gummed-up hair section for a few minutes (or longer, if necessary). Slide out the gum, rinse, and shampoo as usual.

- To remove chewing gum from a coiffure, you can also try mayonnaise. Massage a generous amount of Kraft Mayonnaise into hair. Wait 5 minutes; comb out the gum. Shampoo as usual.

- Remove hairspray and oil buildup from combs and brushes by soaking them in a sink of warm water with 3 tablespoons ARM & HAMMER Baking Soda and 3 tablespoons Clorox Regular-Bleach.

- You can also soak your combs and brushes in a basin of ¼ cup Dawn dishwashing liquid, ¼ cup Parsons' Ammonia, and 2 cups warm water. After 5 to 10 minutes, remove them from the solution. Clean the combs with the brushes and vice versa. Rinse with cool water; air-dry.

- Clean your combs with a weekly wash in 2 cups cold water to which you've added a few drops of Parsons' Ammonia.

- Hairbrushes come clean in a bathroom sink of warm water, ½ cup 20 Mule Team Borax, and 1 tablespoon Tide laundry detergent (liquid or powder). Swish brushes around, rinse in clear water, and let dry.

- Static won't build up on your brushes and combs if you rub them with a Downy dryer sheet every day or two.

- To clean those nasty hairbrushes, fill your bathroom sink with warm water and add a capful of Suave shampoo. Soak your hairbrushes and combs in this for half an hour, then rinse thoroughly.

◆ If you bristle at the thought of cleaning a hairbrush, just read this tip: Cut a 2-inch strip from a No nonsense knee high or the leg section of a pair of pantyhose. Stretch it over a new or just-cleaned brush; use a comb to push the hosiery all the way down to the base of the bristles. When the brush needs a cleaning, simply lift and remove the layer of hosiery and replace it with a fresh piece.

SHAVING TIPS

◆ Who needs shaving cream when you can shave your face or legs with Skippy Creamy Peanut Butter? (We recommend not using the crunchy style.)

◆ Milk also comes through smoothly as a substitute for your usual shaving cream.

◆ In lieu of shaving cream, try lubricating your skin with Crisco Pure Vegetable Oil before shaving.

◆ Ladies, if you're out of shaving cream or gel—or you just want to save some money—use Suave conditioner instead for a smooth, moisturizing shave.

◆ Pamper your freshly shaved legs by using Suave conditioner as a moisturizer after your shower or bath.

◆ Is shaving your legs a painful prospect? Prevent friction burns from an electric shaver by first dusting your legs lightly with Johnson's Baby Powder.

- For instant relief from razor burn, make a solution of 4 tablespoons ARM & HAMMER Baking Soda and 1 quart water and pat it on skin with a Rite Aid cotton ball.

- Use a dab of ARM & HAMMER Baking Soda on a shaving cut to stem bleeding.

- Keep a supply of Melitta Basket Coffee Filters on hand in the bathroom. Tear off a piece and stick it to a nick to stop the bleeding.

- Next time you're careless while shaving, dab Blistex Lip Balm on the nick.

- Men with sensitive skin may find that a solution of 1 tablespoon ARM & HAMMER Baking Soda in 1 cup water makes a great preshave treatment or a soothing aftershave rinse.

- Heinz Apple Cider Vinegar is a great aftershave that will help keep men's skin soft and looking young. Splash on face after shaving.

- Try this homemade aftershave recipe: Mix 2 cups Rite Aid isopropyl rubbing alcohol, 1 tablespoon glycerin, 1 tablespoon dried lavender, 1 teaspoon McCormick Rosemary Leaves, and 1 teaspoon McCormick Ground Cloves. Pour the mixture into a bottle with a tight-fitting cap; refrigerate until chilled. To use, shake well and then strain mixture as you use it. It will keep in the fridge for up to 2 months.

◆ Gals, here's a low-cost way to lighten upper lip hair: Combine 1 teaspoon Parsons' Ammonia and ¼ cup Rite Aid hydrogen peroxide. Dab mixture on the area with a Rite Aid cotton ball and leave on for 30 minutes. Rinse off with cold water.

A MERRY MOUTH

Keeping Your Chompers Clean

◆ Use ARM & HAMMER Baking Soda as toothpaste (or add a little to your child's regular toothpaste) to help take care of plaque buildup. Sprinkle baking soda into your palm, dip a damp Reach toothbrush into it, and brush.

◆ To make your own toothpaste, mix 4 teaspoons ARM & HAMMER Baking Soda with 1 teaspoon Morton Salt. Add a small spoonful of glycerin and mix until it is the right consistency for toothpaste. Add a few drops of McCormick Pure Peppermint, Pure Mint, Pure Anise, or Cinnamon Extract to taste. Spoon into a small, airtight squeeze bottle.

Paste or Powder?

Tooth powders developed by 18th-century British doctors, dentists, and chemists had a base of bicarbonate of soda (today's baking soda). Possible additives included brick dust, charcoal, betel nut, cuttlefish, crushed china, earthenware, sugar, and borax powder (for foaming action).

Today's typical toothpaste tube contains sodium monofluorophosphate, fluoride, foaming agents, detergents, humectants (to prevent hardening), flavoring, and color.

How Did the Toothpaste Get Its Stripes?

Striped toothpaste isn't striped all the way down the tube. The plain, usually white, paste (carrier material) fills the tube to a certain level; above that is the colored "stripe stuff." The nozzle isn't just the hole at the top but a pipe through the center of the tube, ending where it meets the carrier material. Squeeze the tube and the carrier material enters the pipe. Meanwhile, the stripe stuff enters the pipe via small holes very close to the nozzle.

◆ Another way to keep your mouth clean and healthy is to rub a paste made of ReaLime Lime Juice and Morton Salt on your teeth and gums several times a day.

◆ A mixture of salt and baking soda makes an excellent tooth powder, one that can help whiten teeth and remove plaque. To make, first pulverize Morton Salt in a blender or food processor, or spread some on a cutting board and crush it with a rolling pin into a fine, sandlike texture. Then mix 1 part crushed salt with 2 parts ARM & HAMMER Baking Soda. To use, sprinkle a bit into the palm of your hand; dip a dampened toothbrush into the mixture and brush teeth. Keep powder in an airtight container in your bathroom.

Who Invented the Toothbrush?

The first toothbrushing tools appeared more than 5,000 years ago. The Babylonians and Egyptians shredded the end of a twig and— presto!—a toothbrush.

◆ Here's a surprising makeshift toothbrush: Take a piece of lemon or lime peel and rub the inside of it over your teeth and gums. Both contain chemicals that fight gum disease and help whiten teeth.

- A large binder clip placed on the end of a tube of Crest toothpaste or similar packaging will ensure that you'll get all your money's worth.

- Soak toothbrushes overnight in a solution of 4 tablespoons ARM & HAMMER Baking Soda to 1 quart warm water.

Freshening Tips

- All out of breath mints and your breath is less than fresh? Suck on a coffee bean for several minutes, and your mouth will smell clean.

- To freshen breath, use 1 teaspoon ARM & HAMMER Baking Soda in half a glass of water; swish the solution through your teeth, then rinse.

How Is Dental Floss Made?

In 1898, Johnson & Johnson patented dental floss made of silk left over from making surgical sutures. Today's floss is made from nylon or ePTFE (expanded Teflon), with other fibers woven in. Options include wax, flavoring, and whiteners.

- Mix ½ teaspoon Morton Salt and ½ teaspoon ARM & HAMMER Baking Soda into a 4-ounce glass of water. Use this solution to gargle and freshen breath.

- Make a refreshing mouthwash using equal parts water and Heinz Vinegar. Gargle to freshen your mouth and control bad breath. Do not swallow.

- Freshen your breath with lime juice. Mix the juice of 1 lime (or 3 tablespoons ReaLime Lime Juice) and 1 teaspoon Sue Bee Honey in a glass of water. Drink between meals and at bedtime.

- Take care of garlic breath by taking a bite of an apple. Then brush your teeth.

Denture Care

- Soak dentures, athletic mouthguards, retainers, or other oral appliances in a solution of 2 teaspoons ARM & HAMMER Baking Soda dissolved in a glass of warm water. Another option is to scrub these items using an old Reach toothbrush dipped in baking soda.

- To brighten dentures, soak them overnight in pure Heinz Vinegar.

- Cut off a small piece of clean No nonsense pantyhose and use it to polish dentures.

- If your denture splits or cracks when you are away from home, fix the break with Scotch Duct Tape. Cut the tape to size for a more comfortable fit. Remending it with fresh tape every morning can hold it together until you can get to your dentist.

Washington's Chompers

When George Washington became the first U.S. president in 1789, he had only one natural tooth. Did he really have wooden dentures? No. The "inauguration dentures" had a base carved of hippopotamus ivory; the teeth were a combination of human teeth and carved elephant ivory.

HELP IS AT HAND

Washing Up

- Gillette Foamy Shave Foam works as well as soap to clean your hands. This may be an excellent choice if you need waterless cleaning, such as when you're camping or hiking.

- When your hands are greasy or grimy—after pumping gas or working on a project at home—wipe them clean with a Pampers baby wipe.

- A small amount of Tide laundry detergent (liquid or powder) lends a hand when you need a tough cleaner for your hands.

- If you bought some shampoo that nobody in your household likes, pour it into a clean, empty pump dispenser and voilà: You have liquid soap. It's easy on your hands yet gets them nice and clean.

◆ Are your hands a mess from grease, gardening, or generally getting things done? Clean very dirty hands by scrubbing with Quaker Yellow Corn Meal that has been moistened with  a little bit of Heinz Apple Cider Vinegar. Thoroughly scrub your hands—don't miss a grimy finger, knuckle, nail, or palm. Rinse well and dry; repeat if necessary. Your hands will be soft and smooth—and the dirt will be gone!

◆ Wash water-based paint from your hands with a squirt of Suave shampoo.

◆ If your hands are freshly stained with water-based paint, wash and scrub with ARM & HAMMER Baking Soda. Dig your fingernails right into the soda to clean them too.

◆ After working with berries or other fruits that stain, rinse your hands with ReaLemon Lemon Juice to get rid of the color.

Moisturizing Ideas

◆ Johnson's Baby Powder works like a lotion to soften your hands. Just sprinkle a bit on your skin and massage it in.

◆ Mix equal parts Heinz Vinegar and Vaseline Healthy Hand & Nail Lotion to help soothe chapped hands.

◆ When your hands are chapped, you can always turn to Suave conditioner to moisturize and soothe.

- Crisco All-Vegetable Shortening makes a handy hand cream. It softens and is extremely economical.

- Regular use of the following vinegar spray will soften your hands and make them smell nice too! Combine 1 gallon Heinz Vinegar with herbs and spices such as McCormick Ground Cinnamon or Ground Nutmeg. Let mixture sit for 1 month. Strain the fragrant vinegar into an empty, clean spray bottle, or buy a new decorative bottle to keep at your sink. Spray vinegar mixture on your hands after washing dishes.

- Vinegar mixed with onion juice may help reduce the appearance of age spots. Mix equal parts onion juice and Heinz Vinegar and dab onto age spots. After several weeks of this daily routine, spots should lighten and you should smell delicious!

Odor Eaters

- Remove fish, onion, or garlic odor from hands with a solution of 3 parts ARM & HAMMER Baking Soda to 1 part water or Ivory Liquid Hand Cleanser. Rub, then rinse.

- To remove onion odor from your hands, sprinkle on a little Morton Salt, then moisten with a bit of Heinz Vinegar. Rub hands together and rinse.

- If your hands smell like garlic, rub a cut lemon over them.

- Chopping garlic or onions leaves a definite fragrance on your fingers. Rub them with a Pampers baby wipe to counteract the odor.

- Do your hands smell of fish, garlic, or other strong odors? Rub a few coffee beans in your hands; the oil released absorbs the odor. Wash your hands with soap and warm water once the odor is gone.

- If you have a lingering smell on your hands from strong-smelling foods, rub them with a bit of Crest toothpaste. Rinse.

Most Pure and Floatable, Bar None

In 1879, James Gamble developed a pure white bar soap for laundry and bathing and dubbed it "P&G White Soap." His partner, Harley Procter, favored a more distinctive name and was inspired one Sunday morning by a verse from Psalm 45 that described fragrant garments from "out of the ivory palaces." Research results declared Ivory $99^{44}/_{100}$ percent pure soap; "It Floats" was added to the slogan in 1891. The first Ivory television commercial aired in 1939, during the first televised baseball game (the Cincinnati Reds versus the Brooklyn Dodgers).

- Prevent gasoline-scented hands at the pump by slipping a plastic grocery bag over each hand before you pump.

Banish Blisters

- Before you head outside to work in the garden or tackle other chores, rub about a tablespoon of Argo Corn Starch between your hands. The powder absorbs perspiration and prevents blisters.

◆ When the weather is cold and your outdoor chore really can't be done while wearing gloves, protect your bare hands with Johnson's Baby Oil. Put a few drops in your palms and thoroughly massage it all over your hands. The oil closes pores to protect against skin damage.

Nail Care

◆ Don't have a proper nailbrush? Make your own with an old Reach toothbrush. Cut down the bristles to approximately half their original size. The soft bristles will be easy on your fingertips and cuticles but will still get the job done.

Manicure Mysteries Revealed

◆ Stop nail polish from thickening by storing it in the refrigerator.

◆ Rescue nail polish that has become hardened or gummy by placing the bottle into a pan of boiling water for a few seconds.

◆ Quick-dry nail polish by plunging your hands into a bowl of ice water while the polish is still wet.

◆ Clean fingernails (and toenails too) by scrubbing with a nailbrush dipped in ARM & HAMMER Baking Soda. This also softens cuticles.

◆ Fingernails can benefit from the cleansing, mildly abrasive qualities of Crest toothpaste... and it removes unpleasant smells from your hands at the same time. Squeeze some onto a nailbrush and scrub away!

- Soak your fingernails in ReaLemon Lemon Juice for 10 minutes, then rinse well with warm water. This will help strengthen and brighten fingernails.

- To strengthen your fingernails, give them an occasional "bath" in Kraft Mayonnaise. Soak for 5 minutes, then wash with soap and warm water.

Nailed It!

As long ago as 3000 B.C., people impatiently blew on their fingers, urging their nail polish to dry. Egyptians stained their fingernails with henna. The Chinese created varnishes and lacquers with gum arabic, egg whites, gelatin, and beeswax.

Gold and silver were the colors for royal fingernails during the Chou Dynasty (c. 600 B.C.). Later, red and black were assigned the royal role; lower-ranking women could wear nail polish of only pale tones, under penalty of death. Talk about a fatal fashion faux pas!

- Use Instant Krazy Glue to repair a split or torn fingernail in an emergency.

- Use a Lipton Tea Bag and clear Revlon Nail Enamel to repair a badly broken nail. Just cut a small piece out of the tea bag, cover the tear, and apply polish to cover the fabric. Press gently, then repolish the nail with a colored polish.

- The striking portion of a matchbook is an excellent substitute for a nail file or an emery board.

- Moisturize your cuticles with Crisco Pure Vegetable Oil.

- Before your manicure, soak your hands in a solution of 1 cup warm water and 1 teaspoon Dawn dishwashing liquid. This will soften your cuticles as it cleans your fingernails, allowing polish to spread smoothly and adhere better.

- To soften your cuticles, rub in a dollop of Alberto VO5 Conditioning Hairdressing.

- When you can't decide which shade of Revlon Nail Enamel to apply, simply try a few on! Cover 1 or 2 nails with a piece of Scotch Magic Tape and apply the polish to the tape.

- Speed up the drying time for that manicure *and* moisturize your hands: After applying Revlon Nail Enamel, spray your nails with PAM cooking spray.

- Make your manicure last longer by soaking fingertips for 1 minute in 2 teaspoons Heinz Vinegar and ½ cup warm water before applying polish.

- Use a Q-tips cotton swab to fix smudges on cuticles or edges when polishing your nails. If you need a point, tease the end of the swab and twist it into a point before dabbing.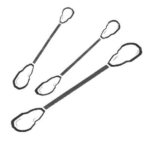

- Before capping your nail polish bottle, use a Q-tips cotton swab to apply a thin coat of Vaseline Petroleum Jelly to the threads inside the cap. This will prevent the cap from getting stuck.

◆ Save some money and do the environment a favor…all in the name of a good manicure! In place of cotton or tissue, use an old pair of No nonsense pantyhose to remove nail polish. Cut the hose into 1-inch rings and dampen with Cutex Quick & Gentle Liquid Nail Polish Remover.

FOOTNOTES

◆ Enjoy a mini "bubble massage": Pour 1½ gallons warm water into a large plastic basin and mix in ¼ cup Morton Salt and ¼ cup ARM & HAMMER Baking Soda. Soak feet for 15 minutes.

◆ Treat your feet to a soothing salt rub after a bath. Add a small amount of Colavita Extra Virgin Olive Oil to a handful of Rite Aid Epsom salts; scrub your feet with the mixture until the salts have dissolved and your skin is soft.

◆ Weary feet will respond to this cool treatment: Mix together 8 mashed strawberries, 2 tablespoons Colavita Extra Virgin Olive Oil, and 1 teaspoon Morton Sea Salt or Coarse Kosher Salt to form a paste. Massage all over your tired tootsies. Rinse off and dry with a soft towel.

Cool Bath for a Hot Day

½ cup ReaLemon Lemon Juice
½ cup ReaLime Lime Juice
5 drops McCormick Pure Lemon Extract
½ cup ARM & HAMMER Baking Soda (if your home has hard water)

Mix ingredients in a bowl; pour into tepid bathwater. Enjoy a soothing soak!

◆ Raid your kitchen pantry to soften really rough, dry feet. First, soak your feet in warm water for 10 or 15 minutes to soften them; pat dry with a soft towel. Next, sprinkle Quaker Yellow Corn Meal onto your hands and rub your feet, scrubbing the calluses; rinse. Then mix 2 tablespoons Colavita Extra Virgin Olive Oil and ½ cup chilled sour cream; massage the moisturizing mixture into your feet. Rinse with warm water; pat dry.

◆ Your feet will love this soothing, smoothing lotion: Combine 1 tablespoon Colavita Extra Virgin Olive Oil, 1 tablespoon almond essential oil, and 1 teaspoon Kretschmer Wheat Germ. Store in a tightly capped bottle. Shake well before using.

◆ Wake up with soft, moisturized feet: Rub on some Crisco Pure Vegetable Oil at bedtime, then put on a pair of clean cotton socks.

◆ Warm some Crisco Pure Vegetable Oil in a double boiler or in a glass measuring cup inside a pan of water on the stove. Apply the warm oil to your feet, wrap them in a warm, damp towel, and sit for 10 minutes or until the towel cools off. Your feet will feel noticeably softer.

◆ Soften your feet overnight. Rub on a light coat of Suave shampoo or conditioner at bedtime, then wear a pair of cotton socks to bed.

IN THE BATH

◆ ARM & HAMMER Baking Soda added to bathwater has a softening effect on the skin (and it will reduce the ring around the tub). Add ½ cup to a full bath. Soaking in this water also helps relieve sore muscles and fatigue.

◆ To relieve itchy skin and/or aching muscles, add 1 cup Heinz Apple Cider Vinegar to a bathtub of warm water. Soak in tub for at least 15 minutes.

◆ Make yourself a soothing milk bath by adding ½ cup Carnation Instant Nonfat Dry Milk to warm bathwater. Milk soothes the skin.

Bubble Bath: Bubble, Bubble... No Toil, No Trouble

1 gallon water
2 cups soap flakes
½ cup glycerin
2 cups Suave shampoo
   Scented oil (optional)

For a relaxing bubble bath, combine the water, soap flakes, and 2 tablespoons of the glycerin in a pot. Stir over low heat until the soap flakes dissolve. Pour into a large bowl; add the rest of the glycerin, shampoo, and (if desired) scented oil. Cool, then store in quart containers at room temperature. As bathtub fills, add 1 cup of mixture.

◆ Mix 3 tablespoons Suave shampoo and 2 cups Crisco Pure Vegetable Oil in a blender. Use as a moisturizing bubble bath.

◆ Suave shampoo can double as a bubble bath. Pour a capful into running water as you fill the tub.

- No, it's not bathtub gin—that's something else entirely. Treat your body to a beer bath to relax you and soften your skin. Pour 3 bottles of Budweiser beer into a tub of hot water, sit back, and relax.

- Relieve itchy skin during the winter by pouring 1 cup ARM & HAMMER Baking Soda and 1¼ cups Johnson's Baby Oil into your bath.

- Make bubbling bath salts with 2½ cups ARM & HAMMER Baking Soda, 2 cups McCormick Cream of Tartar, and ½ cup Argo Corn Starch. Mix ingredients together and store in a covered container. Use ¼ cup per bath.

- Cut off a No nonsense pantyhose leg and make yourself a back scrubber to use in the bath. Insert a bar of Ivory Soap; move it to the middle of the hosiery piece. Tie knots on both sides of the soap. Pick it up by the "handles" and scrub to your heart's (and back's) content!

- Shampoo, conditioner, and body wash bottles can slip right through your hands in the shower. Solve that problem by stretching a couple of thick rubber bands around each one.

Scented Bubbling Bath Mix

2 cups Crisco Pure Vegetable Oil
3 tablespoons Suave shampoo
2 drops perfume or scented essential oil

Pour ingredients into a blender and mix well for 10 seconds. Store in a plastic bottle, and add 2 tablespoons to each bath.

- Blow up a gallon-size GLAD Food Storage Zipper Bag for a handy bath pillow.

- Save money on gifts—or treat yourself— by making your own fragrant bath salts. This project is best done on a day with low humidity, as the salt will absorb moisture from the air. In a large glass or metal mixing bowl, combine 2 cups Rite Aid Epsom salts and 1 cup Morton Sea Salt or Coarse Kosher Salt. Mix well. Add a few drops of McCormick Food Color and stir with a metal spoon until well blended (food coloring will stain plastic or wooden spoons). Add ¼ teaspoon glycerin and, if you wish, 4 to 5 drops of scented essential oil (such as vanilla, citrus, or peppermint). Stir again. Add more food coloring if desired. Spoon colored salts into decorative glass jars (with screw-on metal lids or cork stoppers) or clear gift bags. Add a gift tag with instructions to use ⅓ to ½ cup of the salts in a bath.

SKIN SOLUTIONS

- After you take a shower or bath, and while your skin is still wet, sprinkle Morton Salt onto your hands and rub it all over your skin. This salt massage will remove dry skin and make your skin smoother to the touch. It will also invigorate your skin and get your circulation moving. Try it first thing in the morning to help wake up or after a period of physical exertion.

- Look no further than your kitchen cupboards for excellent skin moisturizers: Crisco Pure Vegetable Oil, Crisco Natural Blend Oil, and Kraft Mayonnaise all work well.

- Freeze skin lotions and gels (such as aloe vera) in plastic ice cube trays. You'll get quick, cool relief for insect bites, rashes, chapped hands, sunburn, and other minor burns.

- Fight cellulite with a homemade herbal wrap. Combine ½ cup grapefruit juice, 1 cup Crisco Pure Corn Oil, and 2 teaspoons McCormick Ground Thyme. Massage mixture into trouble spots such as hips, thighs, and buttocks. Cover areas with GLAD Cling Wrap, and hold a heating pad over each section for 5 minutes.

- Fight cellulite with the same active ingredient found in expensive creams—caffeine. Simply rub some used, cool Folgers coffee grounds on troublesome areas.

- To reduce the appearance of scars, give them a daily massage with a bit of Colavita Extra Virgin Olive Oil.

- Heat got you down…but not out? For a good night's sleep and to prevent heat rash, sprinkle Clabber Girl Baking Powder on your sheets.

- Rub a paste of ARM & HAMMER Baking Soda and water onto elbows to smooth away rough skin.

- Use Kraft Mayonnaise as a treatment for those really tough, rough, dry spots on the skin, such as on the feet, knees, and elbows. Rub a dab of mayo into the area, then rinse clean.

- Here's a remedy for dry or cracked areas—especially elbows, knees, and heels: Mix together 1 part dry Old Fashioned Quaker Oats, 1 part ARM & HAMMER Baking Soda, and 3 parts water. With a clean cloth, apply the mixture in a circular motion to all body parts that require attention.

- Turn your kitchen into a tanning salon...but without the ultraviolet rays. Brew 2 cups strong Lipton tea (black, not green!), allow the liquid to cool, and pour into a spray bottle. Spray the tea onto clean, dry skin; air-dry. Repeat until desired skin tone is achieved.

AROMA ARENA

- Try this inexpensive scented powder when you're fresh out of the bath or shower: Combine Argo Corn Starch with a few drops of your favorite perfume or scented oil. If you prefer a spicy scent, use 1 tablespoon cinnamon oil per ½ cup corn starch. Towel yourself dry, then sprinkle all over your body.

◆ Out of deodorant? Mix equal parts Argo Corn Starch and ARM & HAMMER Baking Soda with a pinch of McCormick Ground Cloves. Apply mixture to your underarm areas. If you're in a real hurry, simply sprinkle on a little Clabber Girl Baking Powder.

◆ Homemade deodorant can be as effective as any commercial brand. Just combine 2 tablespoons Johnson's Baby Powder, 2 tablespoons ARM & HAMMER Baking Soda, and 2 tablespoons Vaseline Petroleum Jelly in a small pan. Stir over low heat until the concoction is creamy and smooth; cool. Store in an airtight container and apply daily to underarms.

◆ For a simple daily deodorant, dust ARM & HAMMER Baking Soda under arms using a powder puff. As an alternative, apply Argo Corn Starch to underarms with a powder puff first, then apply ARM & HAMMER Baking Soda.

Deodorant by Degree: Mum's the Word on a "Soft & Dri" Secret

1888: An unknown inventor from Philadelphia develops the first commercial deodorant, then trademarks it and distributes it under the name "Mum."

Late 1940s: Mum production employee Helen Barnett Diserens envisions a deodorant based on the same principle as the newly invented ballpoint pen.

1955: After several years of tinkering, Bristol-Myers markets a successful new applicator as Ban Roll-On.

1958: Mennen introduces Speed Stick, a gel stick deodorant for men.

1967: The first successful aerosol antiperspirant, Arrid Extra Dry, hits stores (and underarms).

- Dip a few Q-tips cotton swabs in your favorite fragrance—either perfume, cologne, or a scented oil—and carry them in your purse, sealed in a GLAD Food Storage Zipper Bag. Touch a swab to a few pressure points later in the day or whenever you need a pick-me-up.

- To remove the scent from old perfume and cologne bottles, wash with Dawn dishwashing liquid and water, rinse well, and fill with Rite Aid isopropyl rubbing alcohol. Wait a few days, then empty and rinse well with clear water. When the bottle is dry, it'll be ready for a new aroma.

BABY AND CHILD CARE

- Here's a recipe to give baby a soothing bath: Mix together ¼ cup Carnation Instant Nonfat Dry Milk; ¼ cup whole, dry buttermilk; and 1 tablespoon Argo Corn Starch. Store in a covered glass jar. Pour 1 tablespoon of mixture into a baby bathtub or ¼ cup into a full-size tub. This makes a great yet inexpensive gift for new mothers!

- Before diapering baby, apply a coating of Crisco All-Vegetable Shortening directly on baby's bottom to form a moisture barrier.

SOSS!
(Save Old Soap Slivers)

It's a shame to just toss those slivers of Classic Ivory Bar Soap. Whenever a bar becomes too small to handle, cut slits in an O-Cel-O sponge and tuck in the soap pieces. Or, put the slivers in a clean child-size sock to make a soaped-up washcloth. Both are perfect for your child's bath time.

◆ No matter how hard you try, it seems shampoo always gets in baby's eyes. Divert the lather to the sides by applying a thin line of Vaseline Petroleum Jelly above his or her eyebrows.

◆ A quick trick to remove stains on your kids' faces is to rub the spots with Crest toothpaste. Rinse thoroughly.

◆ Clean baby combs and brushes by swishing them in a small basin of water with 1 teaspoon ARM & HAMMER Baking Soda. Rinse well and allow to dry.

◆ Add a little McCormick Food Color to a child's bathwater, and he or she might start begging to take more baths.

◆ If you run out of Johnson's Baby Powder, Argo Corn Starch makes a great substitute and is more absorbent than talcum powder. Your baby will stay comfortably dry and avoid heat rash. Use sparingly, and be sure to keep corn starch away from baby's nose and eyes.

◆ In an emergency, when the tape tabs on a Pampers diaper fail, use small pieces of Scotch Duct Tape instead.

◆ To keep diaper pins handy, stick them in a bar of Ivory Soap. The light coating of soap will allow the pins to go easily through the cloth diaper.

◆ Childproof electrical outlets by covering the openings with Scotch Duct Tape or High Performance Packaging Tape. (Make sure children cannot remove the tape on their own.)

◆ Many families mark each child's height on a wall once a year or so. But what happens when you want to paint the kitchen? Or if you move? Instead, write the name, date, and height on a small piece of Scotch Magic Tape or Masking Tape, placing that on the wall at the appropriate spot. At some point you can put all these records in a scrapbook.

Lost but Not Forgotten

Finding a gemstone, contact lens, earring, hardware, or any very small object on a carpet is challenging. Next time, cut off a No nonsense pantyhose leg (or use a knee high), checking that the toe portion has no holes. Slide it over the nozzle of your vacuum cleaner attachment hose. (Need reassurance? Slip on another piece of pantyhose.) Secure with a tightly wound rubber band. Switch on the vacuum; slowly, systematically move the nozzle over the carpet. The tiny treasure will soon be caught by the pantyhose filter.

◆ Babies and children often are sensitive to loud noises. Use Scotch Duct Tape to cover the speaker on noisy toys, especially those without volume adjustment. (Parents often appreciate this tip as much as their children do!)

ANOTHER TIP OR TWO

◆ Clean your eyeglasses with a drop of Heinz Vinegar and a soft cloth.

◆ Having trouble putting on pierced earrings? Coat the posts and your earlobes with a bit of Vaseline Petroleum Jelly or Crisco Pure Vegetable Oil. The earrings will slip right in.

◆ Can't get your ring or bracelet off? Work up a lather on your hands with Dawn dishwashing liquid and it will soon slide off.

◆ A little Suave conditioner on your finger can free your ring. If you hold your arm straight up for about a minute, the ring will pop off even more easily.

◆ Wish you could turn those slippery slivers of soap into something other than trash? Collect them in a sandwich-size GLAD Food Storage Zipper Bag. When the bag is about half full, place it in a pot of warm—but not boiling—water. Remove when the soap melts. When it cools, you'll have a new bar of soap.

◆ Avoid the frustration of fogged-up bathroom mirrors with the help of Crest toothpaste. Before you shower, spread a small quantity on the mirror and then wipe it off. No more shaving cuts or misplaced mascara from an obscured view.

Why Not G-tips?

In 1923, when Leo Gerstenzang of New York City watched his wife affix wads of cotton to toothpicks, an idea was born. Soon he founded a company to market baby care accessories; the top product was ready-to-use cotton swabs originally called Baby Gays. The labels were changed in 1926 to read "Q-tips Baby Gays" and then, some years later, "Q-tips Cotton Swabs." The letter *Q* stands for "quality."

◆ Create a pouch out of GLAD Press'n Seal to contain leftover soaps, toiletries, Q-tips cotton swabs, and more.

◆ When kept in a drawer, small tubes and bottles tend to tip over and roll around. Cut off the legs from a pair of No nonsense pantyhose. Tack the remaining waist and "girdle" portion to the side of the drawer. Store your cosmetics and other products in the pouch created; your belongings will stay corralled.

◆ Bring some order to that bathroom or bedroom drawer. A plastic ice cube tray is the perfect organizer for small items such as bobby pins, hair clips, safety pins, earrings, rings, and spare change.

Chapter 4: Home Remedies

BETTER GET A BIGGER MEDICINE CABINET

Nothing is more important than the well-being of your family. And nothing is more frustrating than a late-night trip to the drugstore. Nothing except the overwhelming number of over-the-counter medicines...for which you then must overpay.

Some common recipe ingredients, including baking soda, herbs and spices, vinegar, and vegetable oil, have surprising, sometimes even medicinal, properties. Certain cleaning products, such as bleach and hydrogen peroxide, get in on the healing and pain-relieving act too.

People are now finding room in the medicine cabinet for such products. Hair conditioner revives dry skin. Cola calms an upset stomach. Duct tape doubles as a bandage.

Experience how everyday products can bring your family help, healing, and health.

Medical Musts

◆ The basic remedies offered here are never a substitute for professional medical attention.

◆ Call a doctor if the problem is chronic or if you have any concerns about its seriousness; if a home remedy doesn't bring prompt relief; or if you experience severe symptoms or side effects.

◆ Be alert to allergies, paying special attention to hidden ingredients (for example, aspirin is a key ingredient of Alka-Seltzer). Also, never give anything containing honey to a child less than 1 year of age.

COUGHS, COLDS & FEVERS

◆ Drink a cup of warm Lipton tea mixed with ReaLemon Lemon Juice and Sue Bee Honey to soothe a sore throat or as a tonic for laryngitis.

◆ To relieve a sore throat or quiet a cough, mix ¼ cup Heinz Apple Cider Vinegar with ¼ cup Sue Bee Honey. Take 1 tablespoon of this mixture every 4 hours. Vinegar kills bacteria, and honey is soothing.

◆ Gargling with a solution of 1 teaspoon Heinz Vinegar and 1 cup water can help ease the pain of a sore throat.

◆ The simplest remedy for minor sore throat pain is a warm saltwater gargle (no matter how much you dislike the taste!). Just add 1 teaspoon Morton Salt to 1 cup warm water and gargle several times a day. See a physician if sore throat persists longer than 3 days or is accompanied by a high fever.

◆ Gargle (but don't swallow!) with Rite Aid hydrogen peroxide 3 times a day to ease a sore throat.

◆ To alleviate a sore throat and also thin mucus, gargle with Heinz Apple Cider Vinegar that has a little Morton Salt and McCormick Pure Ground Black Pepper added to it.

◆ Lessen the pain of a sore throat with this drink: Mix 3 tablespoons ReaLime Lime Juice, 1 tablespoon Dole Pineapple Juice, and 1 teaspoon Sue Bee Honey in a glass of water.

Feed a Fever...Soak a Cold?

Who can remember the old adage? The folk wisdom, thought to have originated in the 1500s, is "Starve a fever, feed a cold." It assumed a lack of fuel would cool the body; more fuel would stoke the internal fires.

Here's good news: Starving is never advised. For colds or flu, drink plenty of water (and other noncaffeinated beverages) and eat light, healthful food such as fruits and vegetables, whole grains, and protein.

- Make your own cough syrup: Mix ¼ cup Sue Bee Honey and ¼ cup Heinz Apple Cider Vinegar; pour into a jar or bottle that can be tightly sealed. Shake well before each use. Take 1 tablespoon every 4 hours. If cough persists for more than a week, see a physician.

- Another cough syrup recipe: Mix 4 tablespoons ReaLemon Lemon Juice, 1 cup Sue Bee Honey, and ½ cup Colavita Extra Virgin Olive Oil. Heat, then stir vigorously. Take 1 teaspoon every 2 hours.

- Honey promotes the flow of mucus and is great for coughs. Mix 1 tablespoon Sue Bee Honey with 1 cup hot water and 2 drops ReaLemon Lemon Juice. Sip for relief.

- Make a healing honey potion for bronchitis: Slice an onion into a bowl, cover with Sue Bee Honey, and let sit overnight. Take 1 teaspoon of the liquid 4 times a day.

- Try this nighttime cough suppressant. Bring 2 cups water to a boil. Stir in 2 sliced lemons, ½ teaspoon McCormick Ground

Ginger, 2 tablespoons Sue Bee Honey, and 2 tablespoons Domino Sugar. Bring to a boil again; reduce heat and simmer until mixture becomes a thick syrup. If you wish, add 1 ounce liqueur or brandy. Allow to cool, then take 1 to 2 teaspoons.

◆ Tomatoes and tomato products contain the antioxidant lycopene, which can lessen the severity of exercise-induced asthma attacks. You will reap the benefits whether you eat them fresh, cooked in sauces, squeezed into juice, or as an ingredient in Heinz Ketchup.

◆ Attention, asthma sufferers! Lung function can increase with an intake of apples. Researchers think that antioxidants, especially the quercetin found in apples, protect lungs from tissue damage. Eat an apple a day… it may well keep the asthma attacks away.

◆ Onions contain the powerful antioxidant quercetin, which can help relieve bronchitis, chest colds, and asthma attacks. Boost your breathing with onions any way you choose: stir-fried with other veggies, in onion soup, on burgers or sandwiches, or chopped up fresh in a salad. Sometimes, just a whiff of a cut onion at close range can clear the passages!

◆ Too sick to even think about eating an onion? Let one break up your congestion from outside your body. Cut a large onion into thin slices; cook in a small amount of water until they're soft. Wrap slices in a clean hand towel; place on your bare chest for 20 minutes once or twice a day.

How the War Against Polio Was Won

The threat and burden of polio, an infectious disease of the nervous system, was a cloud over generations of families in the United States. Beaches and other typically crowded public places went empty if warnings about the disease ran high. After decades of research by many, the breakthroughs of 2 American physicians changed pediatrics—and parenthood—forever. Microbiologist Jonas Salk developed the inactivated poliovirus vaccine (IPV) in 1955. Ten years later, Albert Sabin, also a microbiologist, created a second type of vaccine, called the oral poliovirus vaccine (OPV). OPV contains live, weakened virus and is given orally. It was initially administered as drops on a sugar cube at central locations such as high schools.

- Spiced or herbal tea is great for treating colds. Brew up a cup with some of these antiviral ingredients: mint, ginger, lemon balm, yarrow, thyme, elder, or bee balm.

- When you feel a cold coming on, the antioxidants in a cup of Lipton tea can boost your immune system to help you fight off the sniffles.

- Spice things up a bit to knock out that cold or flu. In a saucepan, combine 1 McCormick Cinnamon Stick, 3 or 4 McCormick Whole Cloves, and 2 cups water; bring to a boil over medium heat. Allow to boil for 3 minutes. Remove from heat and mix in 1½ tablespoons Brer Rabbit Blackstrap Molasses, 2 shots whiskey, and 2 teaspoons ReaLemon

Lemon Juice. Cover; let sit 20 minutes. Strain out cinnamon stick and cloves, then drink ½ cup every 3 to 4 hours, reheating mixture each time.

◆ Long before there were vaccines against influenza, this potion was a big gun . . . and it can still help today. Cut up 1 large, juicy, tart apple; boil it in 1 quart water until it falls apart. Filter out the solids, then add 2 shots whiskey and ½ teaspoon ReaLemon Lemon Juice. Optional: Sweeten the mixture with Sue Bee Honey. Drink at bedtime.

◆ To treat head or chest congestion, add ¼ cup Heinz Vinegar to a vaporizer and run it for an hour or more. To lessen the pain of a sinus infection, deeply breathe in the steam.

◆ In lieu of a vaporizer, boil a teapot of water and several spoonfuls of Heinz Vinegar. Pour the water into a dishpan or large bowl and cover with a towel. Hold your head under the towel, breathing in the steam, to help loosen chest congestion.

◆ Relieve stuffiness with an aromatic chest rub. Combine 10 drops lavender oil, 15 drops eucalyptus oil, and ¼ cup Crisco Pure Vegetable Oil. Mix and massage onto chest.

◆ Sip this warm elixir to reduce a fever: Combine 1½ teaspoons McCormick Cream of Tartar, ½ teaspoon ReaLemon Lemon Juice, 2½ cups warm water, and ½ teaspoon Sue Bee Honey. Drink slowly.

◆ Get the drop on postnasal drip. In a small saucepan, melt ¼ cup Vaseline Petroleum Jelly. Remove from heat. Add 10 drops each peppermint, thyme, and eucalyptus essential oils; stir. Allow the mixture to reach room temperature, then scoop it into a small, clean glass jar (no need to refrigerate). Place a small amount in each nostril 1 to 3 times a day. The petroleum jelly lets you inhale the essences over time instead of immediately absorbing them into your skin.

◆ Make your own saline drops to control annoying postnasal drip. (People with sleep apnea, a condition that involves a dangerous interruption of breathing while asleep, may also want to try these drops to help keep nasal passages open.) Mix ¼ teaspoon Morton Salt and ¼ teaspoon ARM & HAMMER Baking Soda into 1 cup boiled water. Let cool, then draw liquid into an eyedropper; tilt head back and apply to both nostrils. Hold this position for 15 seconds, then blow nose.

We Get the "Jelly" Part, but "Petroleum"?

When his kerosene business flamed out, Brooklyn chemist Robert Augustus Chesebrough headed to Pennsylvania to try his luck in the oil business. The year was 1859. Chesebrough noticed that the gooey stuff—"rod wax," they called it—that gunked up the drilling rigs also healed cuts and burns when smeared on the skin. He took home some rod wax and was able to extract and purify what he then dubbed "petroleum jelly." By 1870 it was marketed with the name Vaseline, a word Chesebrough came up with from *wasser* (German for "water") and *elaion* (Greek for "olive oil"). Within 10 years, sales were booming and a jar could be found in most American households.

- Irrigating the nostrils and sinuses with salt water is an excellent way to control persistent, annoying allergy symptoms. Dissolve ½ teaspoon Morton Salt in 1 cup room-temperature water. Draw mixture into an eyedropper; squeeze gently, and breathe in the liquid through your nostrils. Repeat several times for each nostril, using 2 or 3 drops of solution each time. When through, blow nose until no discharge remains.

- For a person with severe dust allergies, zipping a plastic cover over the mattress is a smart step. Dust mites, however, are persistent creatures, so seal the mattress zipper tight with Scotch Duct Tape.

SKIN SOLUTIONS

Sunburn Pain and Minor Burns

- For sunburn pain, saturate a washcloth with a solution of 4 tablespoons ARM & HAMMER Baking Soda in 1 quart water. Apply to affected area.

- Mix Argo Corn Starch and water to make a paste; apply directly onto sunburned skin to soothe the pain.

- Old Fashioned Quaker Oats can cool down a sunburn or other minor burn. Wrap 1 cup dry oatmeal in cheesecloth and run cool water through it. Squeeze out any excess water and apply to affected area for approximately 20 minutes every 2 hours. You can use the same poultice again and again for about a day; just rinse it under cold water before each application.

◆ Whole milk can ease sunburn pain. Apply it to sunburned skin, let sit for 20 minutes, then rinse with lukewarm water.

◆ Ease the pain of a minor burn by applying a cold, wet Lipton Tea Bag to the burned area. Keep a wet tea bag in the refrigerator for minor cooking burns.

◆ A gentle rinse of Canada Dry Club Soda cools sunburn pain.

◆ Pampers baby wipes can soothe the pain of sunburn and other minor burns.

◆ Relieve sunburn pain with a generous layer of Kraft Mayonnaise.

◆ Cool a sunburn with diluted Heinz Vinegar in a spray bottle. Spray on affected area.

◆ Sunburned kids (of all ages!) can't get enough of this soothing bath. Mix 1 cup Crisco Pure Vegetable Oil, ½ cup Sue Bee Honey, ½ cup Ivory Liquid Hand Cleanser, and 1 tablespoon McCormick Pure Vanilla Extract (not artificial flavoring). Pour mixture into a bottle with a tight-fitting cap. When you're ready to step into the bath, shake the bottle and pour about ¼ cup under running water.

If You've Wondered About Water...

Since the time of the ancient Romans, bubbly water has had a splashy reputation for encouraging good health. Club soda was sold for the first time in the late 1700s, when North American pharmacists invented a way to inject carbon dioxide into plain water. Today, naturally effervescent water is called "seltzer" and is named for a region of Germany (Nieder-Selters). Club soda is basically the same liquid, but it's manufactured and has a higher sodium content.

- To ease the pain of minor burns, cover area with a piece of cloth or gauze that has been soaked in chilled Heinz Vinegar. Do not use this on any burn where skin is broken.

- For a minor burn, separate a raw egg and gently apply the egg white to remove the heat from the burned area.

- "Beat" sunburn pain with this old-fashioned method: Whip 1 egg white, add 1 teaspoon castor oil, and beat together. Apply to sunburned areas.

- To ease the pain a bit and prevent a blister from forming, hold an ice cube on a minor burn.

- If a burn has already caused a bout of crying, this treatment won't be a bother at all! Run cold water over a minor burn, then apply a slice of raw onion. The chemicals in onions that make you cry also block pain. Onion juice, in addition, is a natural antibacterial agent.

- Use honey to treat a burn. Place a dab of Sue Bee Honey on a sterile gauze bandage and cover the burned area. Change the dressing 4 times a day.

- An oatmeal bath can also relieve the itching of minor burns. Add 1 cup uncooked Old Fashioned Quaker Oats to a lukewarm bath as the tub fills. Soak in the tub for at least 20 minutes.

- Apply Crest toothpaste to soothe a minor burn.

Bug Bites and Stings

Note: If you show any signs of an allergic reaction to a sting or bite, seek immediate medical attention.

- Hold the inside of a banana peel on a bee sting for pain relief. Be sure to go indoors first, so you do not attract more bees!

- Place a slice of onion on a bee sting to ease the soreness.

- To remove a bee's stinger from your skin, rub a wet bar of Ivory Soap on the spot, then gently slide the stinger out.

- Make a soothing paste for a bug bite or sting by combining equal parts Morton Salt and ARM & HAMMER Baking Soda and mixing with a little water. Apply to the affected area with a Rite Aid cotton ball.

- Ease bug bites and stings by applying a paste of Argo Corn Starch and ReaLemon Lemon Juice. Try 3 parts corn starch to 1 part juice; adjust amount of juice as needed to achieve paste consistency.

"One Who Knows"

The word *shamanism* stems from the Manchu-Tungus word *shaman* ("one who knows"). The people of northern Asia practice shamanism in the strictest sense, centered on a shaman who is believed to heal the sick, communicate with the otherworld, and escort souls to the otherworld. Other hunting-and-gathering cultures have practiced their own expressions of shamanism, with various methods of healing. These include Native Americans, Australian Aborigines, and certain Arctic peoples.

- Apply a paste of Heinz Vinegar mixed with Argo Corn Starch to a bee sting or bug bite; let dry. This should alleviate some of the pain.

- A bit of Sue Bee Honey on a bug bite can bring relief from pain and itching.

- Get relief from itching caused by allergies, insect bites, rashes, poison ivy or its relatives, eczema . . . you name it: Use a coffee grinder, blender, or food processor to grind 1 cup Old Fashioned Quaker Oats into a powder. Stir powder into a warm bath and enjoy the soothing soak.

- Work a mixture of Morton Salt and water into a paste that will stick to a bee sting or bug bite. Apply paste to the affected area; let sit until dry and then gently rinse off the paste. This should relieve any itch or pain.

- Soothe the sting of a bee or fire ant with a drop of ReaLime Lime Juice.

- When a fire ant bites, sound the alarm—Clorox Regular-Bleach will come to the rescue. Dab the bite area with a solution of equal parts bleach and water. If treated within 15 minutes of the bite, pain and swelling can be relieved. (Go immediately to a doctor, however, if you've been bitten several times, if the pain is extreme, or if the pain spreads from the original bite spot.)

- Mosquitoes after you? Immediately after one bites—before you start to scratch—dab the spot with a few drops of Parsons' Ammonia on a Rite Aid cotton ball. It will help prevent the itch and swelling.

- Treat a mosquito bite by soaking it in salt water, then applying an ointment made of Morton Salt and Crisco All-Vegetable Shortening.

- Mosquito bites can drive you crazy with itching, but they should also drive you to the medicine cabinet for Listerine Antiseptic mouthwash. Moisten a Rite Aid cotton ball or a Kleenex facial tissue with the mouthwash; cover the bite with it for about 15 seconds.

- Rub a little Crest toothpaste onto a mosquito bite or insect sting to soothe pain and itching.

- Rub a wet bar of Ivory Soap directly onto a mosquito or spider bite, and the swelling and itching will soon vanish.

- Ticks do not just tick us off, and many bugs do not merely bug us. Some pose serious health risks, so don't forget to take precautions to protect your skin—especially at particularly sensitive areas like your ankles and feet. While hiking, fishing, weeding—or any time you're exposed to the elements of the great outdoors—wear long pants and socks. Wrap a length of Scotch Duct Tape securely around your pant cuffs to seal out ticks and other pests.

Rashes

◆ Use your freezer to soothe and cool just about any kind of skin itchiness, be it from sunburn, a bug bite, or a rash. Fill each compartment of an empty, clean foam egg carton with Heinz Apple Cider Vinegar; freeze. When the itch gets insane, pop out a vinegar cube and rub it over the spot.

Beauty and the Bath

Taking a bath, right along with taking a nap, is one of those things most people fought against as kids and now long for as grown-ups. The ancient Egyptians, Romans, and Greeks were *the* bathing experts. Wherever the Roman Empire went, their baths (featuring steaming, cleaning, and massaging) went too. The luxurious Caracalla baths in Rome covered nearly 28 acres. By the Middle Ages, baths were a bit more primitive and sensible. Many people in the 1600s visited spas to take baths for their health . . . and remained underwater for days. Even into the early 1900s public baths were favored over facilities in private residences.

◆ Soaking in a tub of salt water can provide great relief for itchy skin. Just add 1 cup Morton Salt or Sea Salt to bathwater. This solution will also soften skin and help you relax.

◆ Ease windburn or poison ivy irritation with a paste of 3 parts ARM & HAMMER Baking Soda and 1 part water. Do not use on broken skin.

◆ Use ReaLemon Lemon Juice to relieve the itching and alleviate a rash from poison ivy. Apply directly to affected areas.

- Treat poison ivy with a mixture of 1 quart milk, 2 tablespoons Morton Salt, and ice. Apply with a cloth to affected skin 3 times a day, for 20 minutes at a time.

- Listerine Antiseptic mouthwash can interrupt the itch from poison ivy. Apply straight from the bottle with a Rite Aid cotton ball a few times a day.

- To soothe the itch of poison ivy, combine 1 teaspoon Clorox Regular-Bleach with 1 quart water. Dip a Rite Aid cotton ball in the solution and pat it onto the red blotches.

- For immediate relief from the itching of a poison ivy rash, swab the affected area with undiluted Rite Aid isopropyl rubbing alcohol; finish by washing with soap and water.

- Help a poison ivy rash clear up more quickly by soaking irritated skin in very warm salt water.

- Soothe the rash from poison oak or poison ivy by using a vinegar compress. Pour ½ cup Heinz Vinegar into a 1-pint container, then add enough water to fill. Chill in the refrigerator, then dampen a cloth or gauze with the solution and apply to rash.

- Use strongly brewed Lipton tea to dry out a poison ivy rash. Dip a Rite Aid cotton ball in the tea and gently apply it to the rash. Allow it to air-dry, then repeat as needed.

- Rub a rash caused by poison ivy with the inside of a banana peel once or twice a day. Relief from the irritation should arrive within a few days.

- A rash can be a pressing problem, so aim a burst of Niagara Spray Starch at it to stop the itch.

- Calm those itchy hives with milk. Soak a cloth in a bowl of cold milk and apply to affected areas for 10 minutes. Wring out, soak in milk again, and reapply.

- If you think you've tried everything to keep a child (or even a grown-up) from scratching chicken pox or other rashes, try this: Put a pair of mittens on the patient and wrap Scotch Duct Tape around them at the wrists to make sure the mittens stay put.

- If a doctor has confirmed that you have shingles, follow his or her treatment regimen exactly. However, some tips for other rashes may also ease your pain and discomfort. (Note: Shingles sufferers should have someone else apply rash remedies to skin, as any excess movement can stress the inflamed nerve path and make things even worse.) One treatment to try is to soak a clean hand towel in cold milk. Fold it twice lengthwise and gently lay it on the areas of blistery rash. Others find this helpful as well: Apply a paste of ARM & HAMMER Baking Soda and water to dry up and soothe the blisters.

◆ Ringworm is a fungus that results in round, scaly patches on the skin. It's unpleasant and also contagious, so treat it aggressively. Dissolve 1 teaspoon Morton Salt in 2 cups distilled water. Saturate a gauze pad with the solution and apply to the affected area for about 30 minutes. The next day, apply a gauze pad soaked with a solution of 1 part Heinz Distilled White Vinegar and 4 parts distilled water. Alternate days with the salt and vinegar compresses. Most cases clear up in about a week.

◆ Eczema flare-ups are miserable, so sufferers can be glad for this handy, inexpensive, effective form of relief. Mix equal parts milk and water in a bowl; soak a clean cotton cloth or a gauze pad in it. Apply cloth or pad to rash for about 3 minutes. Repeat 2 to 4 times, then rinse area with cool water. Use treatment as needed.

Don't Knock It 'Til You've Tried It

Baltimore pharmacist George Bunting was pretty proud of "Dr. Bunting's Sunburn Remedy," the skin cream he created in 1914. When one of his customers swore that "the cream knocked out my eczema," Bunting changed the name to... Noxema.

◆ Let chamomile calm the skin flare-ups known as rosacea. Steep

either a handful of pure chamomile or several chamomile tea bags in 3 cups boiling water for 10 minutes. Strain the liquid, if necessary, and refrigerate for at least several hours. A clean cotton cloth dipped in the tea makes a cooling compress.

Cuts and Scrapes

◆ Try cleaning minor scrapes, cuts, and abrasions with Pampers baby wipes. They'll get the job done while still feeling gentle on tender skin.

◆ Banana peels heal ... as well as save you money and trips to the drugstore. After you clean up those scraped knees, rub them with the inside of the peel. Bananas contain a natural sugar that has mild antimicrobial properties. They also contain the antioxidant lutein, which will speed up the healing process.

◆ Listerine Antiseptic mouthwash kills germs not only in your mouth but also on your skin. Pour it on to clean cuts and scrapes.

◆ Add spice to your life...and to your cuts and scrapes! After you clean and dry a minor cut or scrape, shake on some McCormick Ground Cinnamon; apply a bandage as usual. Cinnamon provides so much more than a pretty smell: It tends to your cut by numbing pain, stopping bleeding, and killing infection-causing bacteria.

◆ To help loosen an adhesive bandage and remove it as painlessly as possible, rub a drop of Suave shampoo or conditioner on and around the bandage. Let it seep through the air holes. It will pull off easily in no time.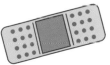

- When you do not have an "official" bandage at hand, you can still provide its key elements: a clean, absorbent material and a way to keep it firmly in place. Clean the cut as well as you can, then cover it with a clean, folded Scott Towel or a piece of fabric. Hold it in place with a length of Scotch Masking Tape or Duct Tape.

- Take preventive action with Scotch Duct Tape. If you are working in a situation in which tools could slip and injure your hand, bandage any exposed areas (knuckles, fingers, palms, etc.) with lengths of tape.

Dry Skin

- To treat chapped hands, coat them with a generous layer of Vaseline Petroleum Jelly. Then place them in a plastic grocery bag (wrapped loosely at the wrists) for 15 minutes.

- Moisturize chapped hands with a small amount of Alberto VO5 Conditioning Hairdressing.

- Moisturize chapped hands and lips by applying a mixture of equal parts ReaLemon Lemon Juice and glycerin.

- Soften dry and cracked heels and feet in a warm bath that is enhanced by grapefruit. Drop a few slices in the tub or squeeze the juice from the tangy fruit into the water. After soaking your feet for 10 minutes, use a washcloth or bath sponge to easily slough off dead skin.

ACHES AND PAINS

Bumps and Bruises

◆ Freeze a wet washcloth in a GLAD Freezer Zipper Bag. You'll be ready for the next burn, teething trial, or knock on the noggin.

◆ Wish you could do more than hop around like a cartoon character when you stub a toe or bang your knee? You certainly can. In a small saucepan, melt 5 parts Vaseline Petroleum Jelly; stir in 1 part McCormick Ground Red Pepper. Let cool, then spoon mixture into a clean glass jar. Apply to bruised area once daily, wearing rubber or plastic gloves to protect your hands from the pepper. (Avoid putting this on your face.) The skin should feel warm but not burning.

◆ Freeze unpopped Orville Redenbacher's popcorn in a pint- or quart-size GLAD Food Storage Zipper Bag. When you place it on a bump or bruise, the bag will conform to the shape of your body, providing maximum comfort. Refreeze as necessary.

◆ Soak a thick slice of onion in Heinz Distilled White Vinegar, then apply onion slice to a bruise. Folk tradition claims this will advance the healing process.

Oh, My Achin' Head

◆ Ease a headache by lying down and applying a compress dipped in a mixture of equal parts warm water and Heinz Vinegar to the temples. Try an herbal vinegar such as lavender to provide aromatic relief.

◆ You may be able to fend off a migraine by taking 1 teaspoon Sue Bee Honey as soon as you feel the warning signs. If you're too late to prevent the migraine, take 2 teaspoons honey with each meal until the pain is gone.

◆ Consuming salt may help lessen the severity of a migraine. Some people get relief by eating a salty snack as soon as they feel headache symptoms coming on.

◆ Ease that throbbing headache. Cut a lime in half and rub it on your forehead.

◆ Caffeine reduces the swelling of blood vessels that causes headaches. For relief, try drinking a cup or two of strong Folgers coffee.

The Buzz on Caffeine

An 8-ounce serving contains the following milligrams of caffeine:

Cola	35–50
Green tea	30–50
Black tea	40–50
Coffee (brewed)	90–100

◆ Have an extreme headache? Let temperature extremes relieve you of it. While the tub is filling for a hot bath, put together an ice pack. Soak in the steamy water while holding the ice pack on the top of your head. The hot-and-cold combo draws blood away from your head and narrows blood vessels in your scalp.

◆ To increase the pain-relieving effectiveness of aspirin or acetaminophen, take them with some caffeinated Folgers coffee or Pepsi rather than water. As always, be sure to consult your doctor and follow safe-dosage guidelines for these over-the-counter medications.

◆ Prevent a hangover (or at least take some of the punch out of it) by ordering French onion soup before going out for a night on the town. The sugar in onions speeds up your metabolism, burning the alcohol more quickly, while the cheese on top will slow the alcohol's flow into your bloodstream.

◆ Get relief from a hangover by taking 1 teaspoon Sue Bee Honey every hour until you feel better.

Sore Muscles and Joints

◆ Keep custom-made ice packs in the freezer for the occasional sprain or aching muscle. To make a small ice pack, pour 1 cup Rite Aid isopropyl rubbing alcohol and 2 cups water into a quart-size GLAD Food Storage Zipper Bag. Squeeze out air and press closed. The mixture will remain slushy, which is helpful for shaping around sprained knees or elbows. For large ice packs, use gallon-size GLAD Food Storage Zipper Bags and double the recipe.

- Make your own massage oil to soothe sore muscles. Mix 1 tablespoon horseradish in ½ cup Colavita Extra Virgin Olive Oil and let mixture stand for 30 minutes. Apply liberally.

- Soaking in a bathtub of hot water and 2 cups Heinz Vinegar for 30 minutes will relieve a minor backache and soothe sore muscles.

- Another remedy for sore muscles is to boil 1 cup Heinz Apple Cider Vinegar and add 1 teaspoon McCormick Ground Red Pepper during boil. Cool this mixture, then apply it in a compress to sore area. Make sure pepper doesn't irritate the skin. The compress should make the area feel warm but not burning.

- Ease the pain of a leg cramp or muscle strain by using a soft cloth soaked in warm Heinz Vinegar as a compress. Apply for only 20 minutes at a time.

- To soothe arthritis pain in your hands, make a paste by mixing 2 cups Old Fashioned Quaker Oats and 1 cup water in a bowl. Warm (but don't cook) the mixture, then apply for quick relief.

- A light coat of WD-40 may help with arthritis pain. Spray it on the troublesome joint or area, then rub it in with a clean, soft cloth or a Scott Towel.

- Try this liniment during a rubdown to relieve achy muscles and arthritis pain: Mix ½ cup Heinz Apple Cider Vinegar, ¼ cup Colavita Extra Virgin Olive Oil, and 2 egg whites.

Massage into the painful parts; use a clean cotton cloth to wipe off any excess.

- Relieve bursitis by massaging the shoulder or upper arm daily with warm Crisco Pure Vegetable Oil or Colavita Extra Virgin Olive Oil.

- A Penn tennis ball inside a sock makes an excellent massager for the lower back. Or, put 3 or 4 tennis balls in a knee sock or sweat sock; knot the end closed.

RELIEF IS HERE

The Eyes (and Ears) Have It

- Flush out pepper or other eye irritants with a few drops of milk.

- An egg makes a nifty hot compress for a cyst, a sty, or other irritation around the eye. Hard-boil the egg but don't remove its shell. While the cooked egg is still warm, wrap it in a clean washcloth and hold it to your eye for 10 minutes. To continue treatment, return the egg to the pot of water to reheat it.

Fashion Spectacle

The 3M Corporation makes a variety of Scotchgard that is used only by the eyeglass manufacturing industry. Scotchgard Protector provides a dirt-, glare-, and scratch-resistant coating for lenses. Other industrial variations include those made for the automotive industry. Just please don't aim your can of Scotchgard at your specs!

- To soothe an earache, put warm (not hot) Colavita Extra Virgin Olive Oil into a dropper and add a few drops into the ear. Then apply a warm heating pad.

- An onion poultice is another remedy to try for an earache. Heat half an onion in the oven (not the microwave) until it is warm, but not hot. Wrap onion in cheesecloth and hold it against the sore ear until the onion cools. The onion's natural chemicals speed up blood circulation (and therefore the delivery of anti-biotics, if prescribed), which in turn helps fight infection.

- Get some relief from the ear pain caused by pressure changes during an airplane flight. Dampen a Scott Towel with hot water, then ball it up and put it in the bottom of a Dixie cup. Tilt your head at a slight downward angle and hold the cup over the hurting ear for about 1 minute. The steam will soften the earwax to lessen the pain.

- Swimmer's ear, an infection of the exterior of the ear and the ear canal often caused by water and damp conditions in the ear, can be treated with vinegar. Combine equal parts Heinz Vinegar and  Rite Aid isopropyl rubbing alcohol in a small jar with a tight-fitting lid. Use an ear dropper to apply 1 to 2 drops of this liquid in each ear 3 times a day during swimming season to prevent infection. Do not use this treatment if you suspect an inner ear infection; instead, see a doctor as soon as possible.

◆ Among the effects of swimmer's ear is a wearing away of earwax, which protects the ear canal and provides a home for good bacteria. Create some "homemade" earwax by dipping a Rite Aid cotton ball in Vaseline Petroleum Jelly and tucking it just inside the ear. Replace daily until condition improves.

◆ Loosen excess earwax with this gentle approach: Warm a small amount of Crisco Pure Vegetable Oil. Use a clean medicine dropper or eyedropper to put 1 or 2 drops of oil into each ear. Do this twice a week; the wax will soon flow out on its own.

◆ If you don't have an eyedropper handy for eye and ear remedies, improvise with a flexible drinking straw. Insert the straw into liquid and cover the open end with your finger; lift and use.

My Mouth Hurts!

◆ As a temporary remedy for a toothache before you can get to the dentist, rinse your mouth with a mixture of 4 ounces warm water, 2 tablespoons Heinz Vinegar, and 1 tablespoon Morton Salt.

◆ Use a rinse of 1 teaspoon Morton Salt in 4 ounces warm water when gums are painful. Swish the solution around in your mouth. If you have an abscess, the salt will draw out some of the infection. Note: See a dentist as soon as possible if you experience pain in your gums.

◆ Reduce the pain of a toothache by holding an ice cube in the V-shape skin area between your thumb and index finger. Apply to the hand that is on the same side of the body as the bothersome tooth. How does it work? The nerve pathways are the same for these 2 places, and nerves can send only 1 message at a time to your brain.

The Flavor of Flavonoids

Brewed teas—made from real tea leaves—contain natural antioxidants called *flavonoids.* According to the American Dietetic Association, both black and green tea promote "reduced risk for coronary heart disease, as well as gastric, esophageal, and skin cancers. Tea and tea flavonoids have also been shown to help strengthen the body's immune system, protect teeth by inhibiting plaque bacteria, potentially fight free radicals produced during strenuous exercise, and possibly increase calories burned during everyday activities." Now that's my cup of tea!

◆ Rinsing with a solution of 2 to 3 teaspoons Morton Salt in 1 cup warm water will also help relieve the pain of a sore tooth.

◆ Gum disease is not an inevitable part of getting older. Fight it by brushing your teeth with a paste made from 3 parts ARM & HAMMER Baking Soda and 1 part Rite Aid hydrogen peroxide. (Consult your dentist about whether to use this method exclusively or alternate with regular toothpaste.)

◆ Stop bleeding gums and soothe the pain after losing a tooth (or having one pulled) by pressing a moist, cool Lipton Tea Bag against the sore spot.

◆ Ease a toothache or other mouth pain by rinsing your mouth with a cup of peppermint tea that's mixed with a pinch or 2 of Morton Salt. Peppermint is an antiseptic and contains pain-relieving menthol.

◆ Soothe a scalded throat or tongue by taking 2 teaspoons Colavita Extra Virgin Olive Oil.

◆ Canker sores are annoying and painful. Put 2 teaspoons McCormick Ground Sage in a cup of hot water; let steep for about 10 minutes. Add ½ teaspoon ReaLemon Lemon Juice. Gargle with the warm solution.

◆ Another canker sore remedy is to soak a Lipton Tea Bag in a hot sugar-water solution (about 1 teaspoon sugar to 1 cup hot water) for about 1 minute. Let cool slightly, then hold it against the sore for a few minutes. Do this a few times a day, and relief is on the way.

Talk About Morning Breath!

Can you believe that most Americans didn't brush their teeth until after World War II, when soldiers brought this habit back home with them?

◆ Canker sores are a painful and hard-to-ignore problem. Mix ½ teaspoon ARM & HAMMER Baking Soda into half a glass of warm water. Rinse your mouth with the solution every few hours until the sores heal.

◆ To clear up a cold sore, hold a warm, wet Lipton Tea Bag on it for about 15 minutes. Do this several times a day until you get relief.

- Dab a little ReaLemon Lemon Juice on that irritating cold sore or fever blister. It acts as an astringent and promotes healing.

- Cold milk helps speed the healing of a cold sore. Apply a milk-soaked Rite Aid cotton ball to the sore to ease the pain.

- When your mouth is on fire from spicy food, water only makes it worse. Instead, drink milk. It dilutes the oils that cause the spiciness.

- Ouch! Who hasn't burned their mouth or tongue by eating something too hot? Get some relief by rinsing with salt water every hour or so, using ½ teaspoon Morton Salt in 1 cup warm water.

- Biting your tongue or cheek can result in a large amount of blood, but it is rarely serious. To ease the pain, rinse your mouth with 1 teaspoon Morton Salt in 1 cup warm water.

Foot Troubles

Attention, diabetics: Always consult your doctor before you soak your feet or apply anything to them.

- Smooth rough and hardened calluses and heels by massaging with a paste of 3 parts ARM & HAMMER Baking Soda and 1 part water.

- Lemon also works to soften calluses and other rough spots on your feet, heels, and elbows. Rub the affected area with half a lemon.

- Remove corns and calluses by covering rough areas with Rite Aid cotton balls soaked in Heinz Vinegar. Secure cotton balls with tape or bandages; leave on overnight. The areas should be softened by morning. Repeat nightly until problem areas disappear.

- To get rid of a corn, soak it in warm Lipton tea for 30 minutes every day. After a week or two, the tea's tannic acid will dissolve the corn.

- You can also soak a corn in Heinz Apple Cider Vinegar for 10 minutes, then place a piece of Scotch Duct Tape over it and leave in place overnight. Peel the tape off in the morning. Repeat this procedure for about a week, and you should see some relief.

- Another way to get rid of a corn is to soak the foot in warm water to soften it, and then place a piece of lemon peel over the corn (with the inside facing the corn). Secure with tape or bandages and leave on overnight.

- Get rid of a plantar wart by holding a hot, wet Lipton Tea Bag on it for 15 minutes. Do this every day until that painful problem shrinks and disappears.

- A banana peel can help remove a plantar wart. Before bed, use Scotch Masking Tape to tape a piece of banana peel (inside part down) over the wart. Cover area with a bandage or wear a clean, tight-fitting sock; leave on overnight. Repeat every night until the wart disappears.

- Fallen arches can hurt quite a bit. If you are waiting for custom-made arch supports—and have your doctor's approval—wrap your arches with Scotch Duct Tape in the meantime. Apply the tape firmly to give support, but not so tight as to impede circulation.

- To relieve your tired and aching feet, combine ¼ cup Old Fashioned Quaker Oats, ¼ cup coarsely ground almonds, 3 tablespoons cocoa butter, and 2 tablespoons Sue Bee Honey. Massage into both feet and wear clean cotton socks overnight. In the morning, remove the socks and rinse feet with cool water.

- Reenergize your tired feet by massaging ReaLime Lime Juice into the skin.

- Relieve aching and tired feet by soaking them in a tub of warm salt water. Just add a handful of Morton Salt to a gallon of water in a plastic dishpan; soak feet for a half hour or more.

- Treat your feet! Roll the bottoms of your feet over Penn tennis balls while you sit in a chair.

Stuck on You

It's hard to imagine the medical field without... Velcro? Yes, the handy hook-and-loop fastener is used in surgical dressings, orthopedic footwear, wrist splints, tourniquets, and much more. George de Mestral, inspired by the way burrs were securely fastened to his dog's fur upon returning from a hike, dreamed up and perfected the design for Velcro in 1955. The name combines the French words *velour* ("velvet") and *crochet* ("hook").

- Keep smelly feet at bay by sprinkling ARM & HAMMER Baking Soda into socks and shoes to control odor and moisture.

- To control foot odor, soak feet in a mixture of 1 gallon warm water and 1 ounce Heinz Vinegar.

- To eliminate stubborn foot odors, steep 4 Lipton Tea Bags in 1 quart boiling water. Pour into a basin and add enough cold water to cool off the mixture and cover feet. Soak feet for half an hour. Dry thoroughly, then apply foot powder. Repeat twice a day, if necessary, until problem disappears.

- If your feet have a tendency to sweat, try Clabber Girl Baking Powder. Wash and dry your feet, then rub them with a little powder before putting on your socks.

- Add 4 tablespoons ARM & HAMMER Baking Soda to 1 quart warm water; soak feet for 10 minutes to relieve foot itch.

- Athlete's foot is a fungal infection that thrives in dampness. Keep your feet dry by sprinkling Argo Corn Starch on your feet, in your socks, and in your shoes to absorb moisture.

- Clorox Regular-Bleach can remove the fungus that causes athlete's foot. Soak your feet twice a day in a mixture of ½ cup bleach per gallon of water. Relief from the itching and burning will arrive in no time.

- Athlete's foot is a common affliction, so it's only fitting that the following treatment uses 2 of the most common things around: salt and water. Fill a basin with warm water; add ½ cup Morton Salt and mix well. Soak your feet in the solution for 5 to 10 minutes once or twice a day. The brine attacks the fungus and also softens your feet, which makes it easier for antifungal cream to penetrate.

- Try this home remedy for athlete's foot relief: Mix 30 minced garlic cloves, 4 teaspoons McCormick Ground Cinnamon, and 4 teaspoons McCormick Ground Cloves in ½ cup Rite Aid isopropyl rubbing alcohol. Put mixture in a sealed jar and let steep for 2 weeks out of sunlight. Apply 2 times a day with Rite Aid cotton balls. Keep feet dry with a dusting of Argo Corn Starch.

- Relieve athlete's foot by soaking feet every night in pure Heinz Vinegar for 10 minutes. (This may sting if the skin is broken. Discontinue soaking if irritation continues.) After soaking feet, soak a pair of socks in a mixture of equal parts water and Heinz Vinegar. Wear the wet socks on affected feet for at least 30 minutes. Remove and pat feet dry. Repeat this procedure nightly until condition improves.

- We don't often think of an onion as having juice, but it does... and it's powerful stuff. Treat athlete's foot by massaging onion juice into and between your toes, twice a day.

- If your feet are prone to fungal infections, soak them occasionally in a tub of warm salt water. Add 2 teaspoons Morton

Salt to 1 gallon water and soak for 5 to 10 minutes. This treatment will also soften callused areas and help control foot odor.

- Soak your toes in Listerine Antiseptic mouthwash to get rid of unsightly toenail fungus.

- Saturate toenails plagued by fungus with a Rite Aid cotton ball that has been soaked in a mixture of equal parts warm water and Heinz Vinegar. Attach cotton ball to problem area and let sit until cotton dries out. Repeat nightly until condition improves. If you don't see a change after 6 weeks, see a physician. Fungal infections are persistent and prone to recurrence, so be sure to wash and dry hands thoroughly after contact with any fungal infection.

- Remove tar stuck to bare feet by rubbing them with Crest toothpaste.

Hand It Over

- You can remove a splinter more easily by first soaking the affected area in Crisco Pure Corn Oil to soften the skin.

- For a pesky splinter, squeeze a drop of Elmer's Glue-All over the tip of the splinter, let dry, and peel off. The splinter will stick to the glue.

- Before using a needle to remove a splinter, hold an ice cube on the spot for several seconds. This will numb the skin and make it easier to perform the delicate procedure—especially on young ones.

◆ Get the upper hand on a painful splinter by covering it with a piece of tape. Any kind of Scotch tape will do—duct, packaging, masking, transparent—though the stickiest varieties may work better on large splinters. Leave tape on for about 1 hour; pull off. If the splinter remains, replace the tape with a fresh piece and keep it on overnight. In the morning, the splinter should slip out when the tape is pulled off.

◆ Splint that injured finger by taping it to its next-door neighbor with Scotch Duct Tape. If you have any doubts about the severity of the injury, go to an emergency room.

◆ To strengthen your grip, squeeze a Penn tennis ball over and over. Start by doing this for 1 minute, then lengthen the time as your hand grows stronger.

BODY OF KNOWLEDGE

◆ Give yourself more energy with a spoonful of Brer Rabbit Blackstrap Molasses, known in folk medicine as a "blood builder." One tablespoon contains 3.5 milligrams of iron.

◆ One "recipe" for remaining healthy and alert well into the golden years combines good nutrition with an unusual beverage. Maintain a well-balanced diet, and drink a glass of water mixed with 1 teaspoon Sue Bee Honey and 1 teaspoon Heinz Apple Cider Vinegar at each of your 3 meals a day.

◆ Curb your appetite by drinking a mixture of 2 teaspoons Sue Bee Honey in a glass of water 30 minutes before each meal.

- Drink plenty of water, especially in hot weather. If your doctor gives the okay, maintain your electrolyte levels (and fend off muscle cramps when exercising) by adding ½ teaspoon Morton Salt to every quart. Remember to keep your fluids up before you become thirsty, because by that time you're likely to already be dehydrated.

- Cinnamon helps your fat cells recognize and respond to the natural chemical insulin. Each day, sprinkle ¼ to 1 teaspoon McCormick Ground Cinnamon on your food.

- Leg cramps catch you when you're down, especially when you're sleeping. When the pain starts, drink 8 ounces of Canada Dry Tonic Water. The key ingredient, quinine, is rather an acquired taste, so feel free to add a squirt of lemon, lime, or orange juice.

Ale's Well that Ends Well

In 1890, Toronto pharmacist and chemist John J. McLaughlin opened a small factory. He manufactured soda water and sold it to drugstores as a mixer for flavored extracts and fruit juices. He fiddled around with various concoctions, determined to make a better product, and his experiments resulted in a drink he named Canada Dry Pale Ginger Ale. Its popularity spread, and in 1919 McLaughlin started shipping his ginger ale to New York City. Two years later, the first Canada Dry plant opened in the United States, on 38th Street in Manhattan. His tenacity and almost-but-not-quite-unquenchable thirst made John McLaughlin a pioneer of mass-bottling technology, so that customers could take their soda pop home in bottles.

INSOMNIA

- The sleep-inducing properties of warm milk are legendary. Zap a microwaveable mug of fresh milk on high for 1 minute; stir and test temperature before drinking. Or, heat the milk in a small saucepan over low heat until it's warm but not boiling.

- Sue Bee Honey has a mild sedating effect and can aid sleep. Add to herbal tea or warm milk before bedtime.

- Here's a more "heavy-duty" recipe to help you sleep: Stir the following into 1 cup warm milk: 1 tablespoon Carnation Instant Nonfat Dry Milk, 2 tablespoons Sue Bee Honey, and 1 tablespoon brewer's yeast. Drink before going to bed.

- Potassium contributes to a deep and restful sleep. If you're going through a patch of insomnia, eat 1 or 2 bananas during the day.

- Prevent snoring with a Penn tennis ball. Attach it to the back of your pajama top to keep yourself from sleeping on your back—the position most conducive to snoring.

HEALTHY HABITS

- Nicotine tends to remain in the body longer in an alkaline environment. People with the opposite environment—who consume a highly acidic diet—tend to smoke more just to get the same effect. Fruits and vegetables promote an alkaline condition, so they are not only nutritious in general but can also help curb your cigarette cravings.

☉ Say Can You (Vitamin) C?

Yes, you probably can. Here are just a few of the many benefits of vitamin C:

- heals capillary walls and prevents bruises
- lowers cholesterol
- boosts immunity to germs
- helps heal wounds
- keeps gums healthy
- fosters good eye health
- eases muscle and joint pain

- Your desire for cigarettes will lessen with this nightly concoction: At bedtime, for 30 days, drink a solution of ½ teaspoon McCormick Cream of Tartar and Tropicana Pure Premium orange juice (enough to fill a medium-size glass). The OJ replenishes your vitamin C, and the cream of tartar flushes out nicotine. By the end of the month, your cravings should be markedly decreased.

- Another way to quiet cigarette cravings is to drink a glass of water with 2 tablespoons ARM & HAMMER Baking Soda added. Have it with every meal, unless you're on a low-sodium diet or have an ulcer.

- If you're trying to quit smoking or drinking, lessen cravings by sucking on a slice of lime. This will also replace some of the vitamins, calcium, and phosphates your system may have lost.

- Drinking a few cups of green tea at each meal can boost your metabolism, which means calories are burned faster. In addition, green tea aids your quest to lose pounds by helping you lose extra water weight.

- If you are trying to curtail your consumption of salad dressing and other high-calorie or high-fat bottled sauces, use toothpicks. (No, you don't sprinkle them over lettuce.) Instead of removing the foil seal on a new bottle, use a toothpick to poke several holes in the foil. Now it's easy to control portions.

- Help yourself to *not* help yourself to more salt. Cut back with this subtle method: Remove the top of a saltshaker and apply clear Revlon Nail Enamel to some of the holes. Let dry thoroughly before using.

Healthy Beverage Guidelines

Nutritional experts, reporting in the *American Journal of Clinical Nutrition,* recommend that beverages compose not more than 10 to 15 percent of an adult's total daily calories. Women should have 9 total servings (8 ounces each); men, 13. Daily servings should be limited as follows:

Soft drinks, juice drinks	1
Whole milk, 100-percent fruit juices, sports drinks	1
Diet soft drinks, calorie-free tea/coffee with sugar substitute	4
Skim/low-fat milk, unsweetened fortified soy beverages	2
Unsweetened coffee (flavored or unflavored)	4
Unsweetened tea (black, green, white, oolong, herbal)	8
Water (women/men)	9/13

- When you are trying to lose weight, try this trick to help curb your appetite: Sniff a banana when you get the munchies. According to a study, dieters who did this lost a "bunch" of weight—an average of 30 pounds in 6 months.

- Make bananas a regular part of your diet. The potassium they contain helps prevent thickening of your artery walls and regulates fluid levels—both important aspects of maintaining healthy blood pressure. Potassium's ability to regulate fluids is also good for fighting fluid retention.

- Tomato sauce contains the antioxidant lycopene, a known cancer-fighter. Studies at Harvard University indicate that eating just 2 servings a week of foods with cooked tomato sauce, such as spaghetti, can help men cut their risk of developing aggressive prostate cancer in half.

TUMMY TROUBLES

Heartburn and Indigestion

Note: People who must restrict salt intake should not use ARM & HAMMER Baking Soda as an antacid. Do not take for nausea, stomachaches, gas, cramps, or distension from overeating.

- Take ½ teaspoon ARM & HAMMER Baking Soda in half a glass of water to relieve acid indigestion or heartburn. Read antacid use information on the ARM & HAMMER Baking Soda package before using.

- The effervescence of Canada Dry Club Soda causes you to burp, which relieves indigestion.

- Cream of tartar is an acid neutralizer. Mix ½ teaspoon McCormick Cream of Tartar with ½ teaspoon ARM & HAMMER Baking Soda in a glass of water; drink to ease heartburn.

- Make a tasty compote of baked pumpkin and apples spiced with cinnamon and Sue Bee Honey to get rid of heartburn. Or, eat the fresh, baked pumpkin by itself.

- Add raw onions to salads, sandwiches, sauces…just about anything that sounds good. The sulfur compounds in the vegetable have been shown to help fight the *H. pylori* bacteria, which is associated with ulcers and stomach cancer.

- Morning sickness varies from woman to woman, even pregnancy to pregnancy. Many find this remedy helps to calm the stomach: Drink a glass of water mixed with 1 teaspoon Heinz Apple Cider Vinegar first thing every morning.

- A few sips of flat Pepsi can calm a bout of vomiting and soothe a minor stomachache.

- Try this elixir as a remedy for nausea: Mix 1 cup water, 10 drops ReaLime Lime Juice, and ½ teaspoon Domino Sugar. Stir in ¼ teaspoon ARM & HAMMER Baking Soda. Sip it slowly.

The Choice of a New Generation

Pepsi gets its name from its use in treating *dyspepsia*, an intestinal ailment more commonly known as an upset stomach.

- Relieve nausea by mixing ½ cup Tropicana Pure Premium orange juice, 2 tablespoons Karo Light Corn Syrup, a pinch Morton Salt, and ½ cup water in a lidded jar or container. Refrigerate. Take 1 tablespoon every 30 minutes until the queasiness quits.

- Bland foods ease nausea, hence the wisdom of this folk remedy: Cover a bowl of unbuttered, unsalted Orville Redenbacher's popcorn (popped without oil) with boiling water. Eat the resulting mush slowly.

Diarrhea

- Drink a cup of hot Lipton tea with 1 or 2 teaspoons ReaLime Lime Juice for fast relief from diarrhea.

Quotable Quote

"Dyspepsia is the remorse of a guilty stomach."
—Alexander Kerr

- Cure diarrhea with this once-a-day remedy: Peel, core, and puree 1 apple in a blender or food processor. Mix in 1 teaspoon ReaLemon or ReaLime Juice, 3 or 4 drops Sue Bee Honey, and a pinch McCormick Ground Cinnamon. Drink the whole concoction.

- Another remedy for diarrhea: Stir 1 teaspoon carob powder into ¼ cup Mott's Classic apple sauce. Eat 2 or 3 times during the day, but slowly.

◆ Drink a big glass of Mott's apple juice in your war against stomach flu. Acting much like penicillin, compounds in apples fight viruses that cause the flu and other illnesses and will help speed up your recovery.

Constipation

◆ Two tablespoons molasses (Grandma's Original or Brer Rabbit Blackstrap) taken before bedtime can help keep you regular. Add the molasses to milk, fruit juice, or even prune juice to dilute its strong taste.

◆ Constipated? Try this drink before breakfast: Mix 1 cup warm water, 4 tablespoons ReaLemon Lemon Juice, and Sue Bee Honey to taste.

◆ Here's a gentle and palatable way to ease con-stipation: Take 1 tablespoon Sue Bee Honey (a mild laxative) 3 times a day. Mix with Brer Rabbit Blackstrap Molasses for more punch.

◆ Get relief from constipation with a mix of ½ cup Mott's Classic apple sauce, 4 to 6 chopped prunes, and 1 tablespoon bran. Eat just before bedtime—things should feel better in the morning.

◆ Vegetable oil lubricates the intestines and helps to get things moving. Take 2 to 3 tablespoons Colavita Extra Virgin Olive Oil or Crisco Pure Vegetable Oil, Pure Canola Oil, or Natural Blend Oil daily until you find relief.

HEAD LICE

◆ Kill head lice with mayonnaise instead of noxious chemical preparations to which lice are becoming more and more resistant. At bedtime, rub a generous amount of Kraft Mayonnaise into the hair and scalp. Cover with a shower cap. In the morning, rinse thoroughly and wash with Suave shampoo. Remove remaining lice and nits from towel-dried hair with a fine-tooth comb. Repeat in 7 to 10 days.

◆ Vinegar can help control an infestation of head lice. First use a medicated head lice shampoo, or follow your doctor's instructions for lice control. After shampooing hair, rinse with Heinz Vinegar and run a comb dipped in vinegar through damp hair. The vinegar will help loosen any remaining nits, or eggs, from the hair. Continue with treatment prescribed on shampoo bottle.

National Inventors Hall of Fame

Every day, amazing discoveries result from "good ol' American know-how," "10 percent inspiration and 90 percent perspiration," or even plain old dumb luck. Whatever the process, U.S. inventors have made daily life better, safer, healthier, cleaner, quieter, more productive, and just about any other comparative you can utter. The National Inventors Hall of Fame salutes the famous (Eli Whitney, Thomas Edison) and the obscure (Ruth Benerito, a chemist who developed wrinkle-free cotton). Linked with the U.S. Patent and Trademark Office, the Hall of Fame sponsors a museum that's both virtual (www.invent.org) and actual (Alexandria, Virginia).

INFECTIONS AND INFLAMMATIONS

◆ Make your own elixir to help heal or prevent a urinary tract infection. Boil 1 cup cranberry juice; reduce heat and add 2 teaspoons powdered echinacea root. Simmer for 15 minutes. Remove from heat, then add 1 teaspoon powdered goldenseal root. Steep for 20 minutes. Strain and add about 1 teaspoon ReaLemon Lemon Juice. Drink warm or iced.

◆ Some bladder infections respond to this vinegar treatment: Three times a day, drink a glass of water mixed with 2 teaspoons Heinz Apple Cider Vinegar. Be sure to consult your doctor first.

◆ Gain relief from the itching of a vaginal yeast infection by drawing a bathtub of warm water and adding ½ cup Morton Salt and ½ cup Heinz Distilled White Vinegar. Sit in tub for at least 20 minutes. See a physician if itching remains after a week.

◆ Yogurt can be applied directly for yeast infections. Mix 1 cup plain (not vanilla) Dannon yogurt with 1 teaspoon McCormick Ground Cinnamon. Use a baster to insert yogurt into the vagina. Be sure yogurt has active *Lactobacillus acidophilus* cultures.

- Here's how to relieve hemorrhoid pain: Make a paste of Argo Corn Starch and water, gradually adding enough of each to measure a pint. Boil, then cool completely and use in an enema.

- To avoid aggravating sensitive hemorrhoids—or after an episiotomy or other surgical procedure—use soothing Pampers baby wipes instead of toilet paper. Baby wipes aren't flushable, however, so remember to toss them in the trash.

- If you're suffering from a boil, make a compress with Contadina Tomato Paste and cover the boil. The acids in the paste will bring the boil to a head and relieve the pain.

- Treat a boil with tea. Hold a warm, wet Lipton Tea Bag on the lump for approximately 15 minutes. Do this several times a day and soon the boil will come to a head or disappear.

Cultural Life: Facts About Yogurt

- Turkey is considered the birthplace of yogurt, and the word *yogurt* is of Turkish origin.

- Yogurt is made from the milk of cows in the United States and north-central Europe, sheep and goats in Turkey and southeastern Europe, and water buffalo in Egypt and India.

- To be considered authentic and healthful food, a yogurt must have live, or "active," cultures of good bacteria—particularly *Lactobacillus bulgaricus* and *Streptococcus thermophilus.*

- After winning the 1908 Nobel Prize in Physiology or Medicine, Ilya Mechnikov of Russia linked yogurt consumption with the longevity of Bulgarian peasants; the live bacteria were later named *Lactobacillus bulgaricus.*

◆ Remove warts with Scotch Duct Tape. Put a piece over the offender, leave it on for 6 days (replace if necessary), and then remove it. Soak the wart in water; dry, then gently rub spot with an emery board or a pumice stone. Leave tape off overnight. Repeat the routine. Treatment can take up to 2 months.

◆ To eliminate warts, rub them with half an onion that has been dipped in Morton Salt. Repeat this twice a day until the warts are gone.

◆ All kinds of fungal infections respond to Listerine Antiseptic mouthwash, including *tinea cruris,* colloquially known as "jock itch." Apply to the clean, affected skin with a Rite Aid cotton ball twice a day.

WHAT ELSE AILS YOU?

◆ When the hiccups just won't go away, cut yourself a small slice of lemon (without the peel). Place it under your tongue and suck once; hold the juice for 10 seconds, then swallow the juice. Many folks swear by this "cure"!

◆ Stop the hiccups with this old-time technique: Add 1 teaspoon Heinz Apple Cider Vinegar to a glass of warm water. Sip very slowly until hiccups cease.

◆ Another hiccup "cure" employs a Q-tips cotton swab. Tickle the roof of your mouth with the swab at the point where the hard and soft palates meet.

◆ Research seems to indicate that people who develop kidney stones on one side of the body also sleep on that same side. Blood flow to the kidneys may be the explanation. If this pattern describes you, try sleeping on the other side. Easier promised than accomplished? A variation on a snoring stopper may help: Sew a Penn tennis ball inside your pajamas on the side of your body you're trying to avoid sleeping on.

Hiccups

Simply put, a hiccup is a spasmodic contraction of the diaphragm. This causes a sudden intake of air, which is cut off by the closing of the glottis (the opening between the vocal cords). Then that sound breaks forth. The most common cause of hiccups is an overdistended tummy, but other possibilities are nerve spasms, gastric disturbances, and an upset somewhere else in the body. The most common treatment for hiccups is holding one's breath. Prolonged, severe hiccups—as in weeks, months, even years—may be surgically treated by crushing the phrenic nerve controlling the diaphragm.

◆ When experiencing a minor nosebleed, apply a vinegar/alum compress to your temples to help stop the bleeding. Dip a washcloth in a mixture of 1 pint Heinz Vinegar and 1 ounce alum and hold cloth to temples.

◆ Slow a nosebleed by soaking a Rite Aid cotton ball in Heinz Apple Cider Vinegar. Insert it gently into the bleeding nostril; hold your nose closed with your fingers. Breathe through your mouth for about 5 minutes. Carefully pull out the cotton. Repeat if your nose is still bleeding.

- Look to your spice cabinet to kill bad breath. Boil 2 cups water; add 3 sprigs parsley, ½ teaspoon McCormick Ground Cloves, and a dash of McCormick Ground Cinnamon. Strain, allow liquid to cool, and use as a mouthwash.

- Cut a hole in 2 Penn tennis balls and fit them onto the back feet of a walker. The walker will move more smoothly and floors will be protected from marks.

- Now you can shower even though you're wearing a cast on your arm or leg! Place a GLAD trash bag over the cast, making sure that it's bigger than the cast (*never* get a cast wet). Secure it with Scotch Duct Tape.

- When you need to strain out any solids from a homemade tonic or other remedy, pour the liquid through a Melitta Basket (or Cone) Coffee Filter.

- Coffee is a natural diuretic. If you tend to retain fluid—and you usually don't drink coffee—have an occasional cup of black Folgers coffee.

- All households should have a first-aid kit stocked and accessible. But ready-made, store-bought kits can be expensive. Instead, take an empty, clean Pampers baby wipes container and wipe the inside with Rite Aid isopropyl rubbing alcohol. Let dry, then stock it with the essentials your family needs (such as adhesive bandages, sterile gauze pads and rolls, antibiotic ointment, small scissors, and tape). Keep a kit in your car as well.

Everyday Wonders

He called himself "an inventor of ordinary, everyday products," but Stanley Mason improved millions of lives. The New Jersey native invented a clothespin fishing lure when he was a boy; some 20 years later, in 1949, he invented the first disposable, pin-free diaper (for his own son's bottom). Mason's 100 inventions and 55 patents include granola bars, stringless adhesive-bandage packaging, dental floss dispensers, instant splints and casts for broken limbs, microwaveable plastic cookware, and the squeezable ketchup bottle. In 1973 he founded Simco, Inc., specializing in food packaging, cosmetics, and medical devices.

◆ Breast-feeding is a healthful and rewarding choice, but nipples can get mighty sore. Brew a cup of Lipton tea, then place the tea bag in a cup of ice for about a minute. Position the bag over a sore nipple, then cover it with a nursing pad held in place under your bra. The tannic acid in the tea leaves heals and soothes.

◆ Inoculations can really hurt, no matter the patient's age. Moisten a Lipton Tea Bag with lukewarm water and hold it gently on the injection site until the pain subsides. Once again, tannic acid comes to the rescue!

◆ Soothe frostbite with warm Colavita Extra Virgin Olive Oil dabbed gently onto affected skin. Then seek medical attention.

- If the label on your prescription bottle is not protected, vital information can be smeared by wet hands or, in the case of liquids, made illegible by drips of the medicine itself. Cover the label completely with a piece of clear Scotch High-Performance Packaging Tape or a few pieces of Scotch Magic Tape.

- Even if the pharmacist adds your child's absolute favorite, surefire, can't-miss flavoring to a medicine, you'll probably still get the reaction of "Yucky!" Instead, have the patient suck on an ice cube before swallowing the prescribed liquid. The taste buds should be numbed enough to help get down a successful dose.

- Use Scotch Duct Tape to make a ball for stroke patients and others in physical therapy. Roll up several lengths (sticky side in) to make the appropriate size for the patient. It will have just the right "give" and "catchability."

- Remind yourself to take your daily dose of medicine by leaving yourself an eye-catching reminder. Brightly colored Post-it Notes fill that bill. Hang a calendar that has big squares on the

Sure, But Did They Have 24-Hour Drive-Throughs?

The pharmacy has its roots in ancient times. The Greco-Roman god of medicine, Asclepius, delegated the preparing of remedies to his daughter Hygieia. She was his apothecary, or pharmacist. Physician-priests in Egypt were divided into 2 classes: those who visited and treated the ill and those who prepared remedies back at the temple.

refrigerator, the kitchen bulletin board, or any other prominent spot. Take 1, 2, or 3 small Post-its (enough for the number of times per day that prescriptions are taken), and write MORNING, NOON, and EVENING on separate notes. Move each note onto today's date right after the medicine for that time has been taken. For example, someone who takes 3 pills with breakfast and 2 pills at bedtime: At 2 P.M. on June 12, the MORNING note would be on the 12th; the EVENING note would be on the 11th.

Quite a Quilt

Patchwork quilts are creative expressions of community and shared history. A famous example of such handiwork, the AIDS Memory Quilt, was created with sewn fabric squares, each memorializing the life of a person lost to AIDS. It has become a symbol of remembrance and honor.

The staff, patients, and visitors at an Arizona hospital reimagined the whole quilt concept, creating one entirely of Post-it Notes. On each square of paper, someone wrote or drew something for which they were thankful. The quilt of brightly colored Post-its eventually filled an entire wall in the hospital and communicated a powerful message of gratitude.

- Mealtimes can be frustrating for stroke victims, arthritis sufferers, and anyone else who has trouble using his or her hands. Make silverware easier to grasp by winding several rubber bands around the handles.

- Oh, she's fainted! Does anybody have some smelling salts? No, but this veggie can do the job: Hold a freshly cut onion under her nose; that distinctive odor will bring her around.

Chapter 5: Help in the Kitchen

HINTS FOR THE HEART OF YOUR HOME

Baking soda, baking powder, and the like...they're not just for baking anymore!

Well-known items from every nook and cranny of your residence will gather in the kitchen just in time for the prep work and hang around until the last dish is washed and returned to the cabinet.

Some everyday products that call this room their home are recipe regulars, but many have at least a few unusual uses up their sleeves and inside their packages. All their qualities come into play, including texture, flavor, aroma, color, carbonation, and alkalinity, as they reduce acidity, tenderize, add fluffiness, increase digestibility, substitute for other ingredients, fix mistakes, clean—and even scrub pots and pans.

Some of the book's most remarkable tips are found in this chapter, utilizing (among many other products) dental floss, duct tape, and denture cleanser tablets. In all kinds of kitchen situations, cover-up experts such as aluminum foil, plastic wrap, plastic bags, paper bags, and paper towels have been repurposed. And wait until you read about the cool new uses for ice cube trays.

When the time (as well as the fresh produce) is ripe, everyday products will come to your rescue. Make more of your time, money, and creativity in the kitchen. Everyday products will help!

RECIPES FOR COOKING SUCCESS

Fruit

◆ Cut fruit will stay fresh in the refrigerator without turning brown if you coat it with ReaLemon Lemon Juice.

◆ Here's another method to keep cut-up fruit and veggies from turning brown: Fill a bowl or container with enough water to cover the pared produce, then add 3 tablespoons ReaLemon or ReaLime juice.

Fruit or Veggie?

Avocados, chilies, eggplants, peppers, tomatoes (they grow above-ground)—these "fruit vegetables" are technically fruits, but we treat them as vegetables. Although they differ greatly from each other, they do have at least one thing in common: They're more perishable than most vegetables.

◆ Juice of 1 lemon or lime = 3 tablespoons ReaLemon or ReaLime juice.

◆ Hold an orange under hot water for a bit before you squeeze it. You'll get twice the juice!

◆ Many fruits ripen more quickly and evenly at room temperature in a paper lunch bag. These include tomatoes, peaches, pears, and avocados. Wrap green bananas first in a damp dishtowel, then place in bag. When the produce is sufficiently ripened, refrigerate as usual.

- Ingredients such as dried fruits won't stick to a knife if you rub a bit of Crisco Pure Vegetable Oil on the blade before chopping.

- When making fresh cranberry sauce, cover cranberries with water in a pot or saucepan; bring to a boil. Add 1 tablespoon ARM & HAMMER Baking Soda, stir, drain, and return to heat. You'll need less sugar than usual to complete the sauce.

- Use up leftover cranberry sauce (say, after Thanksgiving) by making a meatball sauce from 1 cup cranberry sauce and 4 ounces Contadina Tomato Sauce. Heat and stir until fully blended.

- Sweeten tart blackberries with ½ teaspoon ARM & HAMMER Baking Soda before adding any sugar when making pies or cobblers.

- Soak rhubarb in cold water and a pinch of ARM & HAMMER Baking Soda prior to making rhubarb sauce. The water will turn black. Drain. You'll need less sugar in the sauce.

I Guess It Sounds Better than "Orangeys" or "Lemoneys"

Scurvy is one of the oldest recognized nutritional deficiencies. The problem is a lack of vitamin C (ascorbic acid), leading to gum disease, painful and stiff joints, inhibited healing of wounds, and anemia. From the late 1400s on, scurvy became the number one cause of disability and death among sailors. Dr. James Lind, a Scottish naval surgeon, proved in 1753 that scurvy could be prevented and even cured by drinking orange or lemon juice. Citrus juice soon was so common aboard British ships that the sailors were nicknamed "limeys."

240

- Sprinkle ARM & HAMMER Baking Soda on fresh pineapple to improve its flavor, especially if the pineapple is not quite ripe.

Tart Tips

- Before you stow uncut lemons in the refrigerator, put them in a jar of water. They will be juicier and will last longer than lemons stored in the produce drawer.

- If a lemon is too firm to juice, try either of these methods: Microwave it on high in 10-second increments until soft enough, or boil it for a few minutes.

- To get just a few drops of juice from a lemon or lime, pierce the whole fruit with a toothpick. Squeeze out what you need, then use the toothpick to plug the hole. Refrigerate.

Vegging Out

- Salt can help remove gritty dirt from fresh vegetables. To wash arugula, leeks, or spinach, trim them and place in a bowl of lukewarm water. Add a tablespoon of Morton Coarse Kosher Salt, swish vegetables around, and let soak for 20 to 30 minutes. Transfer vegetables to a colander and rinse thoroughly.

- Keep a spray bottle of Heinz Vinegar near your kitchen sink and use it to spritz vegetables before you rinse them with cold running water. The vinegar will help dissolve pesticide residue.

The Pressing Truth About Olives

- ◆ Edible olives were grown on the island of Crete as early as 3500 B.C. They were an important crop of the Romans by 600 B.C.

- ◆ Over the centuries, the cultivation of olives spread to every country that borders the Mediterranean Sea. The craft of turning olives into oil varies from region to region and from grower to grower.

- ◆ Italy is one of the world's largest exporters of olive oil, with production dominated by the areas of Puglia, Sicily, and Calabria.

- ◆ Olive oil is available in the following grades (highest to lowest): Extra Virgin, Superfine, Fine, Virgin, and Pure.

- ◆ To produce 1 liter (approximately 4 cups) of olive oil, at least 10 pounds of olives are needed.

- Don't waste any of that broccoli—even the part you usually throw away. Instead, cut the stalks into 1-inch-thick slices. Stir-fry them with Morton Salt and enjoy as a healthy and delicious snack.

- To ward of discoloration of your cauliflower, keeping it white and bright—as well as keeping its odor under control—when boiling or steaming, add 1 teaspoon ARM & HAMMER Baking Soda to the cooking water.

- When boiling cauliflower, add about 1 tablespoon milk to the water. The veggie will stay white.

- Add a pinch of ARM & HAMMER Baking Soda to the cooking water when boiling cabbage to tenderize and avoid overcooking.

- If you add a small amount of ReaLemon Lemon Juice to the cooking water, beets and red cabbage will retain their color.

- Get rid of the bitter juices in an eggplant by sprinkling eggplant slices with Morton Salt. Stand slices vertically in a rack placed in a shallow pan, and let sit half an hour.

- To poach asparagus, add Morton Salt to a pot of boiling water. Carefully place spears in pot; simmer exactly 5 minutes. Stalks should all be pointing in the same direction. (Some culinary experts insist that asparagus stand upright in the boiling pot.)

- Picking silk from a freshly shucked ear of corn can be a tedious job. Speed up the process by wiping a damp Scott Towel across the ear; it will pick up the strands.

- Dry lettuce faster than you can say "spin cycle"! Wash the leaves and shake off as much water as you can. Place them in a plastic grocery bag lined with Scott Towels. Grasp the bag by the handles (or let your kids have the fun) and whirl it around in circles until the lettuce is dry.

- Slightly wilted produce can be brought back to life if you sprinkle it with cool water, wrap in a Scott Towel, and refrigerate for about an hour.

Quotable Quote

"To make a good salad is to be a brilliant diplomatist—the problem is entirely the same in both cases. To know exactly how much oil one must put with one's vinegar."

—Oscar Wilde

◆ Or you can freshen wilted lettuce by adding a few drops of ReaLemon Lemon Juice to a bowl of cold water. Put lettuce leaves in the bowl and chill in the refrigerator for 30 minutes.

Tomatoes

◆ Tomatoes are easier to peel if you place them in a heatproof bowl and cover them with boiling water. Wait 1 minute, then drain.

◆ Most recipes call for only a fraction of a can of Contadina Tomato Paste...and the rest goes bad in the refrigerator. Prevent wastefulness by measuring 1-tablespoon portions into small paper cupcake liners; place in freezer. Fold over sides of solidly frozen cups, put in a GLAD Freezer Zipper Bag, force out excess air, and freeze. Pull out portions as needed for future recipes.

◆ Tomatoes ripen best when placed stem-side up, not touching each other, and out of direct sunlight. They may look nice on a windowsill, but that may cause soft spots.

Squeeze More from a Squirt Bottle

When you're out of Dawn dish-washing liquid—or any other product that comes in a plastic squeeze bottle—don't toss the bottle in the recycling bin. Rinse it well and let it air-dry. These bottles are just right for storing and dispensing many of the surprising solutions found in this book, such as homemade liquid cleaners and garden tonics.

Potatoes, Rice & Beans

◆ Keep potatoes from sprouting by storing apples with them.

◆ To make a whole spud cook more quickly in the microwave, stick 4 toothpicks into the bottom to serve as "legs." This way, the microwave can hit all surfaces of the potato at once.

◆ A pinch of ARM & HAMMER Baking Soda thrown into potatoes while mashing will make them fluffier.

◆ Keep rice from becoming sticky by cooking it in water with 2 tablespoons ReaLemon Lemon Juice.

◆ Rice won't stick together if you add a bit of PAM cooking spray to the boiling water. This tip works on pasta as well.

◆ Add 1 teaspoon ARM & HAMMER Baking Soda to the water when cooking rice to improve fluffiness.

◆ Reheated, leftover rice rarely displays the steamy fluffiness of last evening's side dish. Before you place the dish in the microwave, place an ice cube atop the rice. It will provide just the right amount of moisture.

◆ Add a pinch of ARM & HAMMER Baking Soda to the water when soaking dried beans. It helps make them more digestible.

◆ Eliminate the gaseous side effects of baked beans by adding a dash of ARM & HAMMER Baking Soda while cooking.

Surf and Turf

◆ Freshen up fish just brought home from the market by returning it to its natural environment for a short time. Add 1 tablespoon Morton Sea Salt to 2 quarts cold water, then add a lot of ice cubes. Soak fish in this salt water for about 15 minutes, then remove and dry it off before preparing as desired.

◆ Return a frozen fish to its original fresh taste. When thawing the fish, cover it with a small amount of fresh milk or with a mixture of ¾ cup water and 1⅓ cups Carnation Instant Nonfat Dry Milk.

◆ Reduce that unpleasant fishy taste by soaking raw fish for at least half an hour in 2 tablespoons ARM & HAMMER Baking Soda and 1 quart water. Rinse and cook.

That Cute Girl with the Umbrella

The Morton Umbrella Girl first appeared in 1914 on the blue table salt packages and in a series of *Good Housekeeping* magazine ads. The concept had been developed 3 years earlier with the copy "Even in rainy weather, it flows freely." Tasked with finding a better slogan, the ad agency thought harder and, remembering an old proverb ("It never rains but it pours"), came up with the now-famous slogan, "When It Rains It Pours." As for Umbrella Girl, she's had a few makeovers over the years, the latest of which was in 1968.

- To get a good grip on a fish while trying to skin it for cooking, sprinkle your hands with Morton Salt.

- Salt will force juices out of meat and prevent it from browning. Wait to salt meat until midway through the cooking process, then salt it lightly, or wait until cooking is complete and salt to taste.

- Marinating any cut of meat in Budweiser beer for an hour adds an interesting flavor and tenderizes just as well as any other marinade.

- Tenderize tough meat by rubbing it with ARM & HAMMER Baking Soda. Let it stand several hours, then rinse and cook.

- To tenderize a pot roast or stew meat, marinate in equal parts strongly brewed Lipton tea and double-strength beef broth.

Baking Soda at Its Best

- Test ARM & HAMMER Baking Soda freshness by pouring a small amount of Heinz Distilled White Vinegar or ReaLemon Lemon Juice over ½ teaspoon of baking soda. If it doesn't actively bubble, it's too old to use. Alternatively, you can put a few teaspoons in a cup of water. If—right away—it fizzes, it's still good.

- A batter using ARM & HAMMER Baking Soda should be mixed and put in the oven quickly to retain the best leavening action.

- Sprinkle ARM & HAMMER Baking Soda on a damp O-Cel-O sponge and scrub your fruits and vegetables to remove dirt, wax, or pesticide residue. Rinse well.

- Neutralize the acids in any recipe with a large amount of fruit by adding a pinch of ARM & HAMMER Baking Soda.

- It's easiest to marinate meats not in a bowl or pan but in a quart- or gallon-size GLAD Food Storage Zipper Bag. The bag allows for full coverage, and you can easily flip the bag at intervals to make sure the marinade reaches all parts of the meat.

- To prevent the roast in the oven from getting tough, place a peeled ripe banana in the pan. The tenderizing ability of the whole fruit is well known in Asia, where meat is wrapped in banana leaves while cooking.

- Before wrapping your meat for the freezer, brush it with a little Colavita Extra Virgin Olive Oil to prevent it from drying out.

- To keep a ham moist while it's roasting, pour a can of Pepsi over it, then follow regular baking instructions or a recipe.

Featuring...Filter Facts!

1908: Melitta Bentz of Dresden, Germany, devises a new coffee-brewing method: pouring boiling water over coffee grounds into a pot lined with blotting paper. She and her husband launch the Melitta Company.

1937: Melitta perfects the filter cone shape.

1941: German chemist Peter Schlumbohm invents the Chemex filter coffeemaker; it is praised by both consumers and the art world.

1972: Mr. Coffee brand invents the first affordable, convenient automatic drip coffeemaker for household use. Through TV commercials, baseball legend Joe DiMaggio becomes the face of Mr. Coffee.

◆ Rub ARM & HAMMER Baking Soda into the fat surrounding pork chops to make them crispier.

Fowl Play

◆ Before cooking whole poultry, rinse it in cold water and sprinkle ARM & HAMMER Baking Soda inside and out to tenderize. Refrigerate overnight. Rinse well.

◆ To make skinning chicken parts easier, use a Melitta Basket Coffee Filter to grab the chicken in one hand. The filter will give you some traction on the slippery skin.

◆ When scalding a whole, fresh chicken, add 1 teaspoon ARM & HAMMER Baking Soda to the boiling water. Feathers will come off more easily, and the flesh will be clean and white.

◆ Before you cook chicken, rub a wedge of lemon over it. The result will be a juicier, more tender dish.

◆ When roasting a turkey, tie its legs together with unflavored Reach dental floss.

◆ Soften the pungent taste of wild game by soaking it overnight in ARM & HAMMER Baking Soda and water. Rinse and dry before cooking.

Dairy

◆ Hard cheeses that are difficult to cut can be tamed by cutting through them with unflavored Reach dental floss.

No-Freeze Ice Cream

You don't need an old-fashioned freezer or a fancy automatic ice-cream machine to make ice cream in a hurry at home.

½ cup milk (whole, 2 percent, chocolate, or skim)
1 tablespoon Domino Sugar
¼ teaspoon McCormick Pure Vanilla Extract (or another flavoring)
6 tablespoons Morton Salt

Combine milk, sugar, and flavoring in a sandwich-size GLAD Food Storage Zipper Bag. Zip the bag shut, then place it inside a quart- or gallon-size GLAD Food Storage Zipper Bag. Add enough ice to the outer bag to fill it halfway, then put in 6 table-spoons salt. Zip the larger bag shut. Now take turns tossing and turning, shaking and mixing the 2 bags in your hands. (It gets cold. You may want to hold a dishtowel while you do this if you don't have helpers.) After about 5 or 10 minutes of shaking, the mix-ture will be the consistency of ice cream.

Note: The ingredient amounts listed do not make very much ice cream, but don't double the recipe. If you need more, make several small batches.

◆ Milk will stay fresh longer if you add a pinch of Morton Salt per gallon. It fights bacteria like a champ.

◆ To prevent milk from scorching on a stove, add a pinch of Domino sugar and do not stir.

◆ Try to soften a block of Kraft Philadelphia Cream Cheese in a microwave and you'll probably make a runny mess. Instead, remove the outer wrapping and seal the cream cheese in a pint-size GLAD Food Storage Zipper Bag. Place the bag in a bowl of hot water until the consistency is right.

◆ Turn yogurt into a low-fat cheese spread: Put plain, nonfat yogurt in a Melitta Cone Coffee

Filter, stand filter in a tall container, cover the filter with GLAD Cling Wrap, and let it drain overnight in the refrigerator. Flavor the yogurt cheese with any herb. Use it on crackers or as a sandwich spread.

- For an easy and affordable fudge pop treat, pour chocolate milk into a 5-ounce waxed Dixie cup, stick in a wood craft stick, and freeze. Once it's frozen, remove the cup and enjoy.

- Add a pinch of Morton Salt to any plain or mild-flavored yogurt to give it extra zing.

- When grating cheese, spray your grater with PAM cooking spray to make it slide better and make cleanup easier.

Toiling with Oil

- Vegetable oils and shortening do not need to be refrigerated. Store them in a cool, dry place, away from direct sunlight, sources of heat, and strong odors.

Garlic Oil

1 cup Crisco Pure Vegetable Oil
1 garlic clove, minced

Mix ingredients in a glass jar with a tight lid. Refrigerate for 1 or 2 days, then open the jar. If your eyes water, it's ready. If not, add another ½ clove of minced garlic; re-cap the jar and refrigerate for one more day. Strain out the garlic pieces. Store the oil in the fridge in a clean jar. Use as indicated in recipes or in the insect repellent on page 325.

- Unopened containers of vegetable oil and shortening (cans or sticks) will keep for 2 years. Opened bottles of oil and cans of shortening last about 1 year; sticks of shortening last about 6 months.

- Don't remove the entire seal on a new bottle of oil—just cut a small slit in it for pouring. No more dripping mess!

- You can reuse oil from frying if you strain it first. Run it through a sieve lined with a Melitta Basket Coffee Filter.

Herbs and Spices

- Grind peppercorns or crush other whole spices by placing them in a snack-size GLAD Food Storage Zipper Bag and smashing with a meat-tenderizing hammer or even a rolling pin.

- Sprinkle peeled garlic cloves with a little Morton Coarse Kosher Salt before attempting to chop them. The salt will absorb the garlic's juice and then dissolve, which will help spread the garlic flavor.

- If you are using whole garlic cloves in a marinade, stick a toothpick through each one before cook-ing. This makes it easy to

Herbs or Spices?

SPICES are the seeds, buds, fruits, flowers, bark, and roots of plants. Among them are cayenne pepper, cinnamon, cumin, ginger, nutmeg, paprika, and turmeric.

HERBS, often less pungent than spices, are the leaves of various herbal plants. Available fresh, dried, or ground, common herbs include basil, dill, mint, oregano, rosemary, sage, and thyme.

locate the cloves after cooking and remove them from the dish at serving time.

◆ Morton Coarse Kosher Salt can be kept in a pepper mill and ground out as needed.

◆ If Morton Salt hardens at the bottom of your box of salt or saltshaker, use a wooden chopstick to loosen it.

◆ Since many recipes call for both salt and pepper, prepare a standby mixture using 3 parts Morton Salt and 1 part McCormick Pure Ground Black Pepper. Keep the mixture in a shaker by your stove.

◆ Preserve fresh herbs with salt. Just spread a thin layer of Morton Coarse Kosher Salt in an airtight container. Layer fresh herbs over salt (works best with basil, sage, or mint). Spread another thin layer of salt over herbs; repeat layering process as needed. Cover the container and store with your spices. When you're ready to use the herbs, gently shake off salt to expose them. Some may be darkened, but their flavor will be fine.

◆ After cutting hot chili peppers, be sure to scrub your hands and nails with soapy water. Then soak your hands in salt water to get rid of the hot chili oil. Rinse.

◆ When cooking with herbs, first marinate the herbs in 2 tablespoons Colavita Extra Virgin Olive Oil for 30 minutes. Marinating brings out the herb flavors.

Popcorn

◆ Unpopped Orville Redenbacher's popcorn will stay fresh longer if stored in the freezer.

◆ Make your own microwave popcorn bag. Put ¼ cup kernels in a paper lunch bag and fold over the top a few times to close tightly. Microwave on high power (or, even better, on the popcorn setting) until the popping stops.

"Or My Name Isn't…"

Orville Redenbacher was a lifelong Hoosier, born and raised in Brazil, Indiana, and a proud alumnus of Purdue University—it's no surprise that corn ran in his blood. The cornfields of northern Indiana inspired him; from age 12 he worked to produce popcorn excellence. In 1965 he and his business partner perfected a popcorn hybrid; 4 years later his first popcorn brand, Red-Bow, appeared on store shelves. The company started running its unique TV commercials in 1976, using the company's own bow-tied, suspendered, and recognizable spokes-popper to market its "gourmet" product. Redenbacher died in 1995 at age 88; he was named to the Madison Avenue Advertising Walk of Fame in 2009.

KITCHEN TRICKS AND TIPS

Prep Work

◆ If you can't see the marks on your measuring cup—either they're faded or your eyes aren't what they used to be— remake the markings by applying red Revlon Nail Enamel.

- Before filling measuring spoons and cups with sticky liquids such as syrup or Sue Bee Honey, apply a light coating of Colavita Extra Virgin Olive Oil or PAM cooking spray. Cleanup just got much easier!

Is Her Real Name Pamela?

The well-known brand of cooking spray is not named after a woman—actually, PAM stands for "Product of Arthur Meyerhoff," who introduced the nonstick spray in the early 1960s with his partner, Leon Rubin. Much of PAM's early success came thanks to the cooking shows of Chicago TV personality Carmelita Pope.

- Add a quick shot of PAM cooking spray to the lip of a measuring cup or pitcher to prevent drips.

- Cover a food scale with GLAD Press'n Seal for quicker cleanup.

- Or, when weighing messy foods on a kitchen scale, put them in a Melitta Basket Coffee Filter to keep the scale clean.

- Mix and dispense in 2 easy steps—no cleanup required! Mix ingredients for deviled eggs or stuffed mushrooms by placing all ingredients in a GLAD Food Storage Zipper Bag. Seal it and knead to blend contents. To dispense the mixture, snip off a small corner of the still-sealed bag. Then just squeeze and stuff! When you're done, throw away your "dispenser."

- Blot meats and vegetables dry with Scott Towels before cooking. They'll brown well instead of simply steaming.

- When you need cracker crumbs for a recipe, put your crackers in a GLAD Food Storage Zipper Bag and squeeze out most of the air. Seal it almost all the way, leaving it open at the corner so air can escape. Crush crackers by rolling a rolling pin up and down the bag. This contains the mess, crushes the crackers, and keeps your rolling pin clean.

- Bunch together produce such as fresh parsley, chives, and scallions with a rubber band for easier chopping.

- Keep the stickiness under control! Spray the pan and also your hands with PAM cooking spray before making crispy rice cereal treats or popcorn balls.

- Apply a light coating of PAM cooking spray to gelatin molds before filling for easy release later.

- Prevent boilovers by spraying the inside of a pot with a little PAM cooking spray before you fill it with water.

Eggstra Info

- How good are those eggs in the grocery store? Some people say the rougher the shell, the fresher the egg.

- Never store eggs in the door of your refrigerator. This is where the temperature fluctuates the most.

- Here's an easy way to separate an egg: Crack it directly into a funnel; the white slides through and the yolk remains.

- Whites last one week when covered and stored in the refrigerator.

- Yolks last only 3 days in the fridge, in a covered container. Submerge unbroken yolks in water to keep them moist; for broken ones, press GLAD Cling Wrap directly on the surface.

- Many casseroles and other baked dishes have a layer of melted cheese on top. Before covering such a dish with a piece of Reynolds Wrap Aluminum Foil, spray the underside of the foil with PAM cooking spray to keep the melted cheese from sticking to it.

- Egg dishes and other casseroles won't stick to the spatula if you spray it with PAM cooking spray before using it to serve.

- Binder clips are a great help in the kitchen. Use them to attach recipes to the oven hood while cooking; close pourable cartons, condiment packages, and snack bags; and clip up long shirt sleeves.

- Before sharpening knives with a whetstone, first dampen whetstone with Heinz Vinegar.

Problem Solving

- Getting peanut butter or other sticky ingredients out of a measuring cup can be frustrating. This should make it easier: Before scooping in the peanut butter, fill the cup with hot water. Dump it out but don't dry the cup, then immediately fill with peanut butter. It will come out easily!

- Spread a sheet of Reynolds Wrap Aluminum Foil on the oven rack below a baking pan if you fear boilovers and spills. (Don't spread the foil on the bottom of an oven.)

- Before you prepare food on a countertop, cover the surface with a large sheet of either Reynolds Cut-Rite Wax Paper or Reynolds Parchment Paper. Put it under any cutting boards too. This is especially important when working with meat, chicken, or fish.

- Cover open bowls and dishes with a Melitta Basket Coffee Filter to avoid splatters in the microwave.

- Use a large rubber band to deal with a stubborn jar lid. Wrap the band around the edge of the lid, and give it a good twist.

- If a challenging jar lid or a twist-off bottle cap just won't budge, cut a Penn tennis ball in half with a box cutter or sturdy craft knife, then use the ball to grip the lid or cap and twist it off.

The Storage Story

- Always check the label on boxed and canned goods to see how they should be stored. If you haven't refrigerated items that should be refrigerated, don't use them! Throw them away.

- High-acid canned foods, such as tomatoes, keep for between 12 and 18 months, while low-acid foods can keep up to 5 years. To be on the safe side, try to use all canned foods within a year of purchase.

- Potatoes and onions should not be refrigerated, but they do need to be kept cooler than most foods stored in cupboards. If you don't have a cellar, make sure you store them in the coolest place possible.

- Don't crowd the refrigerator or freezer. Air needs to circulate to keep temperatures even.

- Use home-frozen fruits and vegetables within a year.

- Place a piece of 3M sandpaper grit-side down on a jar lid that you're having trouble opening. This can be especially helpful when you need to grip a large lid.

- If a piece of cork breaks off into your fine wine while opening the bottle, pour the wine into a glass through a Melitta Basket Coffee Filter. Be sure to stretch the filter tightly over the wine bottle.

- Silence your smoke detector during a cooking disaster by dampening a dishtowel with Heinz Vinegar and waving it in the smoky area.

- When a new bottle of Heinz Ketchup just won't start flowing, insert a drinking straw into the bottle to add air and get it going.

- If you know you'll be in and out of the refrigerator with messy hands, wrap a piece of GLAD Press'n Seal around the door handle before you start cooking.

- The brown sugar is hard as a rock! Don't run to the store for a fresh bag; simply chip off a chunk, wrap it in Reynolds Wrap Aluminum Foil, and bake it at 300°F for 5 minutes to soften.

Straw Man

It's not just kids who think it's fun to sip from a straw! In the late 19th century, beverage drinkers used straws made of rye grass. In 1888, Marvin Stone, a manufacturer of paper cigarette holders, patented a spiral winding process used to manufacture the first paper drinking straws. His prototype was a piece of paraffin-coated manila paper, wound around a pencil and glued together. Hand-winding prevailed in the Stone Straw Corporation until a machine was invented for the job in 1906.

Bubbly Beginnings

In 1846 New Englanders John Dwight and his brother-in-law, Dr. Austin Church, became the first U.S. commercial manufacturers of bicarbonate of soda. They took trona, or soda ash, out of the ground and turned it into what's commonly called baking soda, for use both outside and inside the house. The company was eventually called Church & Dwight Co., Inc.

James A. Church, the son of Dr. Church, joined the company in 1867 and brought his ARM & HAMMER trademark from his own Vulcan Spice Mills (named after the Roman god of fire, skilled at forging armor). The symbol was applied to some ARM & HAMMER Baking Soda packages; it soon became the most popular, and then primary, brand. The ARM & HAMMER symbol is part of the Church & Dwight logo as well.

- Another way to deal with a hardened bag of brown sugar is to put 1 or 2 apple wedges in the bag; seal and store at room temperature. In a couple of days, the sugar should be softened.

- Any time you might have to boil water before drinking it, soften it with 1 tablespoon ARM & HAMMER Baking Soda per gallon of water.

- Clip coupons and then forget them? Hold them together with a binder clip. Hang it on a magnetic refrigerator hook, on the bulletin board—anywhere you'll see the coupons—and grab them on your way to the grocery store.

- On a diet? Try this to curb your appetite: Mix 2 tablespoons grapefruit juice with 1 tablespoon Hain Safflower Oil; take before each meal.

- In a pinch, substitute a Scott Towel for a coffee filter. Roll it into a cone or shape it into a basket, depending on your coffeemaker.

- Before refilling a salt or pepper shaker through a hole on the bottom, cover the top with Scotch Masking Tape. That way you won't make a mess or waste any of the contents when you turn it upside down.

Chef's Secrets

- If you add too much vinegar to a recipe, add a pinch of ARM & HAMMER Baking Soda to counteract it.

- When gravy separates, a pinch of ARM & HAMMER Baking Soda may get oils and fats to stick back together.

- To deepen the color of homemade gravy, stir in 1 teaspoon Folgers Instant Coffee Crystals. The flavor of the gravy will be unaffected, but the color will be enhanced.

The Making of Mayo

In 1756, the chef of the duc de Richelieu invented the recipe for mayonnaise with his particular mixture of egg yolks, vinegar, oil, and seasonings. The chef was inspired by the French victory over the British at Port Mahón in Minorca. Soon the chefs of Paris were serving *mahonnaise* ("sauce of Mahón"). The spelling changed to "mayonnaise" when it arrived in the United States in the 1800s. Not until 1905, however, did mayo meet the masses. That's when Richard Hellmann started selling it in his New York City deli.

Tears from the Joy of Cooking?

Goggles specifically manufactured for the purpose of shielding a chef's eyes from the tear-inducing fumes of onions are sold in kitchen supply stores. But some cooks find it perfectly acceptable to use goggles made for welding or the chemistry lab.

Other tips to curb crying while peeling and cutting: Sharpen your knife, use only fresh onions, soak them in water or freeze them for 10 minutes beforehand, peel them under running water, light a candle nearby, or chew a piece of bread or gum while cutting.

◆ To get rid of some of the fat that has accumulated on the top of poultry or beef broth, strain it through a Melitta Basket Coffee Filter.

◆ Avoid curdling boiled milk by adding a pinch of ARM & HAMMER Baking Soda.

◆ Making a delicate sauce, such as hollandaise, can be tricky. If it begins to curdle, all is not lost. Add 1 ice cube to the saucepan, stir, and watch the sauce turn smooth again.

◆ To test the acidity of canned tomatoes, dip a moist teaspoon in ARM & HAMMER Baking Soda and use it to stir the tomatoes. Bubbling means the acid level is high.

◆ Cut the acidity of tomato sauce or chili by adding a pinch of ARM & HAMMER Baking Soda.

◆ To give an interesting flavor to traditional spaghetti sauce, add ¼ teaspoon Folgers Instant Coffee Crystals. The coffee tones down the acidic flavor and darkens the sauce.

- Add a pinch of ARM & HAMMER Baking Soda to a cup of coffee to reduce its acidity.

- Add ¼ teaspoon ARM & HAMMER Baking Soda to 1 cup orange juice, grapefruit juice, or lemonade. This will add fizz to the drink and reduce its acidity.

- Adding salt to the water for cooking pasta is a good idea, but wait until the water boils. Then add 2 tablespoons Morton Salt for each pound of pasta. If you salt the water before it boils, it will take longer to boil.

- Pots are less likely to boil over when you use this tiny tool: a tiny toothpick laid flat between the lid and the pot. The space allows just enough steam to escape to prevent boilovers. This works when baking covered casserole dishes too.

- The secret to making clear ice cubes is to leave out 1 ingredient: air. Use boiled, distilled water to fill the ice cube tray or another container (such as a ring mold for the punch bowl).

- Omelets get fluffier if you add ½ teaspoon ARM & HAMMER Baking Soda or Argo Corn Starch for every 3 eggs.

Spills

- Picking up the mess from a dropped egg can be tricky. Make it easier by sprinkling the mess with Morton Salt and letting stand 15 minutes. The salt absorbs and solidifies the runny egg. Wipe away with a paper towel.

◆ If you spill a small amount of Crisco Pure Vegetable Oil or other cooking oil, sprinkle it with Morton Salt. Wipe up spill after about 15 minutes.

BAKING BASICS AND BEYOND

Cakes

◆ Cake layers can be baked up to 2 days in advance, individually wrapped in GLAD Cling Wrap, and kept in the refrigerator.

◆ Line an 8-inch round cake pan with a flattened Melitta Basket Coffee Filter to keep the cake from sticking to the pan.

Talk About Time Management

From 1912 to her retirement in 1970 at age 92, Lillian Moller Gilbreth had a remarkable career as an engineer, ergonomics pioneer, and—with her husband, Frank—industrial efficiency expert. She invented an electric food mixer, shelves inside refrigerators, a trash can with step-on lid opener, and various household accommodations for the disabled. She later directed New York University's International Training Center for the Disabled, based on her ergonomically efficient kitchen. Gilbreth is immortalized in the book *Cheaper by the Dozen,* written by 2 of her 12 children.

◆ Cutting 1 layer of a layer cake into yet another thin layer can be tricky, but you can do it with unflavored Reach dental floss. First, insert toothpicks horizontally into the cake at the cutting line. Then, holding a long length of Reach dental floss tightly between your hands, start at the far side and pull the floss toward you, using the tooth-picks as a guide.

- When making sour cream cake, combine the ARM & HAMMER Baking Soda and sour cream before mixing with other ingredients to activate the soda more quickly.

- To prevent homemade frosting from cracking, add a pinch of ARM & HAMMER Baking Soda before spreading it on a cake.

- To make an easy cake-icing tool, put icing in a quart-size GLAD Freezer Zipper Bag. Squeeze the bag to make the icing go to one corner, then snip off a small piece of the bag at that corner. Twist and carefully squeeze the bag to make the icing come out. With practice, you'll be able to make designs and write names. (This trick works for whipped cream too.)

- Decorate that cake with a "pastry bag" made of Reynolds Wrap Heavy Strength Aluminum Foil. Form the foil into a tube with a small opening at the tip, fill it with easily flowing frosting, and pipe your design.

- Make a fancy stencil for powdering the top of a cake: Fold a Melitta Basket Coffee Filter in half, then in half again, and snip a design into it—much the way you would to make a paper snowflake. Apply a light coat of PAM cooking spray to the filter, set it on top of the cake, and sprinkle powdered sugar over it.

- To craft a difficult design on a cake, a toothpick could be just the right tool.

- When you need to cover an iced cake or cupcakes with GLAD Cling Wrap, spray the wrap first with PAM cooking spray so the icing won't stick to it.

- Want to make a cake of a special shape but don't have the exact pan? Create that heart, teddy bear, football, or any other shape you desire by forming the shape with a double thickness of Reynolds Wrap Heavy Strength Aluminum Foil. Place the shape inside a large cake pan; pour in the batter.

Pies

- Cold ingredients are essential to a flaky pie crust. Use cold (even frozen!) shortening and ice water.

- Before rolling out dough, cut a piece of clean No nonsense pantyhose and slip your rolling pin into it. Sprinkle Gold Medal All-Purpose Flour onto the pantyhose; the nylon will hold enough flour to prevent the dough from sticking to the pin.

Getting Cold Feet?

You might get frosty feet if you use this tip—but it will be worth it! Store No nonsense pantyhose in the freezer, and they'll resist runs and holes longer.

- Knead and roll out dough for a pie right inside a GLAD Food Storage Zipper Bag to create less mess.

- When rolling out dough, use Argo Corn Starch instead of flour on your rolling surface. It not only works better but also cleans up more easily.

- To bake a pie to golden-brown without burning the edges of the crust, cover those edges with strips of Reynolds Wrap Aluminum Foil.

Cookies

- Cookies lift off a cookie sheet easily if you run a piece of unflavored Reach dental floss underneath them.

- To grease a pan or cookie sheet with Crisco All-Vegetable Shortening, slip a GLAD Food Storage Bag over your hand and dip it directly into the shortening container. Rub your hand over the pan to spread the shortening. Keep the bag in the shortening container for next time.

- Instead of greasing cookie sheets, line them with Reynolds Parchment Paper. The cookies bake more evenly, they cool right on the pan, and cleanup is minimal.

- What's the secret to perfectly round homemade refrigerator cookies? Cut an old Scott Towel tube lengthwise, open it, and line with GLAD Cling Wrap. Fill with homemade dough, evenly and completely; put the tube edges together; and cover the roll with another layer of plastic wrap. Hold secure with rubber bands or tape. Refrigerate until ready to bake.

- Keep dough from sticking to cookie cutters with a light application of PAM cooking spray beforehand.

Baking Bits

- To bake a perfectly round loaf of bread, use a small coffee can as a pan. Grease the inside of the can. Use 2 cans for yeast breads and fill only halfway; grease the bottom of each lid as well, place them on the cans, and watch the rising dough push off the lid. To bake, place the cans—without the lids—upright in the oven.

- To make an easy-to-use, always-ready flour duster, use a clean, old No nonsense knee high or the foot portion of a pantyhose leg. Fill it with Gold Medal All-Purpose Flour, knot the end, and keep it in your flour canister. When you need to dust flour onto a baking pan or a surface to work with dough, just give it a gentle shake.

- Use a Q-tips cotton swab to remove any yolk that gets into your egg whites. This is especially important when making a meringue.

- Spray your spatulas, spoons, and mixing bowls with PAM cooking spray when tackling a pastry project. This will keep things moving more quickly and make cleanup easier.

Best Thing Since Sliced Bread

During the second half of the 19th century, Minneapolis became America's milling epicenter. In that city on the Mississippi, Cadwallader Washburn, his brother William, and John Crosby joined flour forces in 1877. Three years later the partners entered their finest flours in a competition at the first International Millers' Exhibition in Cincinnati, where they not only won the gold medal but took home the silver and bronze too. Soon after, the Washburn Crosby Company changed the name of its top flour to—what else?—Gold Medal flour. In 1928 the company merged with several other regional millers to create General Mills, Inc.

- Got a bag of marshmallows that are all stuck together? Add at least 1 teaspoon Argo Corn Starch to the bag, then hold it closed and shake. When excess moisture is absorbed, the marshmallows should come apart easily. Repackage in a GLAD Freezer Zipper Bag and store in the freezer to keep them fresh and unstuck.

- Fill open jelly and jam jars with your own flavored syrups. Mix 1 cup Karo Light or Dark Corn Syrup with 4 tablespoons jam or preserves; stir over low heat. Store in the refrigerator.

- Melt chocolate without the messy bowl or pan to wash afterward. Pour chocolate chips, squares, or pieces into a GLAD Food Storage Zipper Bag and squeeze out most of the air. Seal and place bag in a pan of warm (but not boiling) water. When the chocolate is melted, snip off a small corner of the still-sealed bag; squeeze it into a recipe or use it to decorate a cake.

- When kneading dough or performing other messy, hands-on tasks in the kitchen, keep an open GLAD Food Storage Bag near your telephone. You'll be able to pick up the phone even with messy hands by just slipping your hand in the bag.

Keeping Your Cookbooks Clean

- Protect recipe cards and cookbook pages from all manner of messiness by covering them with GLAD Press'n Seal.

- Attach clipped-out recipes to index cards with clear Scotch High Performance Packaging Tape. Cover them completely to protect them from splashes while cooking.

- Keep that cookbook clean while you cook. Open it to the proper page, then cover it with or enclose it in a GLAD Food Storage Zipper Bag.

- Another way to keep your recipes safe from splatters is to spray both sides of the card with Suave hairspray for a spill-resistant gloss.

Well, It's No *Joy of Cooking*...

Not sure what to make for dinner? How about looking for a recipe in this cookbook, published in 1831: *The Cook Not Mad, or Rational Cookery; Being A Collection of Original and Selected Receipts, Embracing Not Only the Art of Curing Various Kinds of Meats and Vegetables for Future Use, but of Cooking in its General Acceptation, to the Taste, Habits, and Degrees of Luxury, Prevalent with the American Publick, in Town and Country. To Which are Added, Directions for Preparing Comforts for the SICKROOM; Together with Sundry Miscellaneous Kinds of Information, of Importance to Housekeepers in General, Nearly All Tested by Experience.* By the time you finish deciphering the title, it might be time for breakfast!

Substitutions

◆ Make self-rising flour with 3½ cups flour, 1¾ teaspoons Clabber Girl Baking Powder, 1¾ teaspoons ARM & HAMMER Baking Soda, and 1¾ teaspoons Morton Salt.

◆ Replace yeast in a recipe with equal parts ARM & HAMMER Baking Soda and powdered vitamin C. The dough will rise during baking.

◆ The recipe calls for buttermilk but there's none in the fridge? No need to change your plans. To make 1 cup buttermilk, put 2 tablespoons ReaLemon Lemon Juice in a glass measuring cup. Add enough low-fat milk (1 or 2 percent) to equal 1 cup. Let sit 15 minutes.

- In a recipe calling for sour milk or buttermilk, substitute fresh milk, adding ¾ teaspoon ARM & HAMMER Baking Soda to each cup needed.

- To substitute honey for sugar in cookies, quick breads, or cakes, use ⅔ cup Sue Bee Honey for each cup of sugar. Add ½ teaspoon ARM & HAMMER Baking Soda for every cup of honey. Reduce liquid called for in recipe by ¼ cup. Bake at 25 degrees less than the recipe recommends.

- If you're out of light brown sugar, stir 1 tablespoon Grandma's Original Molasses into 1 cup Domino Demerara Washed Raw Cane Sugar and use in place of the brown sugar. For dark brown sugar, add 2 tablespoons molasses.

- If you're short 1 egg for a recipe, add a little Argo Corn Starch instead.

- Substitute 1 teaspoon ARM & HAMMER Baking Soda and 2 teaspoons Heinz Distilled White Vinegar for 2 eggs in any fruitcake or ginger cake recipe.

- Whip up an easy sour cream substitute: Add a little ReaLemon Lemon Juice to a tub of Kraft Cool Whip. Let sit for 30 minutes, then serve.

◆ Here's another substitute for sour cream: In a blender or food processor, combine 1 tablespoon ReaLemon Lemon Juice, 1 cup cottage cheese, and ⅓ cup buttermilk. Mix for 2 minutes until the mixture reaches the consistency of sour cream.

◆ Here's an easy way to make low-fat whipped cream: Beat 1 cup Carnation Instant Nonfat Dry Milk with 1 cup ice water for about 5 minutes. When the texture is light and airy, serve it immediately.

Baking Powder Substitutions

If you need 1 teaspoon baking powder but find yourself fresh out, use one of the following substitutions.

◆ ¼ teaspoon ARM & HAMMER Baking Soda plus ⅝ teaspoon (½ teaspoon plus ⅛ teaspoon) McCormick Cream of Tartar

◆ ¼ teaspoon ARM & HAMMER Baking Soda and ½ cup buttermilk or Dannon yogurt (decrease liquid called for in recipe by ½ cup)

◆ ¼ teaspoon ARM & HAMMER Baking Soda plus ½ tablespoon Heinz Distilled White Vinegar or ReaLemon Lemon Juice used with enough milk to make ½ cup (decrease liquid called for in recipe by ½ cup)

◆ ¼ teaspoon ARM & HAMMER Baking Soda plus ¼ to ½ cup Grandma's Original Molasses (decrease liquid in recipe by 1 to 2 tablespoons)

◆ Out of vegetable oil? Crisco All-Vegetable shortening makes an excellent substitute for frying and baking (melt the shortening, let cool slightly, then measure and add according to recipe). Do not use shortening in salad dressings, because it resolidifies when it cools.

Recipe Enhancements

◆ Adding 1 teaspoon ARM & HAMMER Baking Soda to the other dry ingredients in a chocolate cake will give the cake a darker color.

◆ When making a chocolate cake from a box, add a teaspoon of Folgers Instant Coffee Crystals to the water and you'll have mocha cake!

◆ When making fruitcake, add a teaspoon of ARM & HAMMER Baking Soda to darken the cake and soften the fruit a bit.

◆ Add a pinch of ARM & HAMMER Baking Soda to a waffle mix to make the waffles lighter and softer.

◆ For fluffier pancakes, use Canada Dry Club Soda in place of the liquid in your pancake recipe.

◆ When making a boiled syrup, add a pinch of ARM & HAMMER Baking Soda to prevent crystallizing.

STORAGE AND LEFTOVERS

◆ Freeze leftover stock, broth, cooking wine, and other liquids in an ice cube tray. Measure and note the capacity of each compartment. You'll have ready-to-use recipe ingredients.

♦ You can freeze eggs to preserve them, but you have to take them out of their shells first. Save yolks and whites, or just whites, by adding ⅛ teaspoon Morton Salt to every ¼ cup of egg. Make sure you label the freezer container to reflect the date; also indicate that salt has been added so you can adjust future recipes accordingly.

♦ To keep hamburger patties separated in the freezer, place a plastic coffee can lid between each one. Store them all in a GLAD Freezer Zipper Bag. When the time comes to cook them, the patties will separate easily, even when frozen.

How Long Does It Keep?

PRODUCT	STORAGE PERIOD	
	Refrigerator	*Freezer*
Chicken, whole	1–2 days	12 months
Chicken, parts	1–2 days	9 months
Beef, steaks & chops	3–5 days	6–12 months
Beef, ground	1–2 days	3–4 months
Pork, chops	3–5 days	3–4 months
Pork, roasts	3–5 days	4–8 months
Fish, lean (e.g., cod)	2–3 days	6 months
Fish, fatty (e.g., salmon)	2–3 days	2–3 months
Lunchmeat	3–5 days	1–2 months
Sausage	1–2 days	1–2 months
Cheese (most kinds)	3–4 weeks	Do not freeze (if opened)
Milk	5 days	Do not freeze

◆ Extend the life of shredded cheese by storing it in the freezer. It will remain fresh and moisture-free longer. Store the cheese in its original bag, but put the bag inside a GLAD Freezer Zipper Bag.

◆ Prevent a hard cheese from drying out by adding a few drops of Heinz Distilled White Vinegar to a Scott Towel moistened with water. Wrap the cheese in the paper towel and put it inside a GLAD Food Storage Zipper Bag. If the paper towel dries out, add more water or vinegar.

◆ Prolong the life of lettuce in your crisper drawer by wrapping it in a Scott Towel, then in a GLAD Food Storage Zipper Bag before storing it.

◆ Line the bottom of your refrigerator's vegetable bin with Scott Towels. They'll absorb moisture and fend off spoilage.

◆ To distinguish the hard-boiled eggs in the fridge from the raw ones, mark the cooked ones with a Crayola Crayon.

◆ Stop that batch of cookies from drying out: Put a slice of apple or a piece of bread in your airtight cookie jar.

◆ A No nonsense pantyhose leg conveniently stores onions, garlic, and other produce bought in bulk. Drop in 1 item (such as a garlic bulb) and tie a knot. Drop in another item and tie a second knot, and so forth. When a recipe calls for that ingredient, cut just below the knot above it.

◆ Time to pour the leftover Crisco oil or Sue Bee Honey back into its bottle? A sandwich-size GLAD Food Storage Zipper Bag makes a great funnel. Fill a bag with the liquid, seal it, and then snip off a bottom corner over the storage container. Toss the "funnel" when done.

◆ Fold a Melitta Basket Coffee Filter (or cut off the tip of a cone-style filter) and you've got a makeshift funnel. Use it to pour spices or dry ingredients into small bottles, for example.

◆ After they have brought those wonderful herbs and spices to you, the clean, empty bottles have a few more tricks up their caps. With a shaker top, they are perfect for sprinkling cinnamon sugar, powdered sugar, or the like; without, they serve as convenient toothpick holders.

◆ GLAD Cling Wrap won't stick to itself if stored in the refrigerator or freezer. To unsnarl a piece of GLAD Cling Wrap, chill it in the freezer for about 10 minutes.

◆ A large binder clip makes a great "chip clip" for opened bags of snack food.

- Pretzels and their pals will stay even fresher if the package is closed with a piece of Scotch Duct Tape. Choose duct tape rather than packaging tape because duct tape will seal and reseal over and over again.

- Is your life, or at least your pantry, overrun with plastic grocery bags? Try this nifty storage idea. Squeeze the air from each bag, fold, and insert in an empty Kleenex facial tissue box. You won't believe how many bags can fit!

- Save space and keep place mats handy by hanging them inside a pantry or cabinet door. Clip a set together with a binder clip.

- Group cloth napkin sets together in a drawer or hall pantry with a binder clip. When it's time to set the table for company, you'll have a full set at the ready.

- If it seems that nothing short of breaking them will separate stacked drinking glasses, put away that hammer! Pour a bit of Crisco Pure Vegetable Oil around the lip of the bottom glass. Wiggle it gently; the glasses will soon pull apart.

AT YOUR SERVICE

- To create a special warming aid for serving bread, rolls, and baked goods straight from the oven, place a piece of Reynolds Wrap Aluminum Foil under a napkin in a serving basket. This not only keeps the heat in but also keeps grease stains off the basket.

- If you use brass serving dishes for your fancy meals, rub them with a little Colavita Extra Virgin Olive Oil after you've cleaned them. This will prevent tarnishing.

- The foil wrapper on wine bottles is designed to keep air out of the wine and protect the cork from pests. However, it can actually contain lead that is harmful to swallow. To remove lead residue before pouring wine, remove entire wrapper from bottle and discard. Then wipe rim and neck of bottle with a cloth dampened in Heinz Vinegar. The acid in the vinegar will neutralize any traces of lead.

- Clearing the table after a big dinner party can be a challenge. To get a head start on doing the dishes, line a large bowl with a plastic grocery bag, handles overlapping the edges. Place it prominently in your kitchen with a rubber spatula alongside. As the plates are brought into the kitchen, scrape the scraps right into the bowl. Once the plates are clean, it's a snap to pick the bag up by the handles and toss.

Mother of (Nearly) All Grocery Bags

The first recorded reference to paper grocery bags dates to 1630. Not until 1870, however, did Margaret Knight (1838–1914) invent an attachment for paper bag folding machines that created square-bottomed bags. She founded the Eastern Paper Bag Company in Boston and continued her work, which resulted in more than 25 patents. At age 12 she made a safety device for textile looms; among her later inventions were improvements to clothing and shoe manufacturing, a numbering machine, a window frame and sash, and several devices for rotary engines.

- Keep the mess to a minimum! To make ice cream cones and watermelon slices drip-proof, wrap the bottoms with Reynolds Wrap Aluminum Foil.

- Melitta Basket Coffee Filters are also great drip-catchers for frozen treats. Just poke a hole in the middle of the filter and insert the stick.

- If you're dashing out the door with something edible yet messy, wrap it in a Melitta Basket Coffee Filter to avoid drips. This trick works especially well for tacos and pita sandwiches, whether on the go or not.

- No need for paper plates to serve hot dogs fresh from the grill. Just place the bun inside a Melitta Basket Coffee Filter. It's a holder and a napkin all in one!

- Drain grease from fried foods such as bacon, French fries, and onion rings using Melitta Basket Coffee Filters. Put 2 or 3 filters on a plate and they'll soak up the excess grease.

- Use Melitta Basket Coffee Filters as disposable bowls for popcorn or other snacks.

- Lighting a candle that has burned down to almost nothing is difficult and dangerous with a cigarette lighter or a small

Can't Hold a Candle to Him

Thomas Edison is credited with inventing wax paper in the early 1870s. The product is basically moisture-proof paper that has been coated in wax.

match. If you don't have a long lighter or match, light a wooden toothpick to reach the wick easily.

◆ Save yourself some steps and keep your countertops neater. Line a coffee can or Folgers coffee canister with a small plastic bag; place it near the sink and fill it with peelings and scraps. Make just 1 trip to the kitchen trash to toss the bag when you're done rather than traipsing back and forth.

DOIN' THE DISHES

Bottles, Mugs & Jars

◆ To get to hard-to-reach places in vases and bottles, insert a crushed eggshell (the more finely crushed the better) into the vase or bottle, then add warm water plus a drop of Dawn dishwashing liquid. Swirl mixture around to let the shells do the work. Rinse.

◆ Clean the oil out of a salad dressing cruet by shaking ARM & HAMMER Baking Soda inside, then rinsing it clean with warm water.

◆ Deodorize and clean a thermos by dropping in 3 Polident denture cleanser tablets, filling thermos with water, and letting it soak for an hour. Rinse thoroughly.

◆ Sprinkle some Morton Salt into a thermos or any closed container prone to developing odors. Leave overnight, then rinse. Smells should disappear, but repeat if necessary.

- Use Clorox Regular-Bleach to get your travel mug clean and smelling fresh. Wash it as usual, then soak it for 2 minutes in a solution of 1 tablespoon bleach per gallon of water. Rinse and let air-dry.

- Dip a damp O-Cel-O sponge in ARM & HAMMER Baking Soda and rub coffee mug and teacup stains away. Stubborn stains may also require a little Morton Salt.

- Clean mineral deposits and neutralize any acids in old canning jars by shaking a solution of 4 tablespoons ARM & HAMMER Baking Soda per quart of warm water inside. Rinse thoroughly, then sterilize as usual.

What's in a Name?

- "Baking soda" is the common term for bicarbonate of soda, which in turn is more formally called either "sodium bicarbonate" or "sodium hydrogen carbonate." It results when sodium carbonate (soda ash) is treated with carbon dioxide.

- Baking powder is produced from an alkali-acid combination—more specifically, baking soda and cream of tartar (tartaric acid).

- Because it's a source of carbon dioxide, sodium bicarbonate is also used in effervescent salts, carbonated beverages, tanning, wool preparation, and dry-chemical fire extinguishers. When the extinguisher is turned upside down, sodium bicarbonate mixes and reacts with sulfuric acid to propel water.

China and Crystal

- After the dishes are washed and you're ready to store them, insert a flattened Melitta Basket Coffee Filter between china plates and saucers—or other delicate pieces—to protect them.

- Crystal is best washed by hand, very carefully. After washing, dip crystal in a sink full of warm water and 1 tablespoon Heinz Vinegar. Finish with a clear water rinse.

- When washing stemware and other delicate items in the dishwasher, secure them to the top rack with rubber bands.

Life Cycle of the Dishwasher

1886: Josephine Garis Cochran of Shelbyville, Illinois, unable to find a machine to wash dishes more efficiently than her servants, invents one. She receives patent #355,139 for the first practical dish-washing machine.

1893: Cochran introduces her dishwasher at the Chicago World's Fair; when restaurants and hotels express interest, she founds a manufacturing company that eventually becomes KitchenAid.

1926: Kohler Company introduces the Electric Sink, but it's discontinued during the Great Depression.

1949: KitchenAid introduces the KD-10, the first residential dishwasher to distribute water by a pressurized system rather than just splashing water on dishes.

Cutting Boards

- To disinfect a plastic cutting board after it's been washed, place it in a solution of 1 tablespoon Clorox Regular-Bleach per gallon of water. Soak for 2 minutes; drain and air-dry.

- You can keep odors from a clean wood or plastic cutting board by wiping it with an O-Cel-O sponge dampened with a little Heinz Vinegar.

- After cleaning your wood cutting board, rub a bit of ReaLemon Lemon Juice on it to help get rid of garlic, onion, or fish smells.

- Use Clorox Regular-Bleach to keep a wood cutting board free of bacteria. Wash the cutting board in hot, sudsy water and rinse thoroughly. Then mix 3 tablespoons Clorox Regular-Bleach with 1 gallon warm water. Soak or brush the solution onto the cutting board, keep it moist for at least 2 minutes, then rinse thoroughly.

- Clean a wood cutting board with Dawn dishwashing liquid and a little bit of water. Follow cleaning by dipping a damp cloth in Morton Salt and wiping board until salt is gone. The salt treatment will leave the board looking, smelling, and feeling fresh.

- Keep wooden spoons, cutting boards, and butcher blocks well oiled by rubbing them with Crisco Pure Vegetable Oil on a Scott Towel. Wipe away any excess.

- Deodorize and remove stains from wood cutting boards, bowls, or utensils with a solution of 4 tablespoons ARM & HAMMER Baking Soda to 1 quart water.

Glassware

- Get rid of the cloudy film on glassware by soaking items overnight in a tub of equal parts Heinz Vinegar and warm water. Wash glasses by hand the next day.

Like Salt Through the Hourglass

750 B.C. (approximate): The expression "not worth his salt" originates in ancient Greece, where salt was traded for slaves.

500 B.C. (approximate): Soldiers of the Roman Empire are paid *salarium argentum* ("salt money"), from which comes our word *salary.*

1559: Italians discover that ice and salt make a freezing combination...and ice cream makes its debut.

1694: British Parliament doubles salt tax to help fund ongoing war with France.

1777: Lord Howe captures General George Washington's salt supply.

1812: During the war, Americans find salt nearly impossible to obtain from other countries, so commercial production of salt begins in Syracuse, New York.

1820s: The Great Salt Lake in northern Utah is first explored by white trappers.

By 1848: The Erie Canal is known as "the ditch that salt built."

By 1848: Alonzo Richmond moves to Chicago from Syracuse and starts Richmond & Company, Agents for Onondaga Salt.

1863: In key moves of the U.S. Civil War, Union forces cut off the Confederacy from its salt deposits on the Gulf Coast of Louisiana and destroy important saltworks in Florida, North Carolina, and Virginia.

1889: Joy Morton acquires a major interest in Richmond & Company, and he renames it Joy Morton & Company.

1910: The company is renamed the Morton Salt Company.

- You can rub out tiny scratches on your glassware by using a dab of Crest toothpaste.

- Rescue that drinking glass. A small chip in the rim can be smoothed by carefully rubbing it with extra-fine 3M sandpaper.

Plasticware

- Plasticware, especially food containers, often takes on a greasy feeling. Put a capful of Clorox Regular-Bleach in the dishwater along with your usual dishwashing liquid. Problem solved!

- Scrub stained plastic storage containers with a paste of ReaLemon Lemon Juice and ARM & HAMMER Baking Soda.

Papa of Plastics

The modern plastics industry began in 1907, thanks to Leo Hendrik Baekeland. The Belgian American chemist invented Bakelite, a plastic produced from formaldehyde and phenol. Many industrial and household products were made from Bakelite, including early telephones. Baekeland's first great invention was Velox, the first commercially successful photographic paper. He sold his company and rights to the paper in 1899 for $1 million...to George Eastman.

- Avoid red tomato stains on plastic by spraying a container with PAM cooking spray before adding tomato-based food. Before washing the container, rinse with cold water.

- To get rid of red tomato stains or other tough stains from your plastic and rubber containers and utensils, make a paste using ARM & HAMMER Baking Soda and water. Mix to the consistency of toothpaste and apply to the stained areas. Let dry, then rub off. Wash as usual.

- Deodorize plastic bottles, cups, containers, and boxes by brushing them with Crest toothpaste on a Reach toothbrush. Let sit a few minutes, then rinse.

Silver

- Give silverware a quick polish: Sprinkle some ARM & HAMMER Baking Soda on a damp cloth or an O-Cel-O sponge. Rub, rinse, and let dry.

- Shine up your silverware with a banana peel. Remove any leftover "strings" from the inside of the peel, then rub the peel on cutlery and serving pieces. Buff with a clean, soft cloth or a Scott Towel.

> ### After All, They Are Professionals
>
> When you peel a banana, don't you hate those yucky strings running down the sides of it? Turn it over and peel the banana from the bottom. The strings will stick to the inside of the peel! Research shows that the technique works: It's the way monkeys and apes peel bananas.

- Make a paste of Argo Corn Starch and water and apply to tarnished silverware. Let dry; wipe clean with a dry cloth.

◆ Make your silver sparkle! In a bowl, mix 1 tablespoon ReaLemon Lemon Juice (or 1 tablespoon Heinz Distilled White Vinegar), ½ cup Carnation Instant Nonfat Dry Milk, and 1½ cups water. Place your silver in the bowl; let sit overnight. Rinse and dry thoroughly. Double or even triple this recipe if necessary to accommodate your silver.

◆ If you need clean silver now instead of tomorrow morning, pour ReaLemon Lemon Juice over the piece. Polish with a soft, clean cotton cloth.

◆ To clean sterling silver pieces and bring back their shine, rub them with a paste made of ½ cup Heinz Distilled White Vinegar and 2 tablespoons Morton Salt. Dip a clean, soft cloth in the paste, then gently rub silver pieces using a circular motion. Rinse, then dry with another soft cloth.

◆ To remove silver tarnish, bring a medium-size pot of water to a boil and add ½ teaspoon Morton Salt and 1 to 2 teaspoons ARM & HAMMER Baking Soda. Reduce heat. Place tarnished silverware and a piece of Reynolds Wrap Aluminum Foil in the pot. Simmer for 2 to 3 minutes. Rinse the silverware well, then use a soft cloth to buff dry.

◆ Fill a large bowl with Heinz Vinegar and add Clabber Girl Baking Powder until mixture starts to bubble. Dip silver pieces in solution for a few seconds, then buff tarnished areas with a clean, soft cloth. If tarnish remains, repeat process, leaving silver pieces in mixture for a longer period of time. Buff again.

- Remove silverware tarnish by gently rubbing pieces with Morton Salt and a soft cloth; then hand wash with Dawn dishwashing liquid and warm water.

- Coat silver items with a thin film of Alberto VO5 Conditioning Hairdressing to prevent tarnishing. Wash before using.

- Place 1 or 2 pieces of Crayola chalk in your silverware chest to prevent tarnishing.

- Keep silverware shining by storing it on a sheet of Reynolds Wrap Aluminum Foil. To store it for the long term, first wrap each piece in GLAD Cling Wrap (squeeze out as much air as you can). Then wrap in foil, sealing the ends.

Sponges and Scrubbers

- Refresh a fading O-Cel-O sponge by washing it in your dishwasher. Use a clothespin to clip it to the top rack. After cleaning, soak sponge in cold salt water to revive its fibers, using about ½ teaspoon of salt per cup of water.

- Renew old sponges, nylon scrubbers, and scrub brushes— even bottle nipples and bottle brushes—by soaking them overnight in a solution of 4 tablespoons ARM & HAMMER Baking Soda and 1 quart water.

- If a lightly used Brillo Steel Wool Soap Pad still has some oomph left, don't throw it away. Wrap it in Reynolds Wrap Aluminum Foil (so it won't rust) and put it in the freezer.

- Bunch up a pair of old (but clean!) No nonsense pantyhose to create a good scrub pad for doing the dishes. You can also cut off a foot portion, slip it over an O-Cel-O sponge, and knot the end to make a nonscratch scrubber for dishes, cookware, and even walls and other nonporous surfaces. Wrap a piece of hosiery around a bottle brush for extra scrubbing power.

- A retired but clean Reach toothbrush is perfect for getting the grime out of hard-to-get-to places, such as the bars of roasting racks and the bottoms of tall glasses.

Teakettles

- Boil water and ½ cup Heinz Vinegar in a teakettle for 10 or 15 minutes to help remove any mineral deposits inside the pot and spout. Let stand 1 hour; rinse thoroughly.

Mother of All Vinegars

The gooey stuff that forms on vinegar is called "mother" and is actually cellulose. The natural by-product of the harmless vinegar bacteria, mother does not form on pasteurized bottled vinegars.

- To clean a teapot or stovetop percolator, fill it with water, add 2 or 3 tablespoons ARM & HAMMER Baking Soda, and boil for 10 to 15 minutes. After cooling, scrub and rinse thoroughly.

- To remove rust stains and mineral deposits from a teapot, fill the pot with water and add 2 tablespoons each of ARM & HAMMER Baking Soda and ReaLemon Lemon Juice. Boil gently for 15 minutes and rinse.

◆ To clean the inside of a teapot, add the peel of 1 lemon per 2 cups warm water. Soak overnight.

Tea Time

◆ According to legend, in 2737 B.C. Chinese Emperor Shennong brewed the first cup of tea when leaves from a burning tea twig fell into water he was boiling.

◆ Tea was not introduced in England until 1600, when British merchants established the East India Company.

◆ Thomas Sullivan of New York accidentally invented the tea bag around 1908, when to cut costs he sent samples of loose tea in small silk pouches to potential customers.

◆ At the start of World War II, Winston Churchill guaranteed the Royal Navy an unlimited supply of tea; reserves were shipped to hundreds of secret locations.

Utensils

◆ If mineral deposits have built up on your aluminum kitchen utensils, add a few tablespoons Heinz Vinegar to a pot of boiling water. Drop utensils in the water and boil them for about 5 minutes. Rinse with fresh water.

Condiment Complement

When he founded his company in 1869, Henry J. Heinz manufactured vinegar to complement his other products, such as pickles, horseradish, and several sauces. The vinegar was, and still is, 100% pure and natural, made from corn and grapes. The Pittsburgh-based company quickly became the country's first to package and sell vinegar for home use.

◆ Remove streaks on your stainless-steel kitchen utensils or bowls by rubbing them with a little Colavita Extra Virgin Olive Oil. Dampen a cloth with Heinz Vinegar and buff each piece to a shine. This treatment will also work for stains on your flatware.

◆ Try this method for getting rid of stains on a wooden cooking spoon: Wearing rubber gloves, rub a piece of fine steel wool along the grain until the marks vanish. Brush off the resulting dust and dispose of any steel wool residue. Rub about 1 teaspoon Crisco Pure Vegetable Oil into the wood with a soft cloth.

A Helping of Hints

◆ When you can't wash the breakfast dishes immediately, sprinkle plates with Morton Salt to keep eggs from sticking and make dishes easier to clean later.

◆ If you're out of dishwashing liquid—but not out of dirty dishes—Suave shampoo can fill in. It will make short work of grease and oil, but make sure you're not using a shampoo-conditioner combo.

◆ It's certainly convenient and sanitary to run items such as plastic container lids, baby-bottle caps, and other small items through the dishwasher instead of washing them by hand. To ensure that the items don't fall to the bottom of the appliance, put them all in a mesh laundry bag (used to machine wash delicate clothes) on the upper rack of the dishwasher; the items will be protected and washed.

- Soft cheese or other sticky food stuck on a grater? Cut a lemon in half and rub the pulp side on both surfaces of the grater.

- Does your silverware organizer tray, whether plastic or wooden, slide around in the kitchen drawer? It will stay put if you put a few lengths of Scotch Double Sided Tape on the bottom. Or, place 2 loops of Scotch Duct Tape (sticky side out) on the bottom. You will be able to pop out the tray for cleaning, then put it right back in place.

- Place an entire roll or coil of garbage bags in the bottom of your garbage can. When you fill up one bag, remove it and just pull up a new one.

CLEANING COOKWARE

General Cleaning

- Burned-on grease in a pot or pan can be removed by filling the pan with water and adding 6 Alka-Seltzer tablets. Let the pan soak for at least an hour, then scrub it clean.

- To loosen baked- or dried-on food in a pan, gently boil water and ARM & HAMMER Baking Soda in the pan. When food is loosened, allow pan to cool and then wipe clean.

- When you're faced with the challenge of stubborn, baked-on food in a 2- or 3-quart glass casserole dish, fill it with boiling water plus 3 tablespoons Morton Salt. Let stand until the water cools, then wash as usual.

◆ Put down that chisel! Here's an easier way to remove baked-on food from a pan. Pour 1 or 2 teaspoons of Final Touch fabric softener into the pan, then fill it with water, or put the pan in a sink filled with water and a Downy dryer sheet. Let soak overnight, then wipe away the loosened food and wash as usual.

◆ Don't struggle to scrape off burned-on food in a pan. Pour in a can of Pepsi; allow pan to soak for about an hour, then wipe clean.

◆ Get rid of excess grease in a roasting pan by sprinkling it with Morton Salt and wiping with a damp O-Cel-O sponge or Scott Towel. Wash as usual.

What Do You Call a Carbonated Soft Drink?

Throughout the years and across the country, carbonated soft drinks have been known by a variety of names.

Pop: predominantly in the Midwest and Great Plains states, with scattered Mountain and West Coast clusters

Soda: concentrated in eastern quarter of U.S., especially Mid-Atlantic states and New England; also Florida and much of California, with some Midwest and Southwest clusters

Coke (regardless of actual brand): southern U.S.

Soft drink: the Southeast; California

Tonic: upper New England

Soda pop: scattered clusters throughout U.S.

Carbonated beverage: eastern U.S.

Co-cola: primarily Deep South

Sody pop/sodie pop: central U.S.

- Sprinkle ARM & HAMMER Baking Soda over burned-on stains on cookie sheets, then cover with hot water. Let soak for 10 minutes. Next, scour with baking soda and an O-Cel-O No-Scratch Scrub Sponge.

- Reduce the chore of washing a greasy baking dish or pan. After the grease is drained off, rub the pan with a thick slice of lemon or a used lemon half turned inside out. Wash as usual.

- Make cleaning a broiler pan much easier by first pouring used Folgers coffee grounds over it, then rubbing well with an O-Cel-O No-Scratch Scrub Sponge.

Short(ening) Story

In 1911, Procter & Gamble introduced Crisco All-Vegetable Shortening, the first solidified shortening made from vegetable oil. Manufactured from hydrogenated cottonseed oil, by 1923 it was packaged in a can that was opened with an attached key. A magazine ad from that year proclaimed that, of the 117 people who took a taste test, "95 chose the potatoes fried in Crisco because they tasted nicer."

- To remove rust from knives, cast-iron pots, and other kitchen equipment, make a paste with 1 part ReaLemon Lemon Juice and 2 parts Morton Salt. Apply with a clean, soft cloth and rub away the rust. Rinse with clear water; dry well.

- Get rid of rust on a kitchen knife by cutting an onion. Using the rusted blade, carefully cut into (but not all the way through) a large, whole onion. Repeat 2 or 3 times. If there is a large amount of rust on the blade, it may require a few more strokes to clean it off.

◆ Stacked pots and pans can get scratched and soiled. When you put them back in the cabinet, line all but the top one with Scott Towels.

Aluminum

◆ Protect aluminum cookware from being darkened by harsh cleansers. Wipe a clean pot with a cloth dampened with ReaLemon Lemon Juice; rinse well and dry.

◆ To make stains vanish from aluminum or enamel cookware, fill the pot or pan with water and add a cut lime. Boil until the stains are gone. For a small pot, use half a lime; for a larger one, use both halves.

◆ When aluminum pans get dull, return them to their original brightness by boiling apple peelings in them.

◆ Scrub aluminum cookware with 20 Mule Team Borax. Sprinkle a bit on your pots and pans and rub with a damp dishcloth. Rinse completely. Clean...and no scratches!

Johnny Appleseed

Much myth surrounds the legend of Johnny Appleseed. The real-life John Chapman, on whom the legend is based, did collect apple seeds from Pennsylvania cider presses, sell and give them away, and plant what became great apple orchards in the Midwest. Born in 1774 in Leominster, Massachusetts, as a child he met Samuel Wilson...the man who, decades later, became the real-life inspiration for America's Uncle Sam.

Cast Iron

◆ Reynolds Wrap Aluminum Foil helps loosen food cooked onto cast-iron pots and pans. Ball up a piece of foil; use it to rub away the mess. Wipe clean with a soft, dry cloth.

◆ Apply a layer of Crisco Pure Vegetable Oil to rust spots on your cast-iron skillet. Let stand overnight, then wipe the skillet thoroughly. Rust should disappear.

◆ After seasoning a cast-iron skillet with a drop of Crisco Pure Vegetable Oil, store it between 2 Melitta Basket Coffee Filters to help keep moisture at bay.

Fair Enough!

Many products and innovations debuted—or were first introduced to a wider audience—at a World's Fair held in the United States.

World's Columbian Exposition, Chicago, 1893: dishwasher, carbonated soda, Shredded Wheat, Cream of Wheat, Aunt Jemima syrup, Juicy Fruit gum, Ferris wheel

Louisiana Purchase Exposition, St. Louis, 1904: ice cream cone, cotton candy, puffed rice, hot dog, peanut butter, Dr. Pepper, fruit icicle (precursor to the Popsicle), air-conditioning, wireless telegraph

Alaska-Yukon-Pacific Exposition, Seattle, 1909: wireless "telephone" (actually, precursor to radio)

A Century of Progress Exposition, Chicago, 1933–34: Kraft Miracle Whip, automatic fountain soft-drink dispenser

Copper

◆ A combination of ½ cup Heinz Ketchup with 2 tablespoons McCormick Cream of Tartar makes copper cookware and utensils as bright as—you guessed it!—a new penny. Apply to surfaces; wait 1 hour. Rinse in soapy water, then in clear water. Dry completely.

◆ Make a copper-bottom pan worthy of display. Use a spray bottle to spritz the bottom of the pan with undiluted Heinz Distilled White Vinegar. Let sit until you can see the tarnish evaporating. Sprinkle Morton Salt on top of the vinegar and scrub the entire surface with an O-Cel-O No-Scratch Scrub Sponge. Rinse; repeat if necessary.

Popular Types of Vinegar

Distilled White: from alcohol (fermented grains); countless uses

Apple Cider: from apple juice; cooking, pickling, canning, other therapeutic uses

Wine: from fermented wine; salad dressings, marinades, glazes

Malt: from barley and corn malt, earthy; seafood and meat marinades, salad dressings

Rice: light; important ingredient in Asian cooking

Balsamic: from white Trebbiano grapes, made in Modena, Italy, by traditional aging process; cooking and food preparation

Enamel

◆ Enamel cookware can't handle abrasive cleaners. Instead, apply a paste of ARM & HAMMER Baking Soda and water and let sit for an hour. Clean with an O-Cel-O No-Scratch Scrub Sponge and rinse.

- Clorox Regular-Bleach helps remove stains from enamel cookware. Fill a pot or pan with a solution of 2 teaspoons bleach to 2½ cups water. Let soak for 2 hours, then wash with hot, soapy water. Rinse and dry.

Nonstick Surfaces

- Remove stains from a nonstick pan by boiling 1 cup water, 2 tablespoons ARM & HAMMER Baking Soda, and ½ cup Clorox Regular-Bleach in the pan for several minutes. Wash as usual, then use Crisco Pure Vegetable Oil to reseason.

Fire Facts

Note: Do not hesitate to call 911 if you think a fire is out of hand. Once a cooking fire is extinguished, allow pots and their contents to cool before removing and cleaning.

- Keep a box of ARM & HAMMER Baking Soda within reach of the stove (but far enough away to be out of range of a fire). Pour baking soda directly on the flames to extinguish a small fire.

- Do not use ARM & HAMMER Baking Soda to extinguish a fire in a deep-fat fryer; the hot fat may splatter.

- Control the flames when grease drips onto coals during grilling by keeping handy a spray bottle of 1 teaspoon ARM & HAMMER Baking Soda mixed with 1 pint of water. Spray lightly onto coals when flames shoot up.

- Do not use ARM & HAMMER Baking Soda on any fire involving combustibles, such as wood or paper.

- Extinguish a small grease fire with a handful or more of Morton Salt. This method works for a burner fire or a fire inside the oven. (Use caution when putting out fires, and do not hesitate to use a fire extinguisher or call for help if a fire intensifies.)

Porcelain

◆ Sprinkle a bit of 20 Mule Team Borax on porcelain pots and pans, rub with a damp dishcloth, and rinse.

Stainless Steel

◆ Your stainless-steel pans will stay shiny if you rub them with a dry, soft cloth and a little Gold Medal All-Purpose Flour. Buff with another clean cloth.

◆ Remove the "rainbow" from stainless-steel pots by rubbing with a cut lime.

Stoneware

◆ To clean scratches in stoneware, apply a paste of ARM & HAMMER Baking Soda and water to the cracks. Let stand a few minutes, then wash as usual.

FOR BABY

◆ When seemingly clean baby bottles start to smell sour, put a dab of Crest toothpaste on a bottle brush and scrub. Rinse thoroughly.

- Fill baby bottles with warm water and 1 teaspoon ARM & HAMMER Baking Soda. Shake and rinse, then clean as usual.

- Freshen bottle nipples and bottle brushes overnight by soaking them in a solution of 4 tablespoons ARM & HAMMER Baking Soda per 1 quart hot water. Drain, rinse, and clean as usual in the morning.

- To clean baby bottle nipples, add 1 tablespoon Heinz Vinegar to 1 cup water in a glass measuring cup. Add nipples and boil in microwave for 2 minutes. Rinse well.

- Sanitize baby bottles, teething rings, sippy cups, and feeding spoons with bleach. Mix 1 tablespoon Clorox Regular-Bleach with 1 gallon water and soak the prewashed items for 2 minutes. Rinse well, drain, and air-dry. (Before draining, pour the solution through each bottle's nipple. Rinse well.)

- A similar method can disinfect baby's rubber ducks, toy keys, and other plastic toys. Soak the prewashed playthings in a solution of ¾ cup Clorox Regular-Bleach and 1 gallon water for 5 minutes. Rinse, drain, and air-dry.

- Use the same proportions (¾ cup Clorox Regular-Bleach per gallon of water) to sponge down a high chair. Let solution stand for 5 minutes; rinse and let dry.

- Use a generous sheet of GLAD Press'n Seal to cover a toddler's chair at mealtime.

Chapter 6:
Household Tasks & Maintenance

KEEP UP WITH THE UPKEEP

A commonly accepted principle of home ownership is this: To maintain a house, you need either (a) the time and expertise to do the work yourself or (b) the money to pay someone else to do it. Unfortunately, many of us feel that  we're practically running on empty on both options.

What "weekend warrior" couldn't use help?

Everyday products such as masking tape cannot morph into power tools. Repurposing a banana peel won't turn you into a master crafter (or even a promising apprentice). What these and other household products will do is provide readily available and affordable alternatives to household challenges.

You'll wonder at the many uses for paper and plastic bags, the versatility of vegetables and fruits, and the uncommon creativity of common household chemicals. What's more, look forward to fewer interruptions during projects for those (previously) countless trips to the hardware store.

It takes quite a team to keep the homestead operational, the car purring, the painting progressing, and the garden from being swallowed up by nature. Fortunately, you have just such a team at the ready—in the kitchen cabinets, on the shelves of your medicine cabinet, and within the junk drawer.

CAR CARE

Make That Exterior Sparkle

- Buff your clean car to a shine with a bit of Argo Corn Starch on a clean cloth.

- Use ARM & HAMMER Baking Soda to safely clean your car's headlights, chrome, windows, tires, vinyl seats, floor mats, and wiper blades. Sprinkle it onto a damp O-Cel-O sponge, scrub, and rinse.

- Melitta Basket Coffee Filters are perfect for cleaning and polishing the chrome, windows, mirrors, and headlights on your vehicle.

- Alberto VO5 Conditioning Hairdressing makes a good chrome polish. Rub on with a clean cloth, then buff with a second cloth.

- To clean the chrome on your car, pour a small amount of ReaLime Lime Juice on a soft cotton cloth. Buff to shine. Or, use a paste of ARM & HAMMER Baking Soda and water to clean your car's chrome surfaces. Apply, then buff dry.

- Give clean chrome a final buffing with a used Downy dryer sheet. It will remove all streaks and bring out the shine.

- To clean grease and grime from your windshield or chrome trim, pour Canada Dry Club Soda on a clean cloth and use it to polish.

- When windshield wipers leave marks on your clean windshield, wipe them down with a Pampers baby wipe.

- To shine your hubcaps, drop a Polident denture cleanser tablet into water and scrub hubcaps with the solution. Rinse with clean water.

- Trisodium phosphate will remove any stain from a whitewall tire, but if phosphates are banned in your area or you prefer not to use them, substitute ARM & HAMMER Baking Soda. Apply with a damp cloth and use a scrub brush to work it into discolored areas of the whitewall. Rinse with clean water.

- To get rid of rust spots on bumpers, scrub with Pepsi. Use a wadded-up piece of Reynolds Wrap Aluminum Foil as a scrubber.

- Remove sticky tar from your car's bumpers, chrome, and body by covering the affected area with Crisco Pure Vegetable Oil, letting it soak in, and washing it off.

- Another way to remove tar is to cover the spot with Kraft Mayonnaise. Wait several minutes, then scrub away. Mayo is also effective on pine sap.

- Spray WD-40 on tar spots to loosen them before washing.

- Pepsi is an effective cleaning solution for getting rid of bugs splattered on the body of your car. Pour it directly on the critters or apply it to the finish with a car scrub brush.

- Remove splattered bugs and sap with WD-40 without harming your car's finish.

- Once your car's bumpers and grille are clean, spray them with PAM cooking spray to make it easier to clean off rust and bugs the next time.

- Bird droppings drop away when you cover them with a rag soaked in Crisco Pure Vegetable Oil. Once the debris has loosened, carefully wipe off the mess with a Scott Towel.

How Did WD-40 Get Its Name?

In San Diego in 1953, three guys founded the Rocket Chemical Company and attempted to produce rust-prevention solvents and degreasers for the aerospace industry. Success came with the secret formula still used today. They named it WD-40, short for "Water displacement perfected on the 40th try." The aerosol-can version for consumers debuted in 1958; the company was renamed for its only product 11 years later.

The first truckload order for WD-40 was shipped to the U.S. Gulf Coast to aid rebuilding efforts after 1961's Hurricane Carla. The product was used to recondition water-damaged vehicles and equipment.

- To restore the original factory luster of faux-wood paneling on cars, polish with brown Griffin Wax Shoe Polish.

- Use Crayola Crayons to cover scratches on your car's finish. Match the color of the crayon to your car, rub it over the scratches, then buff the area with a cloth.

Simonize Your Car with Simoniz

Back in 1910, George Simons created 2 products for the still-new automobile industry. He and Elmer Rich organized Simons Manufacturing Company to make and sell Simons Cleaner and Simons Paste Wax. Two years later Rich and his brother bought the whole firm, renaming it the Simoniz Company. Their slogan, "Motorists Wise, Simoniz," became well known, and by the late 1930s the trademarked word *simonize* had worked its way into colloquial language (and the dictionary!) as a generic verb, meaning "to shine or polish to a high sheen, esp. with wax: to simonize an automobile."

◆ Make that bumper sticker much easier to remove down the road. Apply a thin coat of Simoniz Original Paste Wax to the bumper *before* you put on the sticker.

◆ Change your mind about that old bumper sticker? Use Cutex Quick & Gentle Liquid Nail Polish Remover to soften the sticker, then carefully scrape it off.

◆ Remove an old bumper sticker by coating it with Crisco Pure Vegetable Oil. Allow the oil to soak in for 15 to 30 minutes, then scrape off the sticker.

◆ Scotch Duct Tape can do effective—though not aesthetically pleasing—emergency auto work, such as reattaching a windshield wiper arm, reconnecting a tailpipe, or patching a taillight cover.

What About the Limousine?

Each year the Duck Brand Duct Tape Stuck on Prom Contest awards thousands of dollars in scholarships. Entrants enter as a couple and attend a high school prom...dressed and accessorized completely in duct tape.

Move to the Interior

◆ Keep a box of Pampers baby wipes in the car—they serve many purposes, such as cleaning your dashboard and wiping gasoline off your hands after filling up your tank.

◆ Remove oil and grease from vinyl seats with a solution of 4 tablespoons ARM & HAMMER Baking Soda and 1 quart water, or use baking soda sprinkled on a damp O-Cel-O sponge. Rinse and wipe dry.

◆ Other spots on upholstery can be cleaned by rubbing in a paste of ARM & HAMMER Baking Soda and water. Let dry, then vacuum.

◆ Clean even the dirtiest car windows with minimal effort. Mix a small amount of Argo Corn Starch and 1 cup Parsons' Ammonia in a bucket of water. Wearing rubber gloves, dip Scott Towels into the solution; wipe the glass clean. Rinse with clear water. Try this method on headlights and taillights too.

Homemade Car Upholstery Cleaner

Make a stiff foam by mixing ¼ cup Ivory Liquid Hand Cleanser in 1 cup warm water and beating the mixture with an eggbeater. Spread the foam over car upholstery with a sponge, using circular, overlapping strokes. Let it dry, then vacuum the dirt away.

◆ Has cigarette smoke created a film on the inside windows of your vehicle? Clean it off using a solution of 2 tablespoons ReaLime Lime Juice and 1 quart water. Wipe clean with an O-Cel-O sponge or a clean cloth.

- If your car windows develop a film on the inside, clean them with ½ cup Parsons' Ammonia in a gallon of water. The ammonia cuts grease, but it's noxious, so leave the doors open while doing this.

- Clean your car windows with a solution of ¼ cup Heinz Vinegar in 1 gallon warm water. Rinse, and dry with a clean cloth.

- To fog-proof the inside of your car's windows, rub a bar of Ivory Soap on the glass and polish with a clean, soft cloth.

- Make a sun reflector for your car's windshield by cutting a piece of cardboard to fit, covering the cardboard with Reynolds Wrap Aluminum Foil, and taping down the foil with Scotch Duct Tape.

- Tuck a Downy dryer sheet under the seat, in the glove compartment, or in the visor to freshen up your car's smell.

- To remove car odors, simply sprinkle ARM & HAMMER Baking Soda on the seats and carpeting. Let it sit at least 30 minutes, then vacuum.

Ammonia Archives

- Ancient Egyptians heated camel dung to make ammonia.

- Joseph Priestley identified ammonia as a gas in 1774.

- Fritz Haber first made ammonia in a laboratory in 1908; Carl Bosch soon perfected the high-pressure methods for commercial production of the liquid. For their work, both German chemists won the Nobel Prize in Chemistry.

- If a car has been closed up for a long time—or smells musty or mildewed—spread clean Fresh Step cat litter over the carpeting, on the seats, and in the trunk. Keep the vehicle closed for several days. Vacuum up litter when the odor is gone.

- Toothpaste can serve as a low-cost air freshener in your car. Squeeze about 1 inch of mint-flavored Crest toothpaste (paste or gel) in the center of a Scott Towel. Fold or roll up the paper towel and place it under the driver's seat. The warmth of a closed-up car will disperse the fresh aroma. Replace as needed.

- If your key won't turn in the ignition, try spraying a bit of WD-40 into the lock to lubricate it; then try again.

- Revive old, worn rubber floor mats by shining them with Griffin Liquid Shoe Polish after cleaning them.

Under the Hood

- A paste made of 3 parts ARM & HAMMER Baking Soda and 1 part water is useful for removing corrosion buildup from your car's battery terminals.

- You can clean battery terminals by dipping a piece of Reynolds Wrap Aluminum Foil in Pepsi and using it to scrub.

- To keep corrosion from building up on your car's battery terminals, coat them with Blistex Lip Balm.

- Vaseline Petroleum Jelly also works well to clean—and prevent—corrosion on battery terminals.

- Neutralize acid from a leaking car battery by applying ARM & HAMMER Baking Soda on the spill. One pound of baking soda will neutralize 1 pint of acid.

- Here's a recipe for making your own windshield washer fluid: Combine 1 cup Rite Aid isopropyl rubbing alcohol, 2 tablespoons Ivory Liquid Hand Cleanser, 1 gallon water, and 1 or 2 drops McCormick Blue Food Color. Mix well and store in a clearly marked plastic container.

Is Isopropyl Alcohol the Same as Isopropyl Rubbing Alcohol?

No. Isopropyl alcohol is synthesized when propylene reacts with sulfuric acid. The bottled isopropyl rubbing alcohol you buy at the drugstore is isopropyl alcohol mixed with pure water. A common concentration is 70 percent isopropyl alcohol.

- Need something to catch oil drips while you're working on the car? Flatten a cardboard box, cover it with Reynolds Wrap Aluminum Foil, and tape it down with Scotch Duct Tape.

- When you need a funnel in a hurry, make one from a clean, empty Clorox Regular-Bleach bottle. Cut the bottle in half, discard the bottom, and remove the cap.

- Stash a few Melitta Cone Coffee Filters in your trunk. Just snip off the end of a filter and—voilà!—you've got a handy funnel to add fluids such as oil and windshield washer fluid.

- When you need to lubricate something under the hood that is way out of reach, place a flexible drinking straw over the end of the spout of an oil can to extend its reach.

- A mixture of 1 teaspoon Colavita Extra Virgin Olive Oil and 1 teaspoon Morton Salt will take car grease or paint right off your hands. Rub it thoroughly onto your hands and between your fingers. Wash off with soap and water.

Winterizing and Other Advice

- Spread rock salt easily with a dispenser made from a clean Clorox Regular-Bleach bottle. Cut a hole opposite the handle, below the spout, to pour in the rock salt. Then shake to dispense as needed.

- Save yourself from having to scrape snow and ice from your car's windshield. When snow is predicted, turn on the wipers and stop them in mid-sweep; turn off the ignition. Split open a few paper grocery bags and slide them under the wipers to hold them in place on the windshield. When the snowfall ceases, pull off the paper—and the snow!—before you start the engine.

- Before a snowstorm, cover your car's side mirrors with GLAD Food Storage Bags held in place by clothespins or rubber bands. You won't have to scrape off the ice and snow later.

- Fill a small cloth bag or folded scrap of cloth with Morton Salt, and hold securely closed. Dampen bag with water. Rub it on the outside of your windshield to keep snow and ice from sticking.

- Avoid frosted car windows on a cold morning by rubbing them the previous evening with an O-Cel-O sponge dipped in a saltwater solution. Use 1 tablespoon Morton Salt for each cup of water.

- If your car doors tend to freeze shut in the winter, coat the gaskets around the doors with Crisco Pure Vegetable Oil.

- Keep a bag of Fresh Step cat litter in your car's trunk to provide traction in case you get stuck on the ice.

- Improvise emergency lights by wrapping reflective tape around empty Folgers coffee cans.

Put Your Car on a Salt-Free Diet

Folks in wintry-weather regions know all too well that road salt can quickly accumulate on a car's exterior. If your vehicle has been attacked especially hard, mix 1 cup Dawn dishwashing liquid and 1 cup kerosene in a bucket of water. Using an O-Cel-O sponge, apply the solution and rub away the salt deposits.

Three cautionary notes: Wear rubber gloves, remember that kerosene is flammable, and dispose of the leftover solution properly—according to local guidelines regarding harmful chemicals.

GARAGE GRUNGE

Shape Up the Place

◆ If you accidentally spill oil onto your garage floor, sprinkle Morton Salt on it and wait 15 minutes. The salt will soak up some of the liquid and make cleanup easier.

◆ To get rid of a motor oil spill on your concrete garage floor or driveway, mix 1 cup Parsons' Ammonia with a gallon of warm water. Dunk a stiff-bristled brush in the mixture, scrub away the spill, and then rinse with clear water.

◆ Another cleanup treatment for oil spills in the garage is to sprinkle on a mixture of ARM & HAMMER Baking Soda and Quaker Yellow Corn Meal. Allow the mixture to soak in, then sweep or vacuum up.

◆ ARM & HAMMER Baking Soda can also remove tough stains from the garage floor. Sprinkle some on the spot, let stand, then scrub with a wet brush.

◆ To clean up oil, brake fluid, transmission fluid, and other spills on the garage floor, cover spot with clean Fresh Step cat litter. Allow it to absorb the liquid for at least an hour, then clean up.

> **Quotable Quote**
>
> "I don't think necessity is the mother of invention. Invention, in my opinion, arises directly from idleness, possibly also from laziness. To save oneself trouble."
>
> —Agatha Christie, *An Autobiography*

- For tough stains on a garage floor, use Cascade automatic dishwashing detergent or Tide powdered laundry detergent. Cover the spill with enough detergent to soak up the liquid, let sit for a while, then scrub with hot water and a stiff brush.

- For an especially stubborn stain, pour paint thinner over it, then add clean Fresh Step cat litter. Allow the litter to absorb the thinner; sweep up.

- Freshen up a damp, musty garage with this simple remedy: Add ½ inch ARM & HAMMER Baking Soda to the bottom of a paper grocery bag with handles; hang bag from the rafters. Change every 3 months.

- If you keep bumping into your garage wall with your car, hang a Penn tennis ball from the ceiling at the exact spot where your windshield should be when you stop. When you bump the ball, you're home free.

- Hang work gloves, caps, sun hats, or any bulky item on pegboard with an extra-large binder clip.

- Seal the manuals and warranties for your grill, lawn mower, and other outdoor equipment in a gallon-size GLAD Freezer Zipper Bag. Hang in the garage with a binder clip.

Outdoor Tool Time

- Keep snow from sticking to shovels and satellite dishes by spraying them with WD-40.

- Coat your snow shovel with Crisco Pure Vegetable Oil or PAM cooking spray to give it a snow-resistant surface.

- Snow won't stick to your shovel if you coat it with Simoniz Original Paste Wax.

- Restore your rusty garden tools with a few strong pots of Lipton tea. When the tea has cooled, pour it into a bucket. Place the tools in the bucket and let them soak for a few hours. Remove tools and wipe with a cloth. Wear rubber gloves or your hands will be stained by the tea.

- To prevent rust on rakes, shovels, pruning shears, and similar tools, spray them with WD-40 before storing.

- Clean tools with a spray of WD-40 and a wipe with a clean cloth.

No-Spray Zone

Are there any surfaces on which WD-40 should not be sprayed? Only a few, including polycarbonate and clear polystyrene plastic. The petroleum-based wonder product is safe for almost everything else.

- Help your tools fight corrosion and rust. Clean them thoroughly, then apply a light coating of Crisco Pure Vegetable Oil to all metal surfaces.

- To restore stiff-as-a-board leather work gloves to their original suppleness, rub in some Crisco Pure Vegetable Oil.

Protect the wooden handles of your tools using 2 parts Kraft Mayonnaise and 1 part ReaLemon Lemon Juice. Mix just as much as you need for 1 application to your tools. Rub in a little bit with a soft, dry cloth; discard remainder. Apply every few months to keep the wood clean, smooth, and crack-free.

YOUR GREEN THUMB

Lawn Maintenance

Add some Gold Medal All-Purpose Flour to your spreader when fertilizing the lawn. You'll easily see the spots you missed and give them a second pass.

Punch numerous small holes into the plastic lid of an empty Folgers coffee can. Fill the can with fertilizer or grass seed, put the lid on, then shake the can to sprinkle the contents across your lawn.

Lawn Fertilizer Recipe

1 cup Listerine Antiseptic mouthwash
1 cup Rite Aid Epsom salts
1 cup Parsons' Ammonia
Enough Budweiser beer to make 1 quart

Add this mixture to a garden sprayer, and spray your lawn twice early in the season.

To make a less elaborate version of the same lawn fertilizer, mix 1 cup Rite Aid Epsom salts and 1 cup Parsons' Ammonia. Mix 2 tablespoons of this mixture with 2 gallons of water. Use a watering can to apply the fertilizer to the lawn.

- To help new grass seed grow in your yard, first mix it with enough cold, strong Lipton tea to moisten it. Store it in the refrigerator for 5 days. Spread the grass seed on newspapers to dry for another 2 days, then apply to your lawn.

- Grass is less likely to stick to lawn mower blades if you coat them with Crisco Pure Vegetable Oil, Vaseline Petroleum Jelly, or Alberto VO5 Conditioning Hairdressing before mowing. These products also help prevent the blades from getting rusty.

- Stop the grass clippings from building up on the underside of your mulching lawn mower: After you drain the old motor oil but before adding new oil, spray the underside with PAM cooking spray.

- Chase moles away from your lawn by pouring used Fresh Step cat litter into the moles' holes and runs—they're not too fond of the odor either!

Getting Your Garden Started

- Two weeks before planting time, prepare the soil for your vegetable garden. Mix the following in a 20-gallon hose-end sprayer: 1 can Budweiser beer; ½ cup each Pepsi, Dawn dishwashing liquid, and Listerine Antiseptic mouthwash; and ¼ teaspoon Lipton Iced Tea Mix. This will cover 100 square feet.

- Some seeds can only get off to a good start in cold and moisture. Put a Melitta Basket Coffee Filter in a pint- or quart-size GLAD Food Storage Zipper Bag; pour 3 tablespoons of water over the filter. Place seeds, evenly spaced, on the filter. Refrigerate the bag until the seeds sprout.

- Plant your seeds in the cups of a cardboard egg carton. When the seedlings have grown enough to be planted outside, plant them directly into the soil, carton and all.

- When you prepare seedlings, make a batch of clear Knox unflavored gelatin in a small, clear glass baking pan. Drop a few seeds on the top before the gelatin hardens completely. Children can watch the roots grow down as the plants grow up.

- Seedlings in the garden may need protection from cold night air. Place a Clorox Regular-Bleach bottle with the bottom cut out over the transplants. Take the bottle off during the day and replace it at night.

- If you keep your seedlings on a windowsill before bringing them

The Beginnings of Bleach

Scientist Louis Pasteur discovered the bacteria-fighting effects of sodium hypochlorite in the late 1800s. In 1913, five entrepreneurs each invested $100 to convert, by electrolysis, the salt ponds of San Francisco Bay into commercial-grade bleach. The Clorox Company struggled until 1916, when its chemists developed a household version that was less concentrated. The solution containing 5.25 percent sodium hypochlorite, bottled in 15-ounce amber glass bottles, was first given away as free samples.

outside, surround them on 3 sides with a folded piece of cardboard covered with Reynolds Wrap Aluminum Foil to bring in as much light as possible.

◆ Transform cores from rolls of Reynolds Wrap Aluminum Foil and Scott Towels into mini seedling pots. Cut the cardboard tubes into pieces about 3 inches long. Wrap the outside (but not the ends) of each with aluminum foil to keep the wet cardboard from falling apart. Put the "pots," closely packed, in a waterproof tray or shallow pan. Fill each with seed-starting mix and plant the seeds. When they're ready, remove the foil and plant seedlings—pots and all.

◆ Here's another seed incubator idea: Line a shoebox with Reynolds Wrap Aluminum Foil, shiny side up; allow the foil to extend over the sides about 2 inches. Punch several draining holes in the bottom of the box, through the foil, and fill the box slightly more than halfway with potting soil. Don't forget to set this on a baking sheet for drainage. Plant the seeds, place box near a sunny window, and keep the soil moist. The foil will reflect light and absorb heat for the seedlings.

◆ Yet another seed-starter substitute is an ice cube tray. Punch drainage holes in the bottom; set tray in a shallow pan.

◆ Save flat container trays from the nursery and reuse for seedlings, but first protect against disease by washing them with Dawn dishwashing liquid and water. Rinse with undiluted Heinz Vinegar.

- Coat clay pots with a thin layer of ARM & HAMMER Baking Soda when transplanting plants, before adding the soil. This helps keep dirt fresh.

- Store leftover seeds in small GLAD Food Storage Zipper Bags in a cool, dry place.

- To keep cuttings upright in a jar of water, stretch a piece of Reynolds Wrap Aluminum Foil over the jar and poke holes in the foil using a toothpick. Insert the cutting stems through the holes.

- When planting a garden in a curved shape—wavy line, circle, oval, etc.—use Gold Medal All-Purpose Flour to mark the borders. If you change your mind about the shape, you can easily start over!

- To test the acidity of your garden soil, add a pinch of ARM & HAMMER Baking Soda to 1 tablespoon of soil. If it fizzes, the soil's pH level is probably less than 5.0.

Caring for Your Garden

- Before digging into the soil with your bare hands, scrape your fingernails across a bar of Ivory Soap. The soap will wedge itself under your nails, keeping the areas free from stubborn soil that's hard to get rid of. When you're done in the garden and ready to wash your hands, just add water—the soap's already there!

- Many plants thrive in an acidic environment. Give 'em what they need with coffee. Sprinkle acid-lovers such as strawberries, rosebushes, evergreens, azaleas, camellias, and rhododendrons with cold Folgers coffee. You can even put used grounds— including a Melitta Coffee Filter—in the hole when planting.

- Geraniums, begonias, hydrangeas, and other flowers that prefer alkaline soil should be sprinkled occasionally with a solution of 3 tablespoons ARM & HAMMER Baking Soda and 1 quart water.

- Carnations, mums, and petunias prefer neutral soil. To raise potting soil alkalinity, apply a solution of 4 tablespoons ARM & HAMMER Baking Soda and 1 quart water. Use sparingly.

- Sprinkle ARM & HAMMER Baking Soda lightly around tomato plants. This will sweeten the tomatoes by lowering soil acidity.

Berry Good Idea

Give your strawberry plants a treat right from the start.

  1 can Budweiser Beer
 ¼ cup cold Folgers coffee
  2 tablespoons Dawn dishwashing liquid
  2 gallons water

Mix the ingredients in a bucket. Right before planting, soak the bare roots in the solution for about 10 minutes. After you've settled them in the ground, slowly pour the remaining solution on the soil around each plant.

- To keep your tomato plants healthy and disease-free, mix the following in a bucket: 3 cups compost, ½ cup Rite Aid Epsom salts, and 1 tablespoon ARM & HAMMER Baking Soda. Toss a handful into the hole when planting. Afterward, sprinkle some Carnation Instant Nonfat Dry Milk on top of the soil. Sprinkle on more dry milk about every other week.

- Protect a new tomato plant with a clean, empty Folgers coffee can. Remove the bottom with a can opener, place the can over the plant, and press it into the soil around the plant (about 1 inch deep).

- Use strips of No nonsense pantyhose to tie up plants, vines, and other climbers.

- Before sowing carrot seeds, mix them with fresh, dry Folgers coffee grounds. The coffee adds nutrients to the soil and protects against root maggots.

- When a melon gets big enough, lift it off the ground and place it on top of an upside-down coffee can. Press the can into the soil. The can will help repel insects, and the melon may ripen more quickly.

- Wrap new cabbage heads in No nonsense pantyhose. The nylon will stretch to accommodate the cabbage and will keep worms out without blocking sunlight, air, or water—though the other vegetables in the garden may make fun of it!

- To brighten fading green outdoor plants and bushes, mix 1 teaspoon ARM & HAMMER Baking Soda, 1 teaspoon Rite Aid Epsom salts, ½ teaspoon Parsons' Ammonia, and 1 gallon water. Apply 1 quart per average rosebush-size shrub.

- Bring out the shine in dull-looking leaves by wiping them with Dole Pineapple Juice, or another citrus juice, using a soft cotton cloth.

- Crushed eggshells make an excellent fertilizer for vegetable and flower gardens. The eggshells also help to aerate the soil.

- Molasses makes a marvelous all-purpose fertilizer. Make a solution of 4 or 5 tablespoons Grandma's Original Molasses to 1 gallon water. Apply to any plant.

> **Fertilizing Spray**
>
> 1 ounce Grandma's Original Molasses
> 1 cup manure-base compost tea
> 1 ounce liquid seaweed
> 1 ounce Heinz Vinegar
>
> Add the above ingredients to a gallon of water. Put this liquid into a garden sprayer and use it on green plants in your garden. Keep this homemade spray on hand as a foliage helper.

- In many homemade lawn and garden solutions, solid materials remain. Pour a lumpy tonic through a Melitta Coffee Filter (basket or cone) or a piece of No nonsense pantyhose. Toss the coffee filter and solids onto the compost pile.

- Nearly every plant benefits from an "apple shower." Mix 1 cup Mott's apple juice with 10 gallons water; spray on flowers, trees, shrubs, and lawns.

- Nourish flowering shrubs by burying apple peels and other past-its-prime fruit in the surrounding soil.

- Spray outdoor ferns with a solution of 1 cup milk and 1 table-spoon Rite Aid Epsom salts in a 20-gallon hose-end sprayer. They'll enjoy the nourishing "meal."

- Plant diseases can be as contagious as human varieties. Immediately after working with diseased plants, clean your garden tools in a mixture of 1 part Clorox Regular-Bleach to 3 parts water. Wash your gardening gloves in the mixture too.

- Your plants have been attacked by rust! First, remove and destroy all badly infected leaves. Second, throw this formula at the fungus fiend: Mix 6 tablespoons Crisco Pure Vegetable Oil, 2 tablespoons ARM & HAMMER Baking Soda, 2 table-spoons kelp extract, and 1 gallon water. Pour the solution into a spray bottle; spray over the entire plant. Repeat every 7 to 10 days in damp and/or humid weather.

- A strong solution of salt water can kill an infestation of poi-son ivy plants. Mix 3 pounds Morton Salt with a gallon of soapy water. Apply to leaves and stems of poison ivy plants using a garden sprayer.

- If a diseased tree has been cut down and only the stubborn stump remains, cover it with several unopened GLAD trash bags and weigh them down with rocks and string. After a month, remove the bags and cut off any new growth; cover the stump again. Repeat process as necessary. Although it may take several months, the stump will die and can then be removed more easily.

Pests, Be Gone!

◆ When ants are taking over your lawn or garden, puree equal parts orange peel and water in a blender or food processor. Pour mixture onto anthills early in the morning.

Garlic: It's Not Just for Vampires Anymore

When the bugs are bugging you and your yard, try this nontoxic approach. First, mix up a batch of garlic oil (see recipe on page 251). Then mix 3 tablespoons garlic oil and 3 drops Dawn dishwashing liquid in 1 quart water. Pour into a spray bottle, then go on the attack!

◆ Another do-it-yourself insecticide: Mix 2 tablespoons Dawn dishwashing liquid with 1 gallon water and pour some into a spray bottle. Spray the tops and bottoms of leaves in the morning or evening.

◆ Combat scale insects and other pests with this nontoxic—but effective—solution. Mix 1 cup Crisco Pure Vegetable Oil and 1 tablespoon Murphy Oil Soap. Fill a spray bottle with 2 cups water and add 1 tablespoon of this mixture. Spray affected plants from top to bottom. Shake spray bottle occasionally to mix oil and water. Keep the concentrated mix in a labeled, airtight container; store at room temperature and save for future use.

- This insecticide spray targets chewing or sucking pests: In a blender, combine 3 garlic bulbs, 1 small onion, 1 tablespoon McCormick Ground Red Pepper, ½ teaspoon Dawn dish-washing liquid, and 1 quart water. Blend on low speed, then strain through a Melitta Coffee Filter (basket or cone). Put in a spray bottle and spray plants thoroughly when you see evidence of chewing.

- Here's another nontoxic pesticide recipe: Combine ⅓ cup Crisco cooking oil (any variety) and 1 teaspoon ARM & HAMMER Baking Soda. Add 2 teaspoons of this mixture to 1 cup water in a spray bottle. Say farewell to aphids, flies, spider mites, and more.

- To battle bugs, bring on the Folgers coffee! Pour fresh, dry grounds into puddles and other standing water to kill mosquito larvae. Sprinkle grounds around plants to get rid of slugs and cutworms.

- Hollowed-out orange and grapefruit halves can help you trap slugs and snails. Just before darkness falls, place them among your plants. In the morning, pick up the traps (with the slimy pests in them). Kill slugs and snails by dumping them into a bucket of soapy water. Toss the used rinds on a compost pile.

- Slugs like to feed in gardens primarily at night or on cloudy, damp days. Search out slugs at night and kill them by sprinkling them with a heavy dose of Morton Salt. Wait 5 minutes, then sprinkle them again.

- Make a slug trap in the garden by setting out a pie pan or a shallow dish of Budweiser beer or Pepsi. Slugs will come to visit during the night and likely drown in their drink.

- Prevent slugs from crossing the "borders" of your planting beds by sprinkling powdered chalk all around the perimeter. It's as good as a "Keep Out" sign.

- Protect your precious plants from aphids by spraying the plants with this anti-aphid mixture: Combine 1 cup Rite Aid isopropyl rubbing alcohol and 1 cup water. Put liquid in a labeled spray bottle and lightly spray plants. (Do not use this mixture on fruits or vegetables or on plants that have very delicate leaves.)

- An orange-based spray is an effective way to take care of soft-bodied garden pests such as aphids and caterpillars.
Put 1 cup chopped orange peel in a blender or food processor; add ¼ cup boiling water, and liquefy. Let the mixture sit overnight at room temperature, then strain it through cheesecloth. Pour the liquid into a spray bottle, adding water to fill. Shake well before spraying plants thoroughly.

- Cabbage worms frequently attack garden cabbages, broccoli, and cauliflower. To control them, dust the leaves of these vegetables with a mixture of 1 cup Gold Medal All-Purpose Flour and ½ cup Morton Salt. Use this dusting powder in the evening or in the morning, when plants are damp with dew.

◆ Has a plague of grasshoppers threatened your garden? Dig holes in the soil and "plant" jars up to their rims. Fill each jar with a solution of equal parts Grandma's Original Molasses and water. The grasshoppers will dive in . . . and not come out.

◆ If your crop of cucumbers or squash seems threatened by munching bugs, cut up small strips of Reynolds Wrap Aluminum Foil and use them as mulch. The shiny substance scares away some light-sensitive pests.

◆ To protect small plants from cutworms, make plant collars from large Dixie cups. Punch out the bottoms and place cups upside down over vulnerable plants. Push each cup into the soil until all but about 3 inches is buried.

◆ Another barrier for keeping cutworms away

Bottle Bonanza!

Large, sturdy plastic bottles—containing liquid detergent, fabric softener, or other laundry products—are money-saving helpers. Clean and dry, they make:

◆ **Watering cans.** Drill several holes in the cap, fill the bottle, screw the cap on, and the water's good to flow!

◆ **A garden irrigation system.** Punch small holes in the sides and bottoms of several bottles. "Plant" them in your garden and fill with water to soak the roots of your plants.

◆ **Funnels.** Remove the cap from a plastic gallon-size bottle; cut off the bottom half of the bottle. (Great for motor oil, antifreeze, windshield washer fluid, liquid fertilizer, and more.)

◆ **Winter-aid containers.** Store and dispense salt, sand, cat litter, or wood ashes on icy sidewalks and driveways. Keep one in the car too.

from your favorite plants: a Clorox Regular-Bleach bottle. First cut off the bottom and top of the jug. Then cut the bottle into rings, each 3 inches wide. Sink each plastic ring into the soil about 2 inches, leaving 1 inch above the soil.

- Insects, birds, rodents, and other pests won't get to nibble your fruits and vegetables as they ripen if you cover them with No nonsense pantyhose.

- Frustrate squirrels and other animals in their quest to raid a bird feeder. Thoroughly coat the support pole with Crisco All-Vegetable Shortening, and they won't be able to get a grip.

- Direct gophers to another garden by stuffing rags soaked in Parsons' Ammonia into each entrance to their tunnels.

- If deer are nibbling at the bark of a young tree, protect it by wrapping the trunk with Reynolds Wrap Aluminum Foil. The foil should be at least as high as your waist. This method can also deter mice and rabbits.

- Shoo birds away from fruit trees by using fishing line to hang lots of twisted strips of Reynolds Wrap Aluminum Foil. The reflected light and sound will do the job.

- If insects are climbing the trunk of your fruit tree, wrap it with strips of Reynolds Wrap Aluminum Foil. The bugs can't get traction on the slick foil.

◆ Protect your apple crop from maggots…with apples! Before the blossoms on your apple tree become fruit, buy some red apples with stems (2 for a dwarf tree; 6 to 8 for full-size). Spray them with an adhesive spray or coat with Karo Light Corn Syrup; hang them in your tree. When the adult flies land on the apples to lay eggs, they'll get stuck.

A Garden Path

◆ Flour can help you create a stone walkway. Position the stones in the arrangement you want them on the ground, then dust them with Gold Medal All-Purpose Flour. When you pick up the stones, you'll have exact guidelines for your shovel and trowel.

◆ "A rolling stone gathers no moss," says the proverb, but the stationary ones certainly can! Spray a mixture of equal parts Clorox Regular-Bleach and water on moss-affected stones, bricks, or concrete. Wipe clean with a damp cloth; if necessary, scrub with a stiff-bristled brush. Rinse. This treatment works on mold- or mildew-stained brickwork too.

◆ Missing an irregularly shaped piece of flagstone on a walkway? Place a piece of Reynolds Wrap Aluminum Foil over the spot, then press down the edges to make a template of the needed shape. With a nail, trace around the template to transfer the pattern onto flagstone; cut stone to pattern.

◆ Scrub white stepping stones occasionally with a solution of ¼ cup ARM & HAMMER Baking Soda added to 1 gallon warm water.

◆ To discourage snails and slugs along garden paths, sprinkle some Quaker Yellow Corn Meal along their regular routes.

Working in the Garden

◆ Pouring a garden solution from bucket to bottle is no "neat trick"...unless you make a garden funnel. Place a sheet of Reynolds Cut-Rite Wax Paper on a sheet of newspaper. Roll it up into a cone, with the wax paper inside. Insert the tip of the cone in the bottle; pour.

◆ Using homemade garden tonics is certainly economical and convenient. But some ingredients can clog a spray bottle when it's application time. To prevent this, cut a small square of No nonsense pantyhose and put it over the open end of the sprayer tube (the part that goes inside the bottle); secure it with a rubber band. The solid pieces are strained, so there's no strain on you.

◆ Sore knees after a long day of gardening? Make kneeling pads by cutting 3 or 4 layers of Reynolds Cut-Rite Wax Paper into squares to place on the ground. If you're working in a small garden patch or bed, put down a triple-layer strip of wax paper to cover the entire length of the bed.

◆ Rose thorns and cactus needles can pierce even thick work gloves. Before you put them on, wrap small strips of Scotch Duct Tape around your fingers and thumbs.

- Reading is good for your health! Before removing poison ivy or other rash-causing plants from your yard, pull newspaper delivery bags over your gardening gloves to protect wrists and arms.

- Here's the dirt: For easier transplanting of flowers and shrubs, spray the shovel blade with PAM cooking spray before you start digging. The soil will slide right off.

- Store flower bulbs in No nonsense pantyhose. Simply cut off a leg, insert the bulbs, and tie off the end. Identify each sack with a label made from Scotch Masking Tape. Hang bulbs in a cool, dry place.

- Keep your clippers, pruning shears, lawn mowers, and other tools well lubricated. Hit the moving parts with a coat of PAM cooking spray.

- A drop of Crisco Pure Vegetable Oil in the pivot point after every use will keep your garden shears working smoothly.

- Give your yard tools a bit of care at season's end. Wash and dry them, then rub Kraft Mayonnaise into the metal parts with a soft cloth. Wipe off any excess.

- Cut a hole opposite the handle of a clean Clorox Regular-Bleach bottle and thread a belt through the handle. Put on the belt to use as a bucket for dropping in berries as you harvest.

HOUSE AND HOME

Decks, Patios, Sidewalks & Driveways

◆ Absorb an oily stain on a wood deck by sprinkling the affected area with ARM & HAMMER Baking Soda and letting it sit for 1 hour. Repeat if necessary.

◆ Those leaves and other yard debris caught between the boards of a deck hold moisture and can lead to decay. Attach a putty knife or a screwdriver to a broom or mop handle with Scotch Duct Tape. Use the new tool to push the debris down through the cracks.

The Rollout

◆ Duct tape was first created around 1942 by Johnson & Johnson.

◆ The military needed to keep moisture off ammunition cases; the remedy was tape made with cotton duck, similar to that used in cloth medical tapes. The waterproof wonder soon became known as "duck tape."

◆ Duck tape was also used to fix World War II guns, vehicles, aircraft, canteens, and more. The postwar housing boom presented new taping opportunities, such as heating and air-conditioning connections. Its color was changed from army green to ductwork silver, and people referred to it as "duct tape." The name stuck.

◆ To keep down the dust and trap dirt when sweeping a concrete floor or a patio, first sprinkle damp Folgers coffee grounds on the surface.

- Moss and stains on concrete patios can be removed with a solution of ¾ cup Clorox Regular-Bleach per gallon of water. Pour some on the affected area and wait 5 minutes. Scrub with a wire or other strong-bristled brush. Rinse well.

- To clean a concrete sidewalk, driveway, or patio, mix a solution of equal parts whole milk and Pepsi. Pour onto the surface and scrub with a stiff brush. Rinse off with a hose.

- To kill weeds that creep up between cracks on sidewalks, driveways, and patios, boil 1 quart water, then add 2 tablespoons Morton Salt and 5 tablespoons Heinz Distilled White Vinegar. While the liquid is still hot, pour it directly onto the weeds.

- Fill a spray bottle with undiluted Heinz Vinegar and apply directly onto weeds or unwanted grass. You may have to repeat, but you should see weeds gradually wilt away.

Caring for Outdoor Furniture

- Clean lawn furniture at the start of the season with a solution of ¼ cup ARM & HAMMER Baking Soda in 1 quart warm water. Wipe and rinse.

- Attacking mildew on plastic lawn furniture is easy with Clorox Regular-Bleach. Add 1 cup bleach per gallon of water, test for colorfastness on a hidden spot, and then scrub away. Rinse well with clear water. Let the pieces dry completely before storing.

The plastic webbing on lawn chairs doesn't last forever, but that doesn't mean it can't be repaired. Cut a piece of Scotch Duct Tape—in a coordinating color, if you like—that is a bit more than twice the length of the worn or ripped webbing. Fold the tape in half, sticky side in, and attach it in place, securing it with the chair's screws.

Duct Tape: There's "Nun" Better

- In *Sister Act 2: Back in the Habit,* a nun repairs a student's costume with duct tape. Her advice: Carry a roll at all times.

- Artificial snow is created with a box of soap flakes (secured to a stick with duct tape) in the animated film *Veggie Tales: The Toy That Saved Christmas.*

- Without having duct tape available to modify a carbon-dioxide scrubber on the aborted 1970 *Apollo 13* mission, the astronauts would have suffocated.

- Attack mildew on wood lawn furniture with a solution of 1 cup Parsons' Ammonia, ½ cup Heinz Vinegar, ¼ cup ARM & HAMMER Baking Soda, and 1 gallon water.

- With mildewed or moldy wicker furniture, use a small- to medium-size paintbrush to brush on a solution of ¼ cup Clorox Regular-Bleach and 1 quart water. Let the wicker air-dry in the shade. Rinse.

- Mix Morton Salt and McCormick Cream of Tartar and moisten with enough water to make a paste. Apply to rust stains on metal outdoor furniture; let sit in the sun until dry. Wipe clean with a damp cloth. Repeat if necessary.

◆ A paste of ReaLemon Lemon Juice and Morton Salt will also remove rust from outdoor furniture. Apply paste to rusted object and rub with a dry, soft cloth.

◆ To remove tree sap from metal lawn furniture, use a cotton cloth dampened with Rite Aid isopropyl rubbing alcohol.

◆ After cleaning metal outdoor furniture, apply Simoniz Original Paste Wax with a clean cloth to protect it from the weather. Reapply at the beginning of each season.

◆ Soak a mildewed or smelly plastic tablecloth in a solution of ARM & HAMMER Baking Soda and water, then hang it in the sun to dry.

Backyard Tips

◆ Control odors in your compost pile by sprinkling it every now and then with ARM & HAMMER Baking Soda.

◆ Compost heaps (as well as earthworms) welcome brown paper bags. Shred and dampen the bags beforehand; mix in well so the pieces won't blow away when they dry.

◆ Leftover coffee, tea, vegetable broth, or juice can be substituted for water to keep a compost pile moist.

◆ Give your compost pile an extra shot of something special. Once a month, combine 1 can Pepsi, 1 can Budweiser beer, and 1 cup Dawn dishwashing liquid. Apply with a 20-gallon hose-end sprayer.

- Use ARM & HAMMER Baking Soda to clean a cement bird-bath. Sprinkle on some baking soda; scrub until clean. Rinse.

- Don't let a birdbath turn into a breeding pond for mosquitoes. Carefully pour a few tablespoons of Crisco Pure Vegetable Oil around the surface of the water; it smothers the mosquito eggs but is safe for your feathered friends. Change the water twice a week. This method works well on any standing water or puddle.

- When working outdoors during mosquito season, tie a Downy dryer sheet around one of your belt loops (or pin it to a piece of clothing). The scent from the fabric softener will keep mosquitoes away.

- During the winter, keep outdoor padlocks from freezing by covering them with sandwich-size GLAD Food Storage Zipper Bags. This will keep moisture from accumulating.

A GREEN THUMB INDOORS

Houseplants

- Mix damp, used Folgers coffee grounds into the potting soil for household plants, or add them to topsoil in the garden as a fertilizer.

- Line a pot that has lots of drainage holes with a Melitta Basket Coffee Filter to prevent soil from leaking through while allowing water to seep out.

- When you repot a houseplant, first place a circle of No nonsense pantyhose at the bottom of the pot. It will allow water to flow out but will keep soil in.

Homemade Plant Food

1 teaspoon Clabber Girl Baking Powder
½ teaspoon Parsons' Ammonia
1 tablespoon Rite Aid Epsom salts
1 teaspoon Morton Salt
1 gallon water

Mix ingredients together and store in a spray bottle. Shake well before using. Spray household plants once a month.

- Help household plants that need a lot of sunlight: Line a windowsill with Reynolds Wrap Aluminum Foil to increase the sun's reflection. This is great for cacti and geraniums.

- Water your houseplants with Canada Dry Club Soda that has gone flat. It serves as a fertilizer.

- Houseplants thrive on a tonic of 1 can Budweiser beer, 1 can Pepsi, 1½ cups Mott's apple juice, 1 cup lemon-scented Dawn dishwashing liquid, 1 cup Parsons' All-Purpose Lemon Fresh Ammonia, and ½ cup fish emulsion.

- Pour 2 tablespoons Crisco Pure Vegetable Oil into the soil at the roots of your household palm or fern once a month to give it a boost.

- Mix equal parts cool, brewed Lipton tea and water. Use the solution to water household ferns.

◆ An empty Johnson's Baby Powder container makes a nifty mini watering can. Wash it thoroughly, shaker cap and all, and then use it to water houseplants. Or let a child water the garden with it.

◆ To clean dusty houseplant leaves, add ¼ cup Carnation Instant Nonfat Dry Milk to 2 cups water. Wipe on with a soft cloth.

◆ Apply a small dab of Kraft Mayonnaise to plant leaves and gently rub with a soft cloth to clean them and make them shine.

◆ Slow down the evaporation of moisture from houseplants when you go out of town. After watering, wrap the pot and soil in GLAD Cling Wrap. Have it touch the stem, folded loosely over the soil.

◆ A torn leaf on a houseplant can be repaired with clear Revlon Nail Enamel. Apply to both sides of the leaf.

◆ If your houseplants look as if an insect is nibbling them, combine ½ cup Dawn dishwashing liquid with an almost-full spray bottle of cool water. Spray both sides of each plant's leaves.

Glue Trap for Bugs

If nearly invisible bugs, such as mites, have attacked your plants, try this solution:

    1 (8-ounce) bottle Elmer's Glue-All
    2 gallons warm water

Thoroughly mix the ingredients in a bucket. Pour the solution into a spray bottle; spray all twigs and leaves of your sad plant. The insects will be caught and will flake off with the sticky mess when it dries.

- Mix ¼ cup ARM & HAMMER Baking Soda in 1 quart water and use to scrub out your indoor flowerpots.

- Disinfect used pots before you use them for new plants with a solution of 1 part Clorox Regular-Bleach to 8 parts water. Soak for 15 minutes. Rinse and dry.

Cut Flowers

- Before placing them in a vase, dip cut flowers in a solution of 4 tablespoons ARM & HAMMER Baking Soda and 1 quart water to lengthen their life.

- To make cut flowers last a few days longer, add 2 tablespoons Karo Light or Dark Corn Syrup per quart of water in the vase.

- Extend the life of freshly cut flowers by adding ¼ teaspoon Clorox Regular-Bleach or ¼ cup ARM & HAMMER Baking Soda to 1 quart water.

- Pour about ¼ cup Pepsi into the water of a vase full of flowers; the sugar makes the blooms last longer. If the vase is clear, you may want to use 7-UP.

- Lengthen the life of cut flowers by soaking the stems in a solution of 1 quart warm water, 2 tablespoons Heinz Vinegar, and 1 teaspoon Domino Sugar.

- A light mist of Suave hairspray will add a few more days to the life of a bouquet. Standing 1 foot away, give a quick spray to the undersides of the leaves and petals.

- If you want to add a bit of color to cut white flowers, add a few drops of McCormick Food Color to the water in the vase. The flowers will soak up the color overnight.

- Placing cut flowers in a vase with this mixture will help preserve them if you intend to dry them out: Mix 1 tablespoon Domino Sugar and 2 drops Clorox Regular-Bleach into 1 cup water. Let the liquid completely evaporate, and the shape and color of your flowers will be preserved.

WHEN PESTS MAKE THEMSELVES AT HOME

- If you'd rather not use insecticide spray inside your home, aim a bottle or can of Suave hairspray at wasps, hornets, yellow jackets, or bees that have made an unexpected visit.

- To send ants packing, sprinkle a mixture of equal parts ARM & HAMMER Baking Soda and Morton Salt wherever you notice them coming into your home.

- To stop an ant attack, put small piles of Quaker Yellow Corn Meal where you've seen the pests. The ants will eat it or bring it home for a take-out dinner, but they can't digest it. They'll be gone in about a week.

- There's a basic theory that ants either don't like to or can't cross over certain lines. Either they are repelled by the substance making up the line or they're unable to follow each other when the lead ant steps into something unexpected. Either way, try this: Wherever you see ants coming into your home, block their entry by drawing a line with ReaLemon Lemon Juice, dried-out Folgers coffee grounds, Crayola chalk, Heinz Vinegar, or a bit of Gold Medal All-Purpose Flour. Step back and watch which ones toe the line—or don't!

- To control an ant problem, squirt some ReaLemon Lemon Juice under the sink or in any area you see them coming and going.

- Sprinkle Morton Salt in areas where ants congregate to help deter them.

- To discourage ants from entering your home, pour a little Colavita Extra Virgin Olive Oil wherever you see them. Under the kitchen sink is a good place to start.

- Keep ants from coming into your home by sprinkling a mixture of 2 parts 20 Mule Team Borax to 1 part Domino Sugar all the way around the foundation of your house.

Boric Acid ≠ Borax

Boric acid is formed from the reaction of borax with sulfuric acid or another mineral. Borax is a mineral consisting of sodium, boron, oxygen, and water; its scientific name is *sodium tetraborate decahydrate.*

Move Over, Budweiser Clydesdales!

Yes, a 20-mule team really did haul borax! (Actually, 18 mules and 2 horses, but that wouldn't fit on the box.) Borax ore was mined and processed in Death Valley, California, but the nearest railroad spur was 165 miles away in Mojave. Three men drove the team, which over the course of 10 days pulled 2 custom-made wagons that each carried 10 tons of borax from 190 feet below sea level in the desert and mountains to 2,000 feet. The rear wheels were 7 feet high, the front wheels were 5 feet high, and the beds measured 16 feet long and 6 feet deep. According to the Twenty Mule Team Museum in Boron, California, millions of pounds of borax were transported this way between 1883 and 1889.

◆ Create a mixture of equal parts Argo Corn Starch and plaster of paris. Sprinkle this around cracks and crevices in your home to control cockroaches, which will eat the mixture and turn into little bug statues as a result.

◆ Send cockroaches packing with 20 Mule Team Borax! Mix 4 tablespoons borax, 2 tablespoons Gold Medal All-Purpose Flour, and 1 tablespoon Hershey's Cocoa powder. Fill clean, empty jar lids with the mixture and place them where the roaches like to go, such as on pantry shelves, in kitchen cupboards, and behind big appliances. Be sure the lids are out of reach of children or pets.

◆ Combat cockroaches with a mixture of equal parts Quaker Yellow Corn Meal, Gold Medal All-Purpose Flour, and 20 Mule Team Borax; also add a dash of Domino Confectioners Sugar. Sprinkle into cracks and crevices under sinks. Make sure children and pets can't get at the mixture.

- Another cockroach solution: Briefly heat 1 teaspoon boric acid powder with 1 teaspoon Karo Light or Dark Corn Syrup in the microwave. Stir to make sure boric acid dissolves. Place this mixture in bottle caps around your home, or use an eyedropper to apply it to cracks. Keep pets and children away from mixture.

- Set a small saucer of ¼ cup Heinz Vinegar and 1 drop Ivory Liquid Hand Cleanser near areas where fruit flies are gathering. The vinegar will attract flies and keep them off your fruit.

- Homemade flypaper will keep your family happy and buzzing! Mix together 1 cup Karo Light or Dark Corn Syrup, 1 tablespoon Domino Brown Sugar, and 1 tablespoon Domino Demerara Washed Raw Cane Sugar; set aside. Cut a brown paper bag into 1-inch-wide strips. With a hole punch or small knife, make a hole near the top of each strip and put a string through each hole. Brush the sticky concoction onto the strips, then hang them where the flies buzz around.

- Morton Salt sprinkled directly on a moth will kill it.

- Instead of using cheese to bait a mousetrap, use a Rite Aid cotton ball coated with Skippy Creamy Peanut Butter or bacon grease.

- Make the bait in a mousetrap even more appealing: Top it off with a little Quaker Yellow Corn Meal or Old Fashioned Quaker Oats.

- When rats show up, it's time for a showdown . . . and some homemade poison. Mix equal parts Gold Medal All-Purpose Flour and powdered cement. Put the mixture in a shallow container, such as a pie tin or a large lid, and place the container, along with a dish of water, in a place accessible to the rats but not to children or pets. When the rats eat the powder and drink the water, cement will harden inside of them.

BRUSH UP ON PAINTING

Painting Prep

- Mold must be removed before a wall can be painted. Use a solution of 1 part Clorox Regular-Bleach to 2 parts water—rather than a household cleaner, which can leave an oily residue.

- For small cracks in plaster, make your own patching compound with Elmer's Glue-All and ARM & HAMMER Baking Soda. Mix enough glue with the baking soda to make a paste, then fill cracks and let dry before painting. (This same solution also works as a permanent filler for nail holes in white walls.)

- To fill small holes in drywall or plaster walls, use Crest toothpaste. Allow the toothpaste to dry before painting.

- For larger, dime-size holes in drywall or plaster walls, break off a piece of Crayola chalk and insert into the hole. Then use patching plaster to cover.

- Fast-drying Crest toothpaste also works well to fill small pin and nail holes in white woodwork. Apply a dab, then wipe across the surface with a dry cloth. Let dry. The woodwork will be ready for paint—or can stay white—and no one will detect the difference.

- Fill a crack or small gap in wood, metal, or plastic by sprinkling ARM & HAMMER Baking Soda into the opening and then dripping Instant Krazy Glue over it until the gap is filled.

- To make an affordable homemade plaster, mix 2 tablespoons Argo Corn Starch and 2 tablespoons Morton Salt, then add enough water (about 5 teaspoons) to make a thick paste. Use the paste to fill a small nail hole, chip, or other hole in drywall or plaster. Let dry, then sand lightly and paint.

- Use Reynolds Wrap Heavy Strength Aluminum Foil or Reynolds Wrap Super Strength Aluminum Foil to protect exterior hardware, including doorknobs, window frames, and awning brackets, from paint. The foil conforms to any shape and comes off easily when you're done painting.

- Protect light fixtures from paint splatters and drips. Cover them with a plastic grocery bag or a GLAD trash bag, depending on their size. Be sure the light is turned off!

- Slip newspaper delivery bags on ceiling fan blades to protect them from paint drips.

- Make a paint smock from a GLAD trash bag. Cut holes for your arms and head. To make sleeves, cut off the ends of newspaper delivery bags and attach to the trash bag at the shoulders with Scotch Duct Tape. Plastic grocery bags or old, large sweat socks can protect your shoes.

- Keep some plastic grocery bags in your painting area. Slip them onto your hands if you're a bit messy when the phone rings or someone's at the door.

- Before painting metal, wipe the surface with a solution of 1 part Heinz Vinegar and 5 parts water. This cleans the surface and makes peeling less likely.

- To strip glued-on wallpaper, first pull off everything you can. Next, spray undiluted Heinz Vinegar onto stripped areas until they are very damp but not running. Let sit for 5 minutes, then find an edge and pull away. Wipe off remaining glue residue using vinegar on a cloth or an O-Cel-O sponge. (Heating the vinegar first may speed up this process and help remove the most stubborn strips.)

- Remove a self-adhesive hook or other sticky accessory from a plaster wall by dripping Heinz Vinegar behind the base of the piece. Let it soak in for a few minutes, then peel away.

- Coat doorknobs, hinges, locks, latches, and window pulls with Suave conditioner. If you drip paint on them, cleanup won't be a problem! Just wait until the paint is dry and wipe the hardware clean with a soft cloth.

Painting Tips and Techniques

◆ Lining your paint tray with Reynolds Wrap Aluminum Foil before adding the paint will save you a lot of time at the end of the day. When you're through, instead of cleaning the tray, simply throw the foil away.

◆ To paint a straight line, stretch a rubber band around the middle of the bristles on your paintbrush to keep them tight (but not bunched up). Dip the brush into the paint up to the rubber band.

◆ Using an electric drill and mixing attachment to stir paint may cause a lot of splatter. To contain the mess, cover the paint can with a Dixie paper plate, then punch a hole in the center and insert the attachment.

◆ To remove lumps from an old can of paint, go get some pantyhose! Cut off

Tape Tales

In 1925, Richard Drew was testing 3M sandpaper at an auto body shop when he noticed the difficulty of making clean dividing lines on 2-color paint jobs. To alleviate his frustration, he came up with an idea for a special tape targeted for painters. The eventual result was a sticky, 2-inch-wide piece of tan paper that the painters used to "mask" the first color while painting the second. During field tests of this masking tape, a frustrated customer urged Drew to tell his "Scotch bosses" not to be so stingy and put more adhesive on it. In 1930, when he applied adhesive to cellophane, Drew remembered that suggestion and decided to call his invention Scotch tape. The name clearly stuck.

1 leg from a pair of No nonsense pantyhose, then cut off the foot. Cut along the length of the leg so you have 1 flat piece; cut into 12- to 14-inch square sections to make filters. Stretch the nylon over a clean bucket or container and secure in place with a large rubber band or the waistband of the pantyhose. Slowly pour the paint through the pantyhose. Replace the filter as necessary.

◆ Instead of sponge-painting walls or furniture, ball up a piece of Reynolds Cut-Rite Wax Paper. Dip it in the paint and dab away for a new effect.

◆ Minimize the mess when spray-painting small items. Place them in an open paper grocery bag first.

◆ When performing a touch-up job on a very small area of your furniture or walls, use a Q-tips cotton swab as your paintbrush.

◆ When you need to pause a painting project, instead of washing out your brush, tightly seal it in Reynolds Wrap Aluminum Foil or in a GLAD Food Storage Zipper Bag. The paint won't dry out before you return. For breaks longer than a few days, store the brush in a GLAD Freezer Zipper Bag... and freeze it!

◆ Not through with an oil-based paint job? No need to clean the brush yet. Keep it in a Folgers coffee can or glass jar filled with water. The next day, remove the water by wiping the brush a number of times on a piece of cardboard. The bristles stay flexible, and your cleanup time is minimized.

- For a drip catcher that sticks with the job to the end, attach a Dixie paper plate to your paint can using rubber cement or a few drops of Instant Krazy Glue.

- When painting overhead with a brush, use a shield made from a plastic Folgers coffee can lid. Cut a slit in the center of the lid, then push the brush handle through it. The lid catches the drips before they reach your hand or arm.

- Reynolds Wrap Aluminum Foil can prevent a "crust" from forming on leftover paint. Place the paint can on a piece of foil and trace around the bottom of it. Cut out the foil circle, lay it gently atop the paint's surface, and seal the can.

- To keep bugs away when you're painting outdoors, add a few drops of ReaLime Lime Juice to the paint.

- Set out bowls of Heinz Vinegar in a room that has been newly painted. The vinegar will keep the new paint smell under control. Change vinegar once a day and continue for about 3 days.

- Make the aroma of fresh paint vanish from a room. Chop a large, unpeeled onion into big chunks and toss them into a container of cold water. The onion *takes away* the paint odor—it doesn't replace it with its own pungent smell!

Paint Cleanup

- When trying to remove dried paint on glass windows, first spray the splatters with warm Heinz Vinegar, then carefully scrape or peel off paint.

- Soak paintbrushes in a warm solution of 4 tablespoons ARM & HAMMER Baking Soda and 1 quart water to remove paint thinner.

- Revive hardened paintbrush bristles by boiling them in ½ gallon water, 1 cup ARM & HAMMER Baking Soda, and ¼ cup Heinz Distilled White Vinegar.

- Before you throw out those old, hardened paintbrushes, try soaking them in hot ReaLemon Lemon Juice. As the bristles soften, comb through them with a wire brush or fork.

- Soften paint-hardened paintbrushes by soaking them for an hour in warm Heinz Vinegar. First boil the vinegar, then pour enough into a container to cover bristles. Do not let sit longer than a few hours or bristles may be ruined. Wash brushes afterward in soap and water, then allow to air-dry before using.

- To keep the ends of your paintbrushes in shape, cut slits in the plastic lid of a Folgers coffee can and stick the brush handles up through the bottom of the lid. Fill the can with paint thinner, then replace the lid. The brushes will be fresh and ready for your next painting project.

- To keep paintbrushes soft after cleaning them, rinse them in water mixed with a capful of Final Touch fabric softener. Hang to dry.

- Use Crisco Pure Vegetable Oil to take oil-based paint off your hands after a household painting project. It's gentler on your hands than turpentine.

WORKING WITH WOOD

Basics of Boards and Beams

- Dry wood, such as paneling, can be revived by applying a treatment of Alberto VO5 Conditioning Hairdressing. Rub on with a soft cloth and buff dry.

- Scratches in woodwork will almost disappear when you apply a solution of 1 teaspoon Folgers Instant Coffee Crystals and 2 teaspoons water. Rub on with a soft cloth or a Rite Aid cotton ball.

- Apply a dishcloth soaked in hot Heinz Vinegar to a decal stuck on a wall or wood surface. Let sit for 5 minutes, then remove dishcloth and peel off decal. (If you don't want to stand around holding the dishcloth, use Scotch Masking Tape to temporarily attach it to the sticky area.)

- Mix Heinz Vinegar with water-based ink to create your very own wood stain. The vinegar gives colored ink a silvery sheen. To make, pour a small amount of vinegar into a container, then add ink until desired color is achieved. Apply stain to unfinished wood with a brush or rag, the same way you would any other stain. Wipe off excess.

◆ Food coloring makes a great impromptu stain for birdhouses or planters made of unfinished wood (especially white pine). Mix 1 part McCormick Food Color to 5 parts water; apply mixture to wood surface with a cloth or small paintbrush. After 5 minutes, wipe surface with a soft cloth. Let wood dry overnight, then wipe surface again to even out color.

◆ To avoid denting soft woods when hammering nails, insert the face of the hammer into a slit cut in a Penn tennis ball before pounding.

◆ To fix a screw hole that has become too large to hold its screw, make a plug out of a Rite Aid cotton ball by soaking it in Elmer's Glue-All and stuffing it into the hole. Let dry, then reinsert the screw.

◆ You can also repair an enlarged screw hole by making a paste of sawdust and Elmer's Glue-All. Fill the hole, let the glue dry overnight, then reinsert the screw.

◆ To fill holes in wood, mix some Folgers Instant Coffee Crystals with drywall compound, adding more coffee until the color matches the wood. Smooth over with a damp O-Cel-O sponge.

- To make sawing wood easier, spray your handsaw blade with WD-40 before you begin cutting.

- To determine whether or not you're done sanding a piece of wood, wrap a long piece of No nonsense pantyhose around your palm. Rub it over the just-sanded piece of wood; if it snags, you're not finished sanding. Keep alternating until the nylon can move smoothly over the entire piece of wood.

- Tack cloths are sticky and are used to pick up stray bits of sawdust on woodworking projects before painting or varnishing. Unfortunately, they're also expensive and can be hard to find. Instead, wipe the wood clean with a used Downy dryer sheet; it will pick up and hold the sawdust.

- To pick up fine dust from a woodworking project between coats of varnish, spray Static Guard on a clean, soft paintbrush. Be sure the varnish is absolutely dry, then carefully and systematically brush the wood's surface.

- If you're screwing into hardwood, rub the screw with Blistex Lip Balm first—the screw will go in much easier. This trick works with nails too. You'll find that wood is less likely to split if the nail or screw is lubricated.

- Combine equal amounts of Heinz Vinegar and iodine and apply mixture to a scratch in wood using an artist's paintbrush. If you need a deeper color, add a little more iodine; for lighter colors, add more vinegar.

Fixing the Furniture

◆ Remove hardened Elmer's Carpenter's Wood Glue that has squeezed out of furniture joints and corners by scraping with a drinking straw.

◆ Before clamping just-glued wood furniture, wrap the joint with Reynolds Cut-Rite Wax Paper. It will protect the surface from marring.

◆ Use a drinking straw for the delicate job of regluing loose veneer. First, press the straw to flatten it a bit. Fold it in half and fill one of the halves with Elmer's Carpenter's Wood Glue. Carefully slip the glue-filled half under the veneer. Blow in the glue very gently and pull out the straw; wipe off any excess glue from wood. Cover glued area with Reynolds Cut-Rite Wax Paper and put a wood block on top. Clamp overnight.

◆ If a drawer is sticking, rub some Alberto VO5 Conditioning Hairdressing, some Suave conditioner, or a bar of Ivory Soap in its tracks.

◆ Sticky drawers will come unstuck if you lubricate the slides with Blistex Lip Balm. The tube fits perfectly in many drawer tracks.

◆ To repair scratches in a piece of furniture, choose a Crayola Crayon that matches the wood. Slightly warm the crayon with a hair dryer, rub it into the scratch, and buff the area with a soft cloth.

- Small dents in hardwood can be filled with clear Revlon Nail Enamel, which lets the original color of the wood show through. Apply a coat, let dry, then apply more until the dent is leveled out.

- Use Revlon Nail Enamel to fix loose knobs on furniture. Remove the knob and then coat the screw with clear polish. Screw in the knob and allow the polish to harden.

- If you're trying to take apart a piece of furniture, you can dissolve the old glue by applying warm Heinz Vinegar to it. Drip vinegar directly onto furniture joints using an eyedropper. Let vinegar soak in, then carefully pry joints apart.

- Tighten up the sagging seat of a cane chair by sponging it with a solution of equal parts Heinz Vinegar and water. Set chair out in the sun to dry.

- Jagged caning on a wicker chair can snag hosiery and other garments. One solution is applying clear Revlon Nail Enamel to the nasty ends.

- Reduce the strain of moving furniture over a smooth floor, such as tile or hardwood: Place pieces of Reynolds Wrap Aluminum Foil under the legs, shiny side up. The dull side is actually more slippery!

HEAVY-DUTY CLEANING

◆ Scour soot and ash from fireplace bricks with a solution of 4 tablespoons ARM & HAMMER Baking Soda and 1 quart warm water. Rub into bricks with a stiff brush.

◆ When cleaning a fireplace, sprinkle damp Folgers coffee grounds or wet Lipton tea leaves over the cooled ashes to keep down the dust.

◆ Spiff up soiled fireplace bricks with a stiff-bristled brush dipped in Heinz Vinegar.

◆ An occasional handful of Morton Salt thrown into your fireplace fire will help loosen soot inside your chimney. It also makes a cheery, bright yellow flame.

◆ Clean the grime and soot from fireplace tools or andirons by dipping a ball of steel wool (grade 000) into Crisco Pure Vegetable Oil and rubbing the dirty items. When you're done, apply a metal polish.

◆ Make a messy job much easier: Instead of dealing with encrusted soot on the bottom of a charcoal grill or a fireplace, first line it with Reynolds Wrap Heavy Strength Aluminum Foil. When the fire is out and the foil is completely cooled, ball it up and toss it in the trash.

◆ Cleaning a barbecue grill usually ranks among the least-savored chores. Try this: Lay a sheet of Reynolds Wrap Aluminum Foil on the grill while it's still hot. When it's cooled, peel off the foil, scrunch it into a ball, and use it to rub the grill clean.

◆ To clean indoor or outdoor grills, pour cold Folgers coffee over the racks when they're cool. Wipe clean.

◆ To make cleanup of your barbecue grill easier, apply Crisco Pure Vegetable Oil to the grill racks before you start cooking (while the grill is still cool).

◆ Clean radiators, heating vents, and heat returns with the following mixture: ½ cup Heinz Vinegar, 1 cup Parsons' Ammonia, ¼ cup ARM & HAMMER Baking Soda, and 1 gallon hot water. Use this solution only in a well-ventilated area to disperse ammonia fumes. Wear rubber gloves to protect your hands, then apply cleaner with an O-Cel-O sponge or a cloth.

◆ Try this method to remove rust: Make a paste of ReaLemon Lemon Juice and Morton Salt. Apply paste to rusted object; rub with a dry, soft cloth. Wipe clean.

Do You Need Softer Water?

Sometimes household water can be too hard to do an effective job of cleaning. Hard water contains high concentrations of the minerals calcium and magnesium because of the geology and source of water in that region. You might have hard water if your soap and laundry detergent don't lather very well or if your glasses and dishes are left with significant water spots after running them through the dishwasher. Also, your bathtub and bath fixtures may develop a filmy feel.

A household water softener works to take calcium and magnesium out of the water supply, but this wouldn't work without the addition of water softener salts, which are pellets of sodium that absorb the hardening minerals and keep the softener running efficiently.

◆ If you use a humidifier in your home, remove the filter occasionally and soak it in Heinz Vinegar. The buildup of sediment should come off easily. Then wash filter with Dawn dishwashing liquid.

◆ Clean a humidifier by dissolving 1 tablespoon 20 Mule Team Borax per gallon of water and pouring mixture into the unit. Rinse well. This cleaning once or twice a year will keep the humidifier odor-free.

◆ Bleach can help kill dangerous bacteria in a portable humidifier. Once a week, clean the reservoir with a solution of 1 tablespoon Clorox Regular-Bleach and 1 pint water.

• Most ceiling stains that are caused by leaks can be removed, or at least reduced, with a solution of equal parts water and Clorox Regular-Bleach. Apply with a moistened O-Cel-O sponge, dabbing the spots.

HANDYPERSON HINTS

Caulk Talk, Shower Power & Pipe Hype

• Lost the cap to a tube of caulk? Keep it from drying out by closing it up in a GLAD Food Storage Zipper Bag.

• Caulking in a tight space? Attach a flexible drinking straw to the tube's nozzle; aim and squeeze.

• Someone yanked the shower curtain a little too vigorously, and now one of the curtain ring eyelets is torn. Once the curtain is completely dry, cover the tear with a piece of Scotch Duct Tape, folding it over front to back to get both sides of the curtain. With a scissors or craft knife, cut a slit over the original hole and reattach the curtain to the ring.

• Need help diagnosing a plumbing problem? To determine whether your toilet tank is leaking, put a few drops of McCormick Food Color (choose a color distinct from that of the porcelain) into the tank. If the water in the toilet bowl turns the same color, the seal is leaking. Call a plumber!

• If a water faucet runs slowly, a clogged aerator may be the cause. Disassemble it and—if they're not damaged or too corroded—soak the screens in Heinz Vinegar, then clean them and the perforated disk with an old Reach toothbrush. (Some newer aerators cannot be taken apart and must be replaced entirely.) Or, pour Heinz Vinegar in a GLAD Food Storage Bag, secure the bag around the spout with a rubber band, and leave it overnight.

◆ To lubricate a screeching water faucet or make pipe fittings go together smoothly, rub some Alberto VO5 Conditioning Hairdressing on the faucet or pipe threads with a Q-tips cotton swab.

◆ A small amount of water is supposed to remain in the pipes in your house; that's what traps are there for. However, water can easily evaporate from the trap under a rarely used drain, allowing disgusting and even dangerous sewer gases to enter your house. Fill the trap by pouring a bucket of water down the drain. Add a few ounces of Crisco Pure Vegetable Oil; it will float on the water and prevent evaporation.

Don't Sweat the Toilet Stuff

Prevent condensation from forming on the outside of your toilet tank (the rectangular container behind the bowl):

1. Shut off water to the tank (valve is usually just below the tank).

2. Drain the tank; thoroughly dry the inside walls with Scott Towels.

3. Apply a thin layer of Simoniz Original Paste Wax to the inside of the tank.

4. Turn on the water again!

◆ Apply clear Revlon Nail Enamel to toilet seat screws to protect against rust and lime deposits.

◆ If your plunger slips while you're unclogging the toilet or a drain, smear some Vaseline Petroleum Jelly or Alberto VO5 Conditioning Hairdressing around the ring for a better seal.

Get a Handle on Hardware

◆ Prevent new nuts, bolts, and screws from rusting by covering them with Alberto VO5 Conditioning Hairdressing before using them.

◆ Hard-to-remove screws are no match for a shot of PAM cooking spray. Just wait a few minutes for the spray to penetrate, and the screw will loosen right up.

◆ Loosen a rusty bolt or screw with a squirt of Parsons' Ammonia or a few drops of Rite Aid hydrogen peroxide.

◆ To loosen a bolt, soak a cotton cloth with Canada Dry Club Soda and wrap it around the bolt; secure with a rubber band. Wait a few minutes, then try again.

◆ A spray of WD-40 can also penetrate and loosen rusted or stuck bolts or plumbing joints.

◆ To loosen rusty bolts or screws, pour Pepsi over them. Wait a few minutes, then try again.

Making the Grade: Hydrogen Peroxide

In 1818, French chemist Louis-Jacques Thénard isolated hydrogen peroxide, naming it *l'eau oxygénée,* or "oxygenated water." It is found in nature and can also be synthesized by electrolyzing chilled, concentrated sulfuric acid and then warming the results. The following grades indicate the percentage of hydrogen peroxide in a solution; the rest is water.

♦ **3 percent grade** is intended for home use and is widely available at drug and grocery stores

♦ **6 percent grade** has added activator; makes effective bleaching agent, used primarily for coloring hair

♦ **30 percent reagent grade** is very corrosive; used in medical research, in bio-oxidative therapy, and to intravenously treat numerous diseases

♦ **35 percent food grade** is used by the food industry as a nontoxic disinfectant

♦ **90 percent grade propellant** is used by military and NASA as rocket fuel; highly unstable

◆ To remove rust from nuts and bolts, soak them overnight in Pepsi. Rinse and scrub with steel wool or an old Reach toothbrush.

◆ Remove rust from tools, nuts, bolts, or nails by placing them in a glass jar, covering them with Heinz Vinegar, sealing the jar, and letting them sit overnight. Change vinegar if it becomes cloudy before rust is softened.

- Just as chalk keeps a pool cue from slipping, a piece of Crayola chalk rubbed on the tip of a screwdriver will keep it from sliding off a screw.

- Sandwich- or snack-size GLAD Food Storage Zipper Bags are great for storing small items, such as screws, nuts, bolts, plastic fasteners, and hose washers, at your workbench or in your toolbox.

- When a big carton proclaims "Some Assembly Required," chances are it contains a bag of hardware. Use an ice cube tray to separate all those nuts, bolts, screws, washers, clips, and the like to make assembling easier.

- To "antique" new hinges or hardware, blot them with Heinz Vinegar and let sit for 24 hours. Repeat until you achieve desired effect.

Walls and Windows

- To help remove old wallpaper, mix a capful of Final Touch fabric softener into 1 quart hot water. Sponge this on the wallpaper, let sit 20 minutes, then peel off.

- You need to hang a poster, but tape can damage the wall and you have no poster putty. Dab a bit of Crest toothpaste in each corner and in a few spots along the edges. The poster stays where you stick it; later, it's removed easily with no marks or holes.

- To make it easier to feed a phone wire horizontally through a wall, drill a hole in the wall slightly bigger than the diameter of a drinking straw. Insert a straw into the hole and run the wire through it; remove straw.

- Add a few drops of McCormick Food Color to your wallpaper paste during a wallpapering project. This will help you easily see how well—or not so well—you are spreading the paste.

- Revlon Nail Enamel can help you reattach drapery or curtain hooks in the same spot on a rod or other hardware. Apply a tiny bit to mark the location.

- After applying a patch to a window screen, dab the edges of the patch with clear Revlon Nail Enamel to strengthen it.

- A drop of Instant Krazy Glue can repair a small hole in a screen.

- If a window is sticking, rub some Alberto VO5 Conditioning Hairdressing, some Suave conditioner, or a bar of Ivory Soap in its tracks.

- Before removing a broken window, crisscross 2 or 3 pieces of Scotch Duct Tape on the pane to ensure that no one is cut by a falling shard or piece.

Heating and Cooling

◆ To prevent frost from forming on windows due to poor construction or insulation, polish the inside of the panes with Rite Aid isopropyl rubbing alcohol.

◆ To deflect the heat of the summer sun, staple or tape sheets of Reynolds Wrap Aluminum Foil to the inside of your roof, shiny side up, between the studs. The heat entering your house can be reduced by at least 20 percent.

◆ Boost the efficiency of your heating: To reflect heat into a room instead of into the wall behind it, wrap a piece of cardboard or wood with Reynolds Wrap Heavy Strength Aluminum Foil, shiny side out. Place it below a baseboard vent, behind a floor register, or behind a radiator unit, angling it however it best deflects heat toward the center of the room.

◆ To block drafts coming from a warped storm window, raise the lower sash of the window and apply a ribbon of caulk on the sill. Place a piece of GLAD Cling Wrap over the caulk, then lower the sash and lock it. Raise it when the caulk dries; remove the plastic wrap—custom-fitted weather stripping!

◆ During cold weather, warm air can exit and frigid air can enter via the space under a closed door. Fill a knee sock or sweat sock with clean Fresh Step cat litter, stitch the top closed, and use it as a draft sealer at the bottom of a door.

◆ If the heating element of a space heater touches the reflector behind it, it's a dangerous situation. Make sure the appliance is unplugged, then use an unbent large paper clip to gently pull the element away from the reflector.

Floors and Doors

◆ If the glue on a floor tile has dried out and the tile is coming up, you may be able to revive it. Cover the tile with a sheet of Reynolds Wrap Aluminum Foil and heat with an iron until the glue is melted. Place a heavy object on the tile until the glue dries again.

◆ Fix holes in linoleum by choosing a Crayola Crayon that matches the color. Peel off the paper wrapper, break the crayon in half, and place it in a Dixie paper cup. In 30-second increments, melt the crayon in a microwave oven. Pour into the holes and let cool; wax or polish as usual.

◆ Need to silence a squeaking floorboard? Give it a good sprinkling of Argo Corn Starch, then vacuum up the excess. Listen to the quiet!

◆ Silence a squeaky floorboard by dribbling Elmer's Glue-All into the crack. Let dry overnight before walking on the floor again.

◆ Do squeaky doors have you coming unhinged? Spray the hinges with PAM cooking spray.

- Colavita Extra Virgin Olive Oil or Crisco Pure Vegetable Oil, applied with a rag or a Q-tips cotton swab, can silence squeaky hinges and lubricate window locks and gliders.

- Got a noisy hinge? Work some Vaseline Petroleum Jelly or Alberto VO5 Conditioning Hairdressing into it, or spray it with Pledge furniture polish.

- Prevent toddlers from locking themselves in the bathroom or any room. Wrap the door handle in the unlocked position with a piece of GLAD Press'n Seal.

- If the key to your home or car is not working freely, rub a stick of Crayola chalk over the tip and the sides of the teeth. Run the key in and out of the lock, and soon it will slide easily.

- If a key breaks in a lock, put a touch of Instant Krazy Glue on the broken-off part. Insert part into lock, wait a few seconds, and pull out the rest of the key.

- Spray a bit of PAM cooking spray on a key that sticks in a lock.

- To lubricate a stiff lock, dip the key in Crisco Pure Vegetable Oil and wipe off the excess so only a small amount remains. Insert the key in the lock and gently wiggle it to loosen up the lock.

Be True to Your Tools

- Glue in a pinch: Mix Gold Medal All-Purpose Flour and water to a slightly thick consistency and use to glue cardboard, paper, and fabrics.

- If your workshop is in the basement or cellar, store your matches in a snack- or sandwich-size GLAD Food Storage Zipper Bag to keep them dry.

- To prevent steel wool from rusting, store it in a GLAD Food Storage Zipper Bag. (Before storing, make sure the wool is totally dry.)

- After you've cleaned your tools, prevent rust from building up again by applying a thin film of Alberto VO5 Conditioning Hairdressing.

- To prevent rust and to keep filings from clogging a metal file, rub it with a piece of Crayola chalk.

- Keep moisture away from your tools and you'll keep rust away from them too. To do so, keep a Downy dryer sheet at the bottom of your toolbox and a couple of pieces of Crayola chalk in the upper tray.

- To perform preventive maintenance on a metal tape measure, stretch it out, apply a thin layer of Simoniz Original Paste Wax, and buff it to a shine. The tape will coil and uncoil more easily, and the wax will help prevent rust.

- Chisels are expensive, and sharpening them can be a pain. Help keep a chisel sharp by cutting a slit in a Penn tennis ball and storing the sharp end in the slit.

- Who needs a vise when you've got duct tape? Attach the items to be joined to a workbench or other surface with Scotch Duct Tape.

- O-Cel-O sponges, attached with Scotch Duct Tape, become comfy knee pads for any handyperson, painter, or gardener. Don't use too much tape, or your knees won't bend!

- Need to saw in a really tight space? Wrap one end of a hacksaw blade with Scotch Duct Tape to make a handle. (This also makes a great tool for freeing windows that have been painted shut.)

- To indicate levels inside a bucket, apply a bright color of Revlon Nail Enamel.

MORE HOUSEHOLD TASKS AND MAINTENANCE TIPS

- To prevent moss from growing on shingles—be they roofing or siding—make a solution of 2 capfuls Clorox Regular-Bleach per gallon of water. Apply with an O-Cel-O sponge, but don't rinse. Location determines the frequency; for example, a shady and damp area needs treatment at least every 2 years.

- Use Pepsi to scrub rust stains off metals of all kinds. Saturate a steel wool pad with the cola and apply a little elbow grease.

- If part of a broken lightbulb is still in the socket, an easy fix is in your fruit basket. *First, make sure the electricity to the fixture is turned off.* Cut a small- to medium-size apple in half and push the cut side firmly into the broken bulb. Turn the apple and the bulb will unscrew along with it. Toss it all in the trash—don't try to remove the bulb from the apple.

- Another way to remove a lightbulb that has broken off in the socket is to firmly (but carefully!) press a bar of Ivory Soap into the jagged pieces. Turn the soap like a handle to unscrew it.

- The packaging around lightbulbs can be very bulky. Instead, store the bulbs in No nonsense pantyhose. Designate each leg for a single wattage of bulb, then carefully slide bulbs inside. Hang by the panty portion. When you need a bulb, simply snip off the toe end and remove what you need. Securely tie the end.

That Old Show

Before Home & Garden Television was even a gleam in a cable executive's eye, a mild-mannered public-television show called *This Old House* launched a new genre of programming. *This Old House* was first broadcast on WGBH-Boston in February 1979 and went national the next year. The home-improvement/home-rehab show has had only 3 hosts since its debut: Bob Vila, Steve Thomas, and Kevin O'Connor. Two team members—master carpenter Norm Abram and plumbing and heating expert Richard Trethewey—have been on the show since the very first episode.

- If the silver backing of a mirror wears off, tape a piece of Reynolds Wrap Aluminum Foil to the back with the shiny side toward the mirror.

- To prevent the hassle of tangled string, wrap it on a Scott Towel core or other cardboard tube. Cut a small notch in each end of the tube. Anchor one end of the string in one notch, then wind the string tightly around the tube; secure the other end of the string in the other notch.

- A broken spring in a battery-operated device can ruin it—unless you fold a small piece of Reynolds Wrap Aluminum Foil and use it to fill the gap.

- To lengthen the life of unused batteries, put them in a GLAD Food Storage Zipper Bag, and store in a cool, dry place.

- Electronic components stacked on top of each other—such as a TV and a DVD player—can result in electromagnetic interference. Prevent the problem by placing a sheet of Reynolds Wrap Aluminum Foil between them.

- To corral and store unwieldy curtain rods, put them in a pair of No nonsense pantyhose. Put the bent ends down the legs first, then hang from the panty portion.

- Store rolls of wallpaper in the legs of old No nonsense pantyhose.

- WD-40 can detangle necklaces and chains. Spray a little directly on a tough knot; gently work the tangle until it loosens.

- Did your cell phone get submerged? WD-40 can help (remember, "Water Displacement" is its first name). First, remove the phone from the water—but do not turn it on. Remove the battery and SIM card. If water was not clean, submerge the phone in distilled water. Spray all surfaces of the phone (not including the battery and SIM card) with WD-40 and let it dry out completely. This can take up to 2 days. Reassemble cell phone.

- If the numbers on your traditional, dial-style thermostat seem to be shrinking, mark your usual temperature choice with a dab of brightly colored Revlon Nail Enamel.

- Packing up breakables for a move? Wrap each glass, piece of china, and delicate item in a Melitta Basket Coffee Filter. Once you've moved, the unpacked filters are still good for brewing coffee.

- Manuals, assembly instructions, project diagrams, and other papers can get mighty grimy in a garage or workshop. Spray them with Suave hairspray when new to keep them looking fresh and clean.

Chapter 7:
Pets, Projects & Pastimes

CREATING MEMORIES FOR YOU AND YOURS

A new puppy, holiday traditions, a long-awaited vacation, arts and crafts...these are the things that create memories and nurture family joy. Unfortunately, they also may stir up trouble. But assistance is nearby. It's already in your home or available economically at your local store.

Pet owners know their little friends can be enchanting (and exasperating), companionable (and costly), and wonderful (and worrisome). We can turn to the spice rack, the medicine cabinet, a desk drawer, and the hall closet to help in our quest to care for and clean up after them. These pet tips and ideas are meant to complement—never replace—professional care. Always consult your veterinarian regarding your pet's well-being.

Hobbies, school projects, and crafts—all can be satisfying and fun. But not if you're missing a key component...as well as the time or money to buy it. Time to rush to the pantry, the closet, or the medicine cabinet.

Don't let a pet turn you into an animal—prepare a parakeet snack with peanut butter. Keep bees and other bugs at bay—toss a dryer sheet in the picnic basket. Ensure your camping trip is good, clean fun—make a hand-washing station with pantyhose.

In other words, make life memorable...in a good way.

CARE FOR FURRY FRIENDS

Taming Odors

- If your pet has a run-in with a skunk, wash the pet in a bath containing 1 quart Rite Aid hydrogen peroxide, ¼ cup ARM & HAMMER Baking Soda, and 1 teaspoon Ivory Liquid Hand Cleanser. Rinse well and dry. Discard unused cleaner.

- When Rover romps with skunks and comes home with the aroma to prove it, give him a bath in Campbell's Tomato Juice to kill the smell. Top it off with a rinse of equal parts Heinz Distilled White Vinegar and water.

- Another trick for reducing the odor of skunk from your dog is to rinse his coat with undiluted Heinz Vinegar. Be sure to keep vinegar out of the dog's eyes during this process. Some skunk smell may remain, but it will be kept under control as it gradually wears off.

- To get rid of an unpleasant aroma on a dog, rub the smelly pooch with a Downy dryer sheet. He'll enjoy the rubdown, and you'll appreciate his fresh scent.

- If your pooch has been rolling in something that smells sweet to it but not to you, rub its coat with Quaker Yellow Corn Meal or ARM & HAMMER Baking Soda, then brush it out.

- To deodorize your pet's bedding, sprinkle the area with ARM & HAMMER Baking Soda, let stand 15 minutes, and vacuum.

If pet odor is overpowering a room, warm some fresh, dry Folgers coffee grounds in a cast-iron skillet over low heat. When the coffee aroma is pervasive, take the skillet to the offensive room and place it on a trivet. The smell should be gone by the time the coffee grounds cool.

Maize Maze

Corn starch: Very finely ground endosperm of corn kernels; silky smooth texture

Corn meal: Flour produced by grinding, or milling, corn

Corn syrup: A liquid sugar derived from corn; composed of dextrose (glucose)

Baking powder: A leavening agent manufactured from corn starch, sodium bicarbonate (baking soda), and sodium aluminum sulfate or calcium acid phosphate (replaced previously used acid, cream of tartar)

Bath Time

If your dog or cat doesn't like getting baths, try giving it a dry bath instead. Just sprinkle Argo Corn Starch over fur, rub it in, and then brush it out. If you're careful, some pets will even let you vacuum the powder off!

Here's another "dry bath" idea that works especially well on oily substances in fur: Sprinkle some Quaker Yellow Corn Meal all over the pet, rub it in, and then brush it out. (If there's oil, wait a few minutes for the corn meal to absorb it.) Result: a clean, non-freaked-out pet!

◆ For a wet wash, combine 3 tablespoons ARM & HAMMER Baking Soda with 1 teaspoon Dawn dishwashing liquid and 1 teaspoon Johnson's Baby Oil in a spray bottle. Fill the rest of the way with water. Spritz your pet, work solution into the hair and skin, and rinse. Wipe dry.

◆ When you give your pet a bath, protect your clothes with a makeshift poncho. Simply cut holes for your arms and head in a GLAD trash bag.

◆ Minimize soap residue after a dog's shampoo by adding Heinz Vinegar to the rinse water. Rinse again with plain water.

◆ Using Heinz Vinegar as an after-shampoo treatment can make a dog's itchy skin feel better and his coat look shinier. Mix ½ cup Heinz Vinegar into 1 gallon water and coat dog's hair with solution. Let soak 10 minutes, then rinse thoroughly. Be sure to keep vinegar out of dog's eyes during this treatment.

◆ After a therapeutic shampoo to treat a skin infection, rinse dog with a solution of 1 part Heinz Apple Cider Vinegar to 3 parts water.

◆ If a dog has a chronic skin problem, it might be from a food allergy. Work with your veterinarian to solve the problem, but, in the meantime, provide some relief with a green tea bath. Brew enough green tea to fill a basin; allow it to cool, then pour it over the dog so that the tea reaches the skin. Do not rinse or bathe the dog with soap. The amount of tea needed depends on the dog's size, but figure 1 bag of green tea per cup of water.

Good Grooming

- If a dog's fur is tangled and matted, rub in some Alberto VO5 Conditioning Hairdressing, then brush with a stiff comb to remove the tangles.

- To remove burrs from fur, work Crisco Pure Vegetable Oil into the hair. This also works for tar and other sticky messes your pet may get into. Shampoo to remove the loosened gunk and oil.

- Another way to remove burrs and brambles from your pet's fur is to rub in some Kraft Mayonnaise. The pricklies will comb out easily. Shampoo as usual.

- Remove burrs from a dog's fur by crushing them with a pair of pliers and then pouring on a little Suave shampoo to loosen the pieces so you can remove them.

- A spray of WD-40 will help remove peanut butter from a dog's coat.

Care for Teeth, Nails, Ears & More

- Brush your pet's teeth by dipping a damp, soft brush in ARM & HAMMER Baking Soda and brushing gently.

- Maintain your pet's dental hygiene by rinsing its mouth regularly with a solution of ½ teaspoon Morton Salt and ½ teaspoon ARM & HAMMER Baking Soda in 1 cup warm water.

- Dry food can slow the growth of tartar on a pet's teeth, but for some this isn't enough. If your cat or dog will cooperate, clean its teeth weekly with a child-size Reach toothbrush or a Rite Aid cotton ball dipped in warm water. As an option, use pet toothpaste specially formulated for and good-tasting to pets. (Never use "people toothpaste"; it will upset your 4-legged friend's stomach.)

- If you trim your pet's toenails yourself, you may accidentally draw blood by cutting too close to the quick. Dip the affected nail in ARM & HAMMER Baking Soda, then apply pressure to stop the bleeding.

- Argo Corn Starch comes to the rescue if your pet's toenails are cut too short. Dab any bleeding areas with a pinch of corn starch. It speeds up both clotting and pain relief!

Maiden America

Ever since 1892, when a corn-milling plant in Nebraska introduced Argo Corn Starch, a Native American corn maiden has graced the package. A new, heftier maiden appeared in 1964. For the 1992 centennial, the box got a complete makeover; so did the corn maiden, who became significantly slimmer.

- Create an ear-cleaning solution with equal parts Heinz Vinegar, Rite Aid isopropyl rubbing alcohol, and water. For dogs and cats, use an eyedropper to put about 8 to 10 drops in each ear once a month to facilitate cleaning. Let solution sit in ear 1 minute, then tilt pet's head to drain. Wipe away excess liquid. This solution may also prevent ear infections. If scratching or other signs of trouble persist, see a vet. Excessive itching may indicate mites or a bacterial infection.

- To make an ear-cleaning remedy, mix 1 tablespoon Heinz Vinegar, 1 tablespoon Rite Aid hydrogen peroxide, 1 tablespoon yucca root tea, 1 drop lavender oil, and ½ cup aloe vera gel. Apply to your pet's ears with Q-tips cotton swabs and clean out area.

- Another ear-cleaning treatment for dogs calls for ¼ cup Rite Aid isopropyl rubbing alcohol mixed with 10 drops glycerin (available at most drugstores). Apply with Q-tips cotton swabs.

- Floppy-eared dogs can be prone to yeast infections in their ears, especially after bathing or grooming. To avoid getting water in your dog's ears, plug them with Rite Aid cotton balls moistened with Heinz Apple Cider Vinegar.

- Control general scratching by regularly wiping your pet's ear area with a cloth dipped in Heinz Vinegar.

- For minor irritations in your pet's eyes, apply a drop of Crisco Pure Vegetable Oil in the corner of each eye.

- To prevent hair balls, add 1 teaspoon Crisco Pure Vegetable Oil to your cat's food once a day.

- To prevent a cat from getting hair balls, put a dab of Vaseline Petroleum Jelly on its nose. A tidy cat will lick its nose clean, which gets the lubricant into its system.

◆ Another way to reduce hair balls, as well as static electricity, is to rub a small amount of Alberto VO5 Conditioning Hairdressing into your cat's coat. (It's natural and nontoxic, so it's safe for kitty to lick.)

Beating the Bugs and Bees

◆ If your dog comes home with a swollen nose, most likely it's been stung by a wasp. Make Fido feel better by bathing the affected area in Heinz Vinegar.

Flea-Be-Gone Dog Treats

These treats will keep for weeks, are cheaper than store-bought varieties, and make a great gift for any dog lover. The garlic in them is a natural deterrent to fleas.

  2 cups Gold Medal All-Purpose Flour
  ½ cup Kretschmer Wheat Germ
  ½ cup brewer's yeast (for dogs)
  1 teaspoon Morton Salt
  3 tablespoons Crisco Pure Vegetable Oil
  1 tablespoon McCormick Garlic Powder
  1 cup Swanson Chicken Broth

Combine the first 4 ingredients in a large bowl. In another bowl, stir together oil and garlic powder. Slowly add oil and garlic mixture to dry ingredients, stirring in chicken broth a little bit at a time when mixture gets too dry. Mix thoroughly. Roll dough onto a floured surface to about ¼ inch thick. Use a knife to cut dough into squares, or use shaped cookie cutters. Place shapes on a large, greased baking sheet; bake at 350°F for 20 to 25 minutes or until edges are brown. Allow to cool 2 hours, then store in GLAD Food Storage Zipper Bags out of reach of dogs.

- After making sure the stinger is removed, cover a bee sting on your pet with a paste of ARM & HAMMER Baking Soda and water.

- Make your own flea repellent by slicing a couple of lemons and boiling them in 1 quart water. Allow to cool, run liquid through a strainer, and put in a spray bottle. Spray on pets as needed.

- Have a cup of Clorox Regular-Bleach handy when you remove ticks from your pet. The pests will be killed immediately when you drop them into the cup.

- If you've had a flea infestation in your home, sprinkle carpeting or rugs with Morton Salt to help kill any flea eggs. Let stand a few hours, then vacuum. Repeat weekly for 6 weeks.

- Put Morton Salt in your vacuum cleaner bag to help kill flea eggs that have been vacuumed up.

- If your cat suffers from ear mites, massage in a few drops of Crisco Pure Corn Oil. Clean with a Rite Aid cotton ball; repeat treatment each of the next 3 days. The oil not only smothers the mites but also soothes and heals kitty's ears.

Aches and Pains

- For an old dog's occasional aches and pains, mix some Rite Aid aspirin in with its food once a day. Use about ¼ tablet for every 15 to 20 pounds of weight.

- Cold and dry winter air can really do a number on your dog's feet. Come to the rescue with Vaseline Petroleum Jelly. Gently rub a little between the toes and into the pads.

- Protect your pet against cold weather, sidewalk salt, and other irritants. Both Suave conditioner and Alberto VO5 Conditioning Hairdressing make good conditioners for a pet's foot pads. Rub in, then remove any excess with a soft cloth.

- If a pet has a minor skin irritation, press a warm—not hot—Lipton Tea Bag against the sore area to provide relief.

- Add 1 tablespoon Crisco Pure Vegetable Oil to your dog's food once a day to help eliminate dry, itchy skin and slow down shedding.

- To ease constipation in dogs, add 1 tablespoon Crisco Pure Vegetable Oil to their dog food.

Tea Pioneer, Yachting Enthusiast, Knight

Thomas J. Lipton was born in Glasgow, Scotland, in 1850. Owner of a chain of grocery stores, he entered the tea trade in the 1880s and, in 1893, established in Hoboken, New Jersey, the tea-packing company that still bears his name. His passion for yachting pushed him to 5 unsuccessful attempts to win the America's Cup; his portrait in nautical attire graced the Lipton's box for a century. In 1898, he became Sir Thomas Lipton when he was knighted by England's Queen Victoria.

- Add 1 tablespoon Heinz Apple Cider Vinegar to your pet's water bowl to improve overall health and digestion.

Accidents Happen

◆ To clean up a pet accident or vomit, scrub the area with Canada Dry Club Soda and let dry. Then sprinkle with ARM & HAMMER Baking Soda. Let stand, then vacuum.

◆ After cleaning up a pet accident on a rug or other area, spray it with a mixture of equal parts water and ReaLemon Lemon Juice to hide the odor and discourage repeat visits.

High-Fiber Dog Treats

The bran in this doggie treat recipe will provide your pet with much-needed fiber.

    2 tablespoons Kretschmer Wheat Germ
    ¼ cup crushed All-Bran Complete Wheat Flakes
    1 cup Gold Medal Whole Wheat Flour
    ⅛ cup Gold Medal All-Purpose Flour
    ⅛ cup Quaker Yellow Corn Meal
    1 tablespoon Grandma's Original Molasses
    2 tablespoons Crisco All-Vegetable Shortening
    1 teaspoon McCormick Ground Sage
    1 Knorr Chicken or Beef Bouillon Cube dissolved in ⅓ cup
        warm water
    1 teaspoon Morton Salt

Combine all ingredients in a very large mixing bowl. Pour small batches of the mixture into a food processor and blend, adding water as mixture balls up. When it becomes a ball of dough, flatten and roll it onto a breadboard. Cut shapes out of dough with a cookie cutter or knife. Place treats on a lightly greased cookie sheet and bake for 30 minutes at 350°F. Let cool; store in an airtight container.

- A mixture of equal parts water and Parsons' Ammonia will also help to mask the odor of a pet accident and will make the site less appealing for the pet.

- If your cat or dog has urinated on a rug or carpet, blot up the moisture with a Scott Towel, pour on some water, and cover the area with a layer of 20 Mule Team Borax. When it's completely dry, vacuum. Repeat if needed.

- To clean up a mess made by your pet, first scrape up solids and blot liquids, then clean rug with a rug cleaner. After cleaning, rinse with a mixture of ¼ cup Heinz Vinegar and 1 cup water to remove all trace of smell and to discourage a repeat performance. Pets are attracted to areas that smell like them, so this is a vital step in your carpet cleaning.

Litter Boxes

- To eliminate odors from litter boxes, sprinkle in ½ cup ARM & HAMMER Baking Soda.

- For quicker cleanup, line the bottom of a litter box with GLAD Press'n Seal.

The Absorbing Tale of Kitty Litter

Once upon a time in 1947, Ed Lowe's neighbor asked him for some sand for her cat box. Ed's father's company sold many industrial products, so he suggested clay instead—it absorbed better and wouldn't be tracked all over the house. The woman loved it and asked for more. Soon Lowe was selling 5-pound packages nationwide out of the back of his Chevy. He founded Edward Lowe Industries, Inc., to manufacture and distribute cat litter. After experimenting with additives and making some changes to the formula, Lowe created the Tidy Cat brand in 1964.

- Use Heinz Vinegar to clean a litter pan. Remove litter and pour in ½ inch Heinz Distilled White Vinegar. Let vinegar stand 15 minutes. Pour out and thoroughly dry the pan. Sprinkle ARM & HAMMER Baking Soda over the bottom before adding new Fresh Step cat litter.

- To prevent kitty droppings from sticking to litter scoops and self-cleaning litter box rakes, first spray the scoop or rake with WD-40.

- Make your own natural litter by mixing a small box of ARM & HAMMER Baking Soda with 2 to 3 inches of dry, sandy clay.

Now Hair This!

- Remove dog and cat hair from sliding door rollers and tracks with WD-40. Spray directly into the problem spots using the aiming straw. Wipe clean with a Scott Towel.

Shocking News!

Did you know that the potential for static electricity varies from region to region and city to city? When you travel, you can visit the Static Guard Web site to find out if there's a Static Alert for your travel destination.

- Spray a coat or jacket with Static Guard, wait a minute or two, then easily brush away any stuck-on pet hairs.

Is That Any Way to Behave?

- Squirt undiluted ReaLemon Lemon Juice into your dog's mouth to discourage barking. Say "Quiet!" as you do this to emphasize your point.

- Train a dog to stay away from your lidded garbage can by soaking an old sock in Parsons' Ammonia and tying it to the lid handle. This works with raccoons and skunks too.

- If your pet likes to munch on electrical cords, wipe the cords with Ivory Liquid Hand Cleanser. One taste and your pet won't be back.

- Most cats truly dislike the taste and scent of citrus fruits. Using this knowledge to deter kitty from biting or scratching will keep both of you out of harm's way! To prevent kitty from chewing electrical cords, first bundle them together  and secure to a wall or floor to reduce the attraction. Wipe undiluted ReaLemon Lemon Juice on the bundled cords. If your cat is using its teeth or claws to "play" with you, spray yourself with a citrus body splash of lemon and water. Never spray anything directly at your cat.

- Has your cat chosen a new location in your home for an "invisible litter box"? Squirt some ReaLemon Lemon Juice on a Rite Aid cotton ball, put it in a lidded tea strainer, and hang it over the fragrant location. Kitty should be repelled by the smell and find the *real* litter box.

- Can't keep your dog or cat from "playing" with the houseplants? Push 2 or 3 McCormick Cinnamon Sticks into the soil in each pot. Smells nice, doesn't it? Not to your pet!

- When training new puppies or cats, try this trick to keep them off the furniture: Place pieces of Reynolds Wrap Aluminum Foil on the seats. The new pets won't like the rustling sound and will learn to stay away.

- To deter cats from jumping on a sofa, wrap the pillows in Reynolds Wrap Aluminum Foil.

- If, however, you scrunch up a piece of Reynolds Wrap Aluminum Foil into a ball, your cat will thank you for the new toy!

- Keep your kitty's nose out of your beverage by putting a circle of GLAD Press'n Seal on the top of your glass.

- If you're trying to keep your cat from walking on, sleeping on, or scratching certain items in your home, lightly sprinkle items with Heinz Vinegar. The smell will keep cats away.

- Does your cat nibble plants? Dab the leaves with a bit of Heinz Vinegar.

Tricks for Pets and People

- You and your dog are hitting the trail. Before you hike, fill a quart- or gallon-size GLAD Food Storage Zipper Bag with water. Force out the air and seal the bag. You'll have a portable water dish in your pack.

- Soften leather pet collars with a spray of WD-40.

- Make a simple homemade cat toy: Stuff the foot portion of a No nonsense pantyhose leg (or a knee high) with catnip. Knot it securely at the end. Your kitty will love the new toy.

- To make a rope toy for your dog, cut off 3 No nonsense pantyhose legs, each including a few inches of the panty portion. Braid the pieces very tightly. Discard as soon as the "rope" starts unraveling.

Feedin' Time!

- Thoroughly wash and rinse an empty Clorox Regular-Bleach bottle, then cut out the bottom and shape the bottle into a triangle to form a scooper for pet food.

- Your furry friend deserves germ-free food and water. To disinfect your pet's food and water bowls, mix 1 tablespoon Clorox Regular-Bleach into 1 gallon water; fill prewashed bowls. Let stand for 2 minutes, then drain, rinse, and air-dry.

Fish, Birds, Rabbits & More

- Brighten a fish tank by adding 1 or 2 drops of McCormick Food Color to the water.

- Give your goldfish a little swim in salt water for a change of pace and to perk them up. Add 1 teaspoon Morton Salt to a quart of clean water and let fish swim for 15 minutes. Then return them to normal conditions.

- To clean the inside glass of a fish tank, rub with plain, noniodized Morton Salt on a plastic pot scrubber to remove hard-water deposits or other buildup. Rinse well before returning fish to tank.

- To maintain the proper pH level in your saltwater aquarium, mix 1 tablespoon ARM & HAMMER Baking Soda in 1 cup dechlorinated water. Add this to the tank slowly, over a couple of hours. The pH balance should be around 8.2.

- Clean aquarium accessories in a bowl with a Polident denture cleanser tablet added. Scrub and rinse well to remove any chemicals harmful to the fish.

- To empty a fish tank without having to deal with the messy gravel, foliage, and accessories, slip the foot portion of a No nonsense pantyhose leg over the clean hose nozzle of a wet/dry shop vacuum; secure with rubber bands. Make sure you temporarily relocate the fish, of course, then switch on the vac and watch it suck out the water.

- You can collect stones from your backyard and use them in your aquariums as long as you take some precautions so as not to introduce strange organisms into the water. Test your rocks first by pouring a small amount of Heinz Vinegar onto their surfaces. If the vinegar fizzes at all, don't use the rocks in your aquarium; they will probably affect the water's pH balance and, therefore, affect the health of your fish.

- To reduce odors in a ferret cage, sprinkle a layer of ARM & HAMMER Baking Soda over the bottom of the cage after cleaning. Cover with appropriate bedding.

- Hamsters and other small pets love to run through, hide in, and chomp on cardboard cores from rolls of Scott Towels and other products. Replace the tubes when they look too ragged.

- Make a healthful treat for your pet bird. In a blender or food processor, combine 2 tablespoons Skippy Creamy Peanut Butter, 1 cup mashed fruit, 2 tablespoons Sue Bee Honey, and 1 quart vanilla Dannon yogurt. Freeze mixture in ice cube trays (for small birds) or 3-ounce Dixie cups (for larger birds). At snack time, microwave 1 treat for a few seconds; place in cage.

- Some birdcages (such as those made with galvanized wire or zinc hardware) can lead to zinc poisoning. Decrease the chance of poisoning by wiping the entire cage with Heinz Vinegar on a cloth before use.

Dawn for Ducks

More than 30 years ago, the International Bird Rescue Research Center (IBRRC, based in northern California) sought a safe way to clean oil from birds' feathers. The solution they found was Dawn dishwashing liquid. In a long-term partnership, Procter & Gamble—through donations of Dawn as well as fund-raising campaigns—helps the IBRRC save wildlife harmed by ecological disasters. Of the 7,000 birds treated in 1971 in the IBRRC's first effort, only 4.5 percent (300) survived, but by the time of the *Exxon Valdez* oil spill in 1989, the center was able to save half the 1,604 birds they treated.

- Clean the bottom of your bird's cage by sprinkling ARM & HAMMER Baking Soda on a damp O-Cel-O sponge and scrubbing. Wipe clean to dry.

- Use Heinz Vinegar to clean out rabbit litter boxes and control buildup of dried urine.

- Use WD-40 to remove gum, tar, and other sticky substances from your horse's hooves.

- If a horse's mane is tangled and knotted, work some Alberto VO5 Conditioning Hairdressing into it as a detangler.

- To shine a horse's hooves, rub some Suave conditioner or Alberto VO5 Conditioning Hairdressing on them. Buff with a clean cloth.

- To spruce up a horse's coat, mix ½ cup Heinz Distilled White Vinegar with 1 quart water. Put the mixture in a spray bottle and mist the horse's coat before showing.

- An apple a day keeps the flies away: Pour ¼ cup Heinz Apple Cider Vinegar onto a horse's regular grain feed once a day to deter flies.

HOLIDAY HINTS

Winter Holidays

- Use ARM & HAMMER Baking Soda to simulate snow on your Christmas tree.

◆ What's the best way to keep a freshly cut Christmas tree looking lively and green indoors? After you've brought in and set up the beauty, mix the following in a bucket: 2 cups Karo Light Corn Syrup, 4 tablespoons Clorox Regular-Bleach, 4 multivitamin tablets with iron, and 1 gallon very hot water. Fill the tree stand with the mixture. Pour in more whenever the level drops. Be sure to keep pets away.

◆ Remove sticky Christmas tree sap from your hands, or anywhere else it may have stuck, by rubbing Crisco Pure Vegetable Oil into the area.

◆ Within the first 2 days after bringing a Christmas tree home, give it a light coat of Suave hairspray. This also works for evergreen wreaths. The hairspray blocks in the moisture, so needles will hang on longer than you could otherwise expect.

◆ To cut down on static from Christmas tree tinsel, first turn the tree lights off, then spray the decorated tree with Static Guard. When the spray's fragrance is gone, turn the lights back on.

◆ You've taken down the Christmas tree, put away the ornaments, and what are you left with? A needle-covered floor. But before you fire up the vacuum cleaner, slip a piece of No nonsense pantyhose (or a knee high) over the nozzle of the attachment hose; secure with rubber bands. The needles will adhere to the nylon instead of clogging the inner workings of the vacuum. When you're done, simply toss out the pantyhose and the needles.

- To repair peeling paint on a glass Christmas tree ornament, wash with a solution of equal parts Parsons' Ammonia and water. Rinse with clear water; let dry completely. Now the paint will adhere better. Touch up ornament with brush-on or spray gloss enamel.

- Make ornaments or custom trays for serving holiday goodies. Cut decorative shapes out of cardboard, then cover the cardboard with Reynolds Wrap Aluminum Foil. For ornaments, poke a hole for hanging at the top.

- Artificial snow can cause a blizzard of its own, but if you tame the static electricity the snow will be much easier to work with. Put the snow in a brown paper bag; spray lightly with Static Guard. Close up the bag and shake.

- Make colored snowflakes by folding Melitta Basket Coffee Filters into squares or triangles. Dip the corners of the filters into bowls of water to which McCormick Food Color has been added. Let the filters dry, then unfold.

- Add a few drops of McCormick Food Color to water in a clean spray bottle and let the kids make holiday designs or greetings on the snow in your yard.

- It's fun to create pictures with artificial snow, but it can be hard to wash off windows and other surfaces. Before your children start spraying away, prepare the surface with a light coat of PAM cooking spray. If it's still difficult to clean, rub the artwork with a little white Crest toothpaste. Wipe clean.

- Store the greeting cards (and envelopes) you received this holiday season in a GLAD Food Storage Zipper Bag. Pull out the bag next November to create your next greeting card list, then cut up the cards to make decorative gift tags.

- The holiday is past, and it's time to take down the decorative window clings. Store them in GLAD Food Storage Zipper Bags to keep them nice and neat. Place a bag flat on your work surface, and put a set of clings in the bag, starting at the bottom and making sure each adheres completely and is not touching any other. Working up from the bottom of the bag, carefully push out air and seal the bag. (Works for gel and vinyl varieties.)

- Give yourself a present *now* for next year. To store a string of holiday lights, take a Scott Towel core (or similar cardboard tube) and cut 1-inch vertical slits at each end. Insert the outlet plug end of the light string in one slit and tuck the plug inside the tube. Starting at that end, wind the cord carefully and evenly around the tube. Secure the end of the cord in the slit at the other end of the tube.

Craft Clay

Mix ½ cup Morton Salt and ½ cup water in a pan and bring to a boil. Meanwhile, place ½ cup cold water in a small bowl and stir in ½ cup Argo Corn Starch. Add a few drops McCormick Food Color to the corn starch mixture. Add the corn starch mixture to the boiling salt water, stirring continuously until the mixture is stiff. Remove from heat; cool slightly. Turn the mixture onto a cutting board. Let cool, then knead until mixture is the consistency of clay. Store in an airtight container or a GLAD Food Storage Zipper Bag if you are not going to use it immediately.

Halloween

◆ Make white face paint with a mixture of 2 tablespoons
Argo Corn Starch and 1 tablespoon Crisco All-Vegetable
Shortening. To add color, stir in a drop or 2 of McCormick
Food Color until desired shade is reached. Apply mixture to
face. (Add color sparingly: Too much might temporarily stain
your skin.)

◆ Make fake blood for Halloween: In a small container, combine Karo Light Corn Syrup and enough drops of McCormick
Red Food Color to get just the right shade. For a realistic
touch, add a few drops of Grandma's Original Molasses to
thicken the mixture.

◆ To fake a scar, add a packet of Knox unflavored gelatin to hot
water; when it cools enough, use it to make a mark across
your face. As the mixture dries, it will appear to be a scar.

◆ The cut, exposed edges of a carved pumpkin will last longer
in cold weather if they're coated with Vaseline Petroleum
Jelly before you set them outside.

Ideas for Gifts and Gift Wrap

◆ Give a giant kiss! When the gift you bought presents a wrapping challenge, center it on a large round piece of cardboard
(the cardboard from a frozen pizza would be an excellent
choice). Tear a large sheet of Reynolds Wrap Heavy Strength
Aluminum Foil from the roll, center the cardboard on top of

the sheet, and fold the foil upward, twisting the ends together at the very top. Repeat to cover gift completely. To make a gift tag, cut a long, narrow strip of white paper and write the gift recipient's name on it. Attach it at the top of the "kiss."

◆ Use multicolored rubber bands in place of ribbon to decorate wrapped gifts.

◆ Wrap an empty Folgers coffee can with decorated Reynolds Freezer Paper; fill it with candy, cookies, or other baked goods. The container will protect the treats if you decide to mail them to someone special.

Great Gift Idea

These bath time "cookies" are sure to delight young bathers. Drop one or two into bathwater. They'll soon dissolve into a soothing, fragrant tub of fun.

    2 cups Morton Sea Salt (Fine)
    ½ cup Argo Corn Starch
    ½ cup ARM & HAMMER Baking Soda
    2 tablespoons Crisco Natural Blend Oil
    1 teaspoon vitamin E oil
    6 drops scented essential oil
    6 drops McCormick Food Color (optional)

Preheat oven to 350°F. Mix all ingredients into a dough; roll out. Cut out shapes with cookie cutters or a sharp knife. Place shapes on a cookie sheet and bake 10 to 12 minutes (do not overbake). Cool cookies completely; place in a glass jar or other attractive container. Add a decorative label that reads: "Bath Cookies / Feed 1 or 2 to your tub. / Have fun!"

◆ Whether you're packing or unpacking a box, those foam "peanuts" can turn on you and go wild with static electricity. Before you begin, rub a Downy dryer sheet over your hands (and arms if you're wearing a short-sleeve shirt). The little critters will be corralled and calmed.

◆ Here's a very handy, inexpensive, and fun alternative to store-bought wrapping paper. Spray the color comics section from the Sunday newspaper with a light coat of Suave hairspray. When it dries, it will seal in the ink and give the paper a gloss. Wrap a gift with the hairspray side facing out.

◆ Store rolls of leftover wrapping paper in a convenient, protective "container." Use the legs of a pair of No nonsense pantyhose as tubes—simply slide in the rolls. Use just 1 leg for a couple of rolls. For a bigger supply, keep the pantyhose intact, fill both legs, and hang from the panty portion on a hanger.

ARTS, CRAFTS & CREATIVITY

Flower Power

◆ Try this trick for displaying flowers in a vase or other container that is not watertight: Fill a GLAD Freezer Zipper Bag about ⅓ full with water; place it in the container. Arrange cut flowers in the bag, zipping as needed to hold the stems in place.

◆ Use Morton Salt to hold an arrangement of artificial flowers in a vase or container. Just pour in salt, add a little cold water, and arrange flowers as desired. As salt dries out, it will solidify around stems and create a stable base.

- Clean artificial flowers using a paper grocery bag and Morton Salt. Pour ¼ cup salt into the bag, then put in the flowers, blossom ends first. Close top and shake well. Carefully remove the flowers from the bag over a sink (or outside), then shake off the salt.

- Lengthen flower stems that are too short for your vase by inserting the stems into straight drinking straws and cutting to the appropriate length.

- Dry out and preserve your last bouquet from the garden. To dry flowers and leaves, find a lidded cardboard box that's big enough to contain your plant pieces. Mix 1 part 20 Mule Team Borax and 2 parts Quaker Yellow Corn Meal; pour mixture into the box to a 1-inch depth. Lay  your plant pieces on top, then gently cover them with more mixture. Lightly sprinkle mixture into blooms of flowers with many petals. Make sure there are no air spaces around the pieces. Close and tape the box shut; keep in a dry spot at room temperature for 7 to 10 days. After opening the box, carefully brush away mixture and lift out pieces. To reuse mixture, strain out debris, cover, and store in a cool, dry place. (Note: This method may not work on cut flowers that have been in a water solution or other preservative.)

◆ Dry flowers by placing them between 2 Scott Towels and inserting between the pages of a telephone book. Add weight by placing another telephone book or other heavy object on top. Let dry several weeks.

◆ Display dried leaves or pressed flowers by affixing them to Reynolds Parchment Paper with Elmer's Glue-All. Add a colorful mat; frame.

◆ Store dried flowers and pinecones in a GLAD Food Storage Zipper Bag. Add McCormick Bay Leaves, Ground Cloves, a Cinnamon Stick, and a few drops of cinnamon essential oil. Keep the bag sealed for a few weeks, then add the potpourri to decorative dishes throughout your house.

Decorative Details

◆ Here's an idea for an unusual centerpiece: Fill a vase ¾ full with water, add a few drops of McCormick Food Color and ¼ cup Heinz Distilled White Vinegar, and then pour in 3 teaspoons ARM & HAMMER Baking Soda. Drop in buttons, rice, or pasta and watch them rise and fall like magic.

◆ When making a centerpiece out of helium balloons, you can create a table weight that coordinates with the theme of the party. Using a funnel, pour enough Morton Salt into an uninflated balloon to weigh it down. Wrap the weighted balloon with tissue paper and secure with a ribbon. Tie helium balloons to this weighted balloon with long ribbons, then add any other decorations you desire.

- Use Melitta Basket Coffee Filters when making goodie bags. Fill each filter with small toys, candy, or other goodie bag favorites. Bring up the sides to form a bag; tie with colorful ribbon. If you like, attach helium balloons or add name tags to make place cards.

- Simulate a lava lamp by filling a glass with Canada Dry Club Soda and raisins. The raisins will float up and down with the carbonation. Even better, add McCormick Food Color and pour the liquid into a decorative bottle.

Crafty Tips

- Not sure where to hang a mirror or picture? Trace around it on a paper grocery or lunch bag, cut out the shape, and affix it to the wall with Scotch Masking Tape, moving it around to determine the best spot. When you've decided where to hang the art object—but before you remove the cutout—mark on the wall where the nail should go.

- When working on small woodworking crafts, you can hide a scratch or touch up a smudge by mixing 1 teaspoon Folgers Instant Coffee Crystals with 2 teaspoons water. Use a Q-tips cotton swab to apply the liquid to the mark.

- Sharpen craft scissors by cutting a piece of Reynolds Wrap Aluminum Foil several times.

- Nails, screws, and brads go into wood easier if you first stab them into a bar of Ivory Soap to lubricate them.

- When you've used up your Pampers baby wipes, keep the plastic containers. They are perfect for storing all the odds and ends of craft projects, such as string, ribbon, glue sticks, beads, and so on. Use a permanent marker to label each container for easy identification.

- Don't forget about other packaging, such as the cylindrical plastic containers in which other wipes and cleaning cloths are sold. Once empty, clean, and dry, they are perfect dispensers for yarn, twine, or string. Remove the cap, put in the roll, and thread the end through the slot in the lid. Replace lid.

- Model builders will be glad for this fix: Remove model glue from clear plastic pieces by applying a dab of Simoniz Original Paste Wax and rubbing it into the glue.

- Use Suave hairspray as a light adhesive for your next craft project.

- Attention, rubber stamp fans! Before you apply embossing powder to your paper or card stock, wipe the paper with a used Downy dryer sheet. This reduces the static, which cuts down on the amount of powder that sticks where you don't want it to.

- If you'd like to add an extra artistic touch to a letter, melt a Crayola Crayon and use it as sealing wax on the envelope. Place a crayon (without its wrapper) in a Dixie paper cup. In increments of 30 seconds, melt the crayon in a microwave oven. Pour the melted crayon onto the envelope, but be careful not to touch the hot wax. Press an object into the warm wax to leave an imprint.

What fun it is to see the names or photos of the people you love in the newspaper. Wish you could keep clippings from getting brittle and yellowed? Pour 1 tablespoon Phillips' Milk of Magnesia into a quart of fresh Canada Dry Club Soda; let it sit overnight. Stir the solution well in the morning and pour it into a shallow pan. Insert the clipping; wait 2 hours, then carefully remove it and lay it flat on a soft towel. When it's dry, mount it in a scrapbook (with adhesive photo corners or other archival methods, not glue or tape).

The Colorful Company Called Crayola

- Cousins Edwin Binney and C. Harold Smith took over the family business, pigment manufacturer Peekskill Chemical Works, in 1885.

- The first box of 8 Crayola Gold Medal School Crayons debuted in 1903. Edwin's wife, Alice Binney, coined the name "Crayola" from *craie* ("chalk" in French) and *ola* (from *oleaginous*, meaning "containing oil").

- A box of 64 crayons, featuring a built-in sharpener, debuted in 1958 and was immediately a much-sought-after item.

- In 1993, 16 consumer-named colors were introduced, including shamrock, denim, and mauvelous.

- Only 3 color names have been changed over the years: Prussian blue to midnight blue (1958), flesh to peach (1962), and Indian red to chestnut (1999).

Candles

- Stop new candles from dripping by soaking them for several hours in a solution of equal parts water and Morton Salt. Let dry, then burn as usual.

A Household-Hints Classic by 1830

The American Frugal Housewife: Dedicated to Those Who Are Not Ashamed of Economy, written by Lydia Maria Francis Child, was first published in Boston in 1829. When the book went out of print in 1850—due in part to Child's growing antislavery work, as well as the appearance of more modern cookbooks—it had gone through 35 printings. The book included recipes, information about buying and storing food, household hints, and home remedies.

"The true economy of housekeeping," she wrote in the introduction, "is simply the art of gathering up all the fragments, so that nothing be lost. I mean fragments of *time,* as well as *materials.* Nothing should be thrown away so long as it is possible to make any use of it, however trifling that use may be...."

- Pretreat wicks for homemade candles to reduce ash and eliminate smoke problems. Combine 1 cup warm water, 3 tablespoons 20 Mule Team Borax, and 1 tablespoon Morton Salt. Soak twine or string in the solution for at least 24 hours. Let dry completely before making candles.

- Make your own oil lamp: Pour Crisco Pure Vegetable Oil into a metal or heatproof ceramic bowl. Insert a cotton wick (available at craft stores).

Air Fresheners

- You know Argo Corn Starch makes a great carpet freshener. With a few extra touches, it also makes a great gift! In a large bowl, thoroughly mix 32 ounces of either corn starch or ARM & HAMMER Baking Soda (or a combination of both) with 20 to 40 drops of your favorite essential oil blend. Spoon into a clean, dry Parmesan cheese shaker. Make a colorful label that includes these directions: "Sprinkle on carpet. Wait 30 minutes, then vacuum."

- To make a refreshing air freshener, mix 4 packages Knox unflavored gelatin in a saucepan with 1 cup near-boiling distilled water; stir to dissolve. Remove from heat and add another cup of water. Add 10 drops of a scented essential oil and a bit of McCormick Food Color. Pour mixture into clean baby food jars and let sit overnight. Add a cap if giving the air freshener as a gift or place around your home for a fresh scent.

HOBBIES

Photography

- To make a light-reflecting panel for photography, apply a light coat of rubber cement to heavy cardboard or mat board and cover with Reynolds Wrap Aluminum Foil, shiny side out. A handy approach is to make 3 panels and join them with silver Scotch Duct Tape. They'll fold up for storage and carrying as well as stand by themselves.

- To create a starburst effect when shooting a sunrise, sunset, or any bright or reflective object, stretch a small square of No nonsense pantyhose over your camera lens and secure with a rubber band.

- Q-tips cotton swabs are perfect for cleaning fine optics such as camera lenses, binoculars, or a magnifying glass. They're gentle, 100 percent cotton, and the perfect size and shape.

- Before you pass around those great new photos of your kitten, your children or grandchildren, or last week's trip, seal each one in its own GLAD Food Storage Zipper Bag. They'll be safe from smudges or spills.

Music to Our Ears

- Lubricate the fretboard on a guitar with WD-40. This product also helps clean, polish, and protect chrome on electric guitars.

- Here's an idea that should be music to your ears: Polish your guitar with Crest toothpaste. Rub some on, let it dry, and then buff it. The notes and your guitar will really shine!

- Lubricate and clean the valves and hardware of brass and woodwind instruments with WD-40.

- To free stuck organ and piano keys, spray them with a little WD-40. Wipe with a clean cloth.

Kept in Stitches

- To make it easier to thread a needle, stick the end of the thread into Revlon Nail Enamel and let it dry. Red polish will make the thread easier to see and will provide a slick end for threading.

- To prevent thread from breaking, spray it with WD-40.

- Sewing projects become easier when the thread doesn't tangle. Wipe both the needle and thread with a Downy dryer sheet.

- When removing stitches from black or very dark fabric, run a line of white Crayola chalk around the stitch path. This will make it much easier to see when you resew the fabric. The chalk will wash right out.

- If you're out of dressmaker's chalk—or any kind of chalk, for that matter—a bar of white Ivory Soap can take its place.

Stitching in Time

1833: Walter Hunt invents the first workable sewing machine but never obtains a patent; in 1849 he invents (and patents) the safety pin.

1845–46: Elias Howe invents a similar sewing machine but does patent it; others copy and manufacture it, but in 1854 Howe's patent is declared "basic" and others must pay royalties.

1857: Isaac Singer opens a mass-production facility and cuts production cost to about $10 per sewing machine. Within 3 years, his company is the biggest manufacturer of sewing machines worldwide.

1863: With Edward Clark, Singer incorporates the Singer Manufacturing Company; the company holds 22 patents.

1894: Sears sells its own brand-name sewing machine, the "Minnesota"; the first Kenmore model appears in 1913 catalog.

1940: Beulah Henry invents the first bobbinless sewing machine.

- Wrap a piece of fabric around a bar of Ivory Soap, tightly tape it on the bottom, and you have a nifty pincushion. The soap helps pins and needles move smoothly through any fabric, while the cover looks neat and keeps the pincushion in place.

- Why struggle to cram used sewing pattern pieces back into their original envelope? Fold the pieces, then store them and the envelope (front facing out) in a quart- or gallon-size GLAD Food Storage Zipper Bag.

- Prevent stains from a just-oiled sewing machine by stitching several rows on a Scott Towel or two before sewing fabric.

- Machine-stitching a piece of slippery material can be maddening. Put a piece of Reynolds Cut-Rite Wax Paper on the seam. Tear off when finished sewing.

- Save fabric remnants in an old Scott Towel core or other cardboard tube. Cut an unused tube lengthwise, insert the rolled-up fabric, and close with rubber bands or tape. On the tube, write information such as fabric type, color, yardage, and date.

- An empty box from Reynolds Wrap Aluminum Foil or another roll product—minus the cutting strip—is the perfect place to store knitting needles.

- Store knitting needles in an old Scott Towel core. Cover one end with strips of Scotch Magic Tape; pinch the other end closed and tape it securely with Scotch Duct Tape. Slide the needles into the tube through the transparent tape to hold them in place.

PROJECTS WITH THE KIDS

Clay Day

Play Clay Recipe

2 cups ARM & HAMMER Baking Soda
1 cup Argo Corn Starch
1¼ cups cold water
McCormick Food Color (optional)

Mix baking soda and corn starch in a saucepan. Add food coloring to the water to make colored clay. Add water to the pan, stir to combine, then cook over medium heat, stirring constantly, 10 to 15 minutes. Don't overcook. Clay should have the consistency of mashed potatoes. Spread the mixture on a plate or cutting board and cover with a damp cloth until it's cool enough to handle. Knead until smooth. Make Play Clay ahead of time, and store unused clay in an airtight container in the refrigerator for up to 1 week. Bring clay to room temperature before using.

To dry finished clay pieces, let them sit, uncovered, for a few days; alternatively, bake them for about 30 minutes in a warm (not hot) oven. Check the oven often to make sure the clay is baking evenly. When items are dry, decorate with acrylic paint.

- Smooth rough or cracked edges of Play Clay sculptures with a Cutex Emery Board.

- Paint dry Play Clay pieces with watercolor, poster, or acrylic paints. Draw on them with a felt-tip pen or waterproof marker. Apply glitter to wet paint.

- Protect finished Play Clay objects with clear acrylic spray or clear Revlon Nail Enamel.

- Capture a child's handprint by pressing into damp Play Clay. When it's dry, paint the piece and add the child's name and date on the back, then attach a picture hanger.

- Make fancy napkin rings out of Play Clay by rolling out long, narrow rectangles of clay, then piecing the ends together into rings.

- Cut a square or rectangle from Play Clay, then cut a frame opening the size of a photograph. The frame should be at least ½ inch wide. Use another piece of clay for a stand to attach to the back. Decorate frame when dry.

How to Dry Play Clay

Here are three ways to dry Play Clay art:

Air-dry: Set on a wire rack overnight.

Oven: Preheat to 350°F, turn off oven, then place finished objects on a cookie sheet. Leave in until oven is cold.

Microwave: Place objects on a paper towel, bake at medium power for 30 seconds, turn over, and bake for another 30 seconds. Repeat until dry.

- Create a name plaque for a child's room by cutting out the shapes of letters and pressing them onto a rectangular piece of Play Clay as the background. Paint and finish when dry.

- Shape beads for a necklace by rolling Play Clay into oval or round shapes. Poke a toothpick through the shapes to make holes for stringing. Let dry, then string beads on thread, shoelaces, yarn, kite string, or fishing line. Tie knots between beads to hold them in place, and tie both sides of the string together to finish.

- To make jewelry such as earrings or brooches, create small shapes with flat backs out of Play Clay; glue to earring or pin backings.

Works of Art

- Give an older child a chance to take up sculpting. Have him or her carve figurines using bars of Ivory Soap and a dull table knife. Even with a dull knife, children should take care.

Soap Sculpture

The first Ivory Soap sculpture contest was held in 1924, a tradition that continued through 1987. The first event bubbled into the hobby of soap carving. Over the years entries included countless replicas of the Empire State Building. The Ivory Web site includes detailed guidelines for soap carving, as well as photos of record-setting sculptures.

- If you'd like to save your child's artwork for posterity, spray it with a thin layer of Suave hairspray to protect it from smudging or fading.

- Line work surfaces with Reynolds Freezer Paper to prevent paint and glue stains.

- Create finger paints in custom colors. Add ¼ cup Argo Corn Starch to 2 cups cold water; boil until mixture thickens. Let cool slightly, then pour mixture into small containers to make various paint colors. Add a few drops of McCormick Food Color to each container. Also add a few drops of Dawn dishwashing liquid to each bowl to help with cleanup later. Make sure the paints are completely cool before using.

- Make a disposable palette for paints by wrapping a piece of cardboard in Reynolds Wrap Aluminum Foil.

- An ice cube tray makes a perfect paint palette, especially for very young artists.

- Cut a hole in a clean, empty Clorox Regular-Bleach bottle and use it to store your children's crayons or small toys. Sand down any sharp edges with a Cutex Emery Board.

- Use Reynolds Parchment Paper in place of tracing paper for any project.

- Increase the fun and save money by making your own paste. Combine 3 teaspoons Argo Corn Starch

Stuck on You

Before the advent of the glue stick, school supply lists nationwide included a very special item: "1 jar school paste." Preferred brands were Elmer's, LePage's, and Pogo. Each of the 3 brands came in a white jar, emitted a memorable aroma, and were nontoxic (in kidspeak, "edible"). Elmer's and LePage's featured an orange cap with an applicator brush attached; Pogo's cap was red, and the "pogo stick" brush nestled in a center well. With school paste, every sense was engaged and every grade-schooler was an artist.

with 4 teaspoons cold water; stir until mixture has paste consistency. Apply with fingers or wooden craft sticks.

◆ Make your own colorful glues by adding a few drops of McCormick Food Color to Elmer's Glue-All.

◆ Have a child dip a Q-tips cotton swab in ReaLemon Lemon Juice and use it to write or draw on plain white paper. To make the design appear, hold the paper near a hot lightbulb. (Supervise children as they do this.)

Notes on Post-it Notes

1968: A senior scientist in 3M's Corporate Research Lab discovers an adhesive you can pick up and put down again.

1974: Another 3M scientist, who sings in his church choir, wishes he had a hymnal bookmark that was only semi-adhesive. He remembers his coworker's discovery.

1977: Enough Post-it Notes are manufactured to supply 3M's corporate headquarters. Employees are soon stuck on them.

1978: 3M marketing floods the Idaho office supply industry with samples—the famous "Boise Blitz"—and the reaction is amazing.

1979: Post-it Notes are introduced in 11 states. Consumers start mailing the product to their friends and coworkers in the other 39 states.

1980: The Little Sticky that Could is introduced nationwide. Everyone, from mail clerks to CEOs, loves Post-it Notes.

1981: Post-it Notes migrate to Canada and Europe.

2009: Post-it Notes are available in 62 colors, 25 shapes, and 8 standard sizes.

- Make your own mosaic art with Post-it Notes in a variety of colors and sizes.

- Give kids a sheet of Reynolds Cut-Rite Wax Paper for sticker creations. They can arrange and rearrange to their hearts' content before putting stickers in a scrapbook or album.

- Cover your child's art project or photos with GLAD Press'n Seal to protect and preserve.

- Reach dental floss makes a handy hanger for children's artwork. Apply Elmer's Glue-All to attach the floss to the back of the paper, or punch a small hole in the artwork and thread the floss through.

- Here's a project from yesteryear—creating place mats, bookmarks, book covers, or other decorative pieces. Arrange items such as colorful autumn leaves, flowers, or magazine pictures on a sheet of Reynolds Cut-Rite Wax Paper. Cover with another sheet. Put the whole stack inside a paper grocery bag or between 2 sheets of cloth. Iron on a low setting to melt the wax, creating a seal. Carefully remove the bag or cloth from the wax paper. Let cool, then cut the wax paper to the shape and size you wish. Pinking shears and other craft scissors make interesting edges.

- To make a sun catcher, shave Crayola Crayons or colorful candle pieces onto a sheet of Reynolds Cut-Rite Wax Paper. Place another sheet on top, then put the whole set inside a paper grocery bag or between 2 sheets of cloth. Using a low setting, iron the "sandwich" until the shavings melt (try 10 seconds at first). Carefully peel bag or cloth off the wax paper. Let it cool, then cut the wax paper art into a fun shape. Poke a hole in it and use ribbon to hang it near a window.

Salt Painting

This cool art project will take your children a couple of days to complete, but the resulting artwork will be well worth the wait! Here's what you'll need:

Clear self-adhesive vinyl
Scissors
Morton Salt
Pencil
Crayola watercolors
Paintbrush
Construction paper
Elmer's Glue-All
Coloring book or plain white paper

Cut self-adhesive vinyl into a size suitable for painting a picture (8"×10" is a good size). Peel backing; sprinkle entire sticky side with salt. Hold up vinyl and gently shake off any excess salt. Let sit for 2 days.

Place sheet of vinyl, salty side up, on top of a coloring book picture to trace an image, or place over a plain piece of paper and draw a design. Using a set of watercolors and a paintbrush, paint salty side of vinyl. Paint lightly; rubbing too hard could ruin the paintbrush. Let dry, then remove coloring book page (or plain paper) from underneath the sheet of vinyl.

Glue painted salt image to a piece of construction paper to make it sturdy. You can glue it either salty- or smooth-side up.

Bedecked and Bedazzled

- Use Reach dental floss to string beads for necklaces, bracelets, and other homemade bead projects. Floss can also be used to restring a broken beaded necklace.

- Cut colorful drinking straws into ½-inch sections and string the pieces on Reach dental floss to make necklaces.

- Fill small bowls with water and a few drops of McCormick Food Colors. Drop macaroni noodles into the water until they change color, then remove, drain, and dry the noodles on a Scott Towel. String them on Reach dental floss to make a colorful necklace.

- When a costume jewelry gem needs to be reset, put a small amount of clear Revlon Nail Enamel in the base, set in the stone, and let dry.

How Does Your Garden Grow?

Who said a garden is only made of flowers or vegetables? This cool project—a crystal garden—is a sparkling alternative. It's educational too! You'll need the following: 6 tablespoons Morton Salt, 6 tablespoons liquid bluing (a laundry whitening product), 6 tablespoons water, 1 tablespoon Parsons' Ammonia, a medium-size bowl, small rocks or rock pieces, a shallow bowl, McCormick Food Color, and a tray or breadboard (optional). Mix salt, bluing, water, and ammonia in the medium-size bowl. Place rocks in the shallow bowl. Pour mixture over rocks, then drip food coloring on top of rocks. Crystals will grow in about 3 weeks. After that time, keep adding water and they'll continue to grow. Place bowl on a tray or breadboard if crystals begin to grow over edges of bowl.

- Before hand-painting T-shirts and other fabrics, cover the backing board with Reynolds Cut-Rite Wax Paper. It will keep the mess to a minimum.

Fun and Games

- Put green eggs and ham on the menu for all the Dr. Seuss fans in your house. Before scrambling the eggs, simply add a few drops of McCormick Blue Food Color.

- Cut the bottom off a clean, empty Clorox Regular-Bleach bottle, remove the cap, and encourage your child to shout through the spout for a fun megaphone.

Oobleck!

Bartholomew and the Oobleck is a classic from Dr. Seuss, first published in 1949. Bartholomew Cubbins encounters the weird substance called "oobleck"—liquid and solid at the same time—and for decades science classes have too. Create it at home: Mix 2 cups Argo Corn Starch, about 3 drops McCormick Green Food Color, and enough water to give the mixture the texture of pancake batter (start with 2 cups water, adding a little at a time). Observe the surface, then watch how it changes when you touch it! Make a ball out of oobleck and toss it in the air, then try to make it bounce (it won't). Or mold oobleck in assorted shaped containers. Oobleck is a great example of a non-Newtonian fluid.

- Have your kids make their own kazoos. Cut 3 small holes, aligned vertically, in the middle of an empty Scott Towel core. Cover one end of the cardboard tube with Reynolds Cut-Rite Wax Paper and use rubber bands to hold in place. Have the kids hum into the open end and cover 1, 2, or 3 holes with their fingers to change the pitch.

◆ Use a flexible drinking straw as a bubble blower. Cut one end on a diagonal and dip that end into bubble liquid. Have a child blow into the other end.

◆ A pack of Post-it Notes can lead to a game of tic-tac-toe. Tailor the size of the notes to the playing surface as well as the child's age (bigger notes for younger kids). Each "X" or "O" gets its own note.

◆ When housing fireflies, caterpillars, and other insects in a glass jar, don't cover the jar with the metal lid. Instead, cut a 5- or 6-inch square of No nonsense pantyhose and secure it over the top of the jar with a rubber band. The nylon not only lets in plenty of air but also makes for easy access to the bugs.

◆ Children who are tall enough and can keep their balance will enjoy these homemade "stilts." Punch 2 holes in the bottoms of 2 empty Folgers coffee cans and string a length of rope through them. Have the child stand on the cans and grab the ropes, holding tight. Time for a walk!

◆ Remove the bottom from an empty Folgers coffee can, then nail the can above your garage door for a mini basketball hoop. (Use with Penn tennis balls instead of basketballs.)

◆ Empty 2-liter bottles from Canada Dry Club Soda, Pepsi, or any soft drink can become pins for lawn bowling. Rinse out the bottles, allow them to dry, then pour in a few inches of Fresh Step cat litter, pebbles, sand, or soil. Arrange the pins and use any hard ball to knock them down.

Grains of Science

You may not be able to find fossils in your backyard, but you can make your own with this super science project. You'll need the following: ½ cup cold Folgers coffee, 1 cup used coffee grounds, 1 cup Gold Medal All-Purpose Flour, ½ cup Morton Salt, Reynolds Cut-Rite Wax Paper, an empty can and/or butter knife, small objects (such as beads, coins, jewelry pieces, or shells), and yarn or string (optional).

To make a plaster, stir cold coffee and coffee grounds together in a bowl. Add flour and salt; mix well to form a dough. Knead dough, then flatten onto a sheet of wax paper. Use the empty can to cut circles in the dough; use a butter knife to cut squares, rectangles, or other shapes. Each shape should be large enough to hold the object or objects you are going to use to make a fossil impression. Make a pattern or indentation in each piece of dough by firmly pressing small objects into it. Be sure not to press too hard, or your object will poke through the back of the plaster shape. Remove the object. If you're going to hang your creations, poke a hole in the top of each shape—when they harden you'll be able to thread a piece of string through the holes. Let dough dry overnight.

- Make a playing-card holder for young children with an empty box of Reynolds Wrap Aluminum Foil, Reynolds Cut-Rite Wax Paper, or GLAD Cling Wrap. Simply remove the cutting strip and close the lid. The cards stand up between the flap and the side of the box. Paint or decorate the box with your child if desired.

- Separate sticky playing cards by dropping them into a brown paper bag and adding a small amount of Johnson's Baby Powder. Shake the bag vigorously.

- To prevent playing cards from sticking together, apply a small amount of Simoniz Original Paste Wax to the backs.

- If the slide on your backyard swing set isn't slippery enough for your crew, apply 2 coats of Simoniz Original Paste Wax. Buff with a soft cloth after each coat.

- Make some slime! Put ⅓ cup Elmer's Glue-All (not Elmer's Washable School Glue), 6 drops McCormick Food Color, and ⅓ cup water in a small covered container. Seal container and shake mixture until well blended. Set aside. Put ⅓ cup water in a small bowl and add 20 Mule Team Borax 1 teaspoon at a time until it settles. Pour off excess water. Add first mixture to borax mixture, then pour new combination onto waxed paper. Knead the slime to blend well and remove air bubbles.

Volcano Alert

Shape cardboard into a cone. Insert a Dixie cup in top of cone to make crater. Stand cone on baking sheet. Cover cone with plaster of paris, but don't get any in the cup. Let cone dry completely, then paint or decorate it to look like a volcano.

Making the Eruption

Mix ¼ cup Heinz Distilled White Vinegar with 1 teaspoon Dawn dishwashing liquid and a little McCormick Red Food Color. Put 1 teaspoon ARM & HAMMER Baking Soda into the crater cup. Pour in the vinegar mixture.

Volcano Variation

Make a mini volcano in a sandbox. Fill a Dixie cup with 1 tablespoon ARM & HAMMER Baking Soda and set it in a mountain made of sand. When you're ready for the eruption, pour in ¼ cup Heinz Distilled White Vinegar.

TIPS FOR TYKES

- To track whose toy is whose, use red Revlon Nail Enamel to mark the bottom of each toy with the child's name or initials.

- Run the string of a pull toy through a straight or flexible drinking straw and knot it at the end. This will prevent tangling.

- Make your own baby wipes for a fraction of the cost of store-bought. Mix 1 tablespoon Ivory Liquid Hand Cleanser (antibacterial), 1 teaspoon Johnson's Baby Oil, and ⅓ cup water. Fold several Scott Towels to fit inside a sandwich- or pint-size GLAD Food Storage Zipper Bag. Pour enough of the mixture into the bag to get the towels damp but not dripping. Seal the bag.

- Go ahead . . . let your kids show off their first lost tooth. Just first put it in a snack-size GLAD Food Storage Zipper Bag so it doesn't get misplaced.

- Help a child just learning to dress on his or her own by packing a gallon-size GLAD Food Storage Zipper Bag with a complete outfit, from shirt to socks. The child can pick a bag for the day, then get dressed all alone.

- Help students keep track of school supplies: Punch 2 holes along the bottom edge of a quart-size GLAD Freezer Zipper Bag to align with the rings in a three-ring binder. Although this pencil pouch doesn't have unlimited capacity, it will hold a small supply of pencils, pens, erasers, paper clips, index cards, and Post-it Notes.

◆ Store and protect items such as diplomas, keepsake papers, certificates, and your children's artwork. Roll them up and insert into an empty Scott Towel core, gift wrap tube, or similar cardboard packaging. Write pertinent information on the tube to identify its contents at a glance.

◆ Keep a few old Scott Towel cores in the car. They'll come in handy when your student gets in the car with a test paper or piece of artwork that's a keeper.

PACKING AND TRAVEL TIPS

◆ Put brightly colored strips of Scotch Duct Tape on your luggage. You'll ID your bags from a distance at the baggage claim. (Duct tape does double duty on luggage repair as well, if necessary.)

◆ Roll up your clothes and you'll be able to pack a lot more into your suitcase. Bulky items tend to unroll, so pack them

Packing Tips

◆ Label luggage both inside and out with your name and address. Include your phone number on the inside identification, but not on the outside.

◆ Stuff small items, such as rolled socks, into shoes and purses to save room.

◆ As you pack, jot down what you're taking. The list can make it easier for your luggage to be identified if lost and will help you with any insurance claim if your bags are permanently lost.

◆ Because post earrings are easy to lose, keep them together by poking them through an index card and fastening them on the other side.

in hosiery. Cut off the legs of a pair of No nonsense pantyhose; cut off each foot portion and stretch the nylon over the rolled-up clothing.

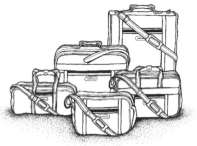

- Protect your shoes from scuffs and your clothes from dirt: Wrap the shoes in GLAD Press'n Seal before packing them in your suitcase.

- Store liquid toiletries in GLAD Food Storage Zipper Bags so they won't ruin clothes if the containers break or spill.

- Use 2 small pieces of GLAD Press'n Seal to carry vitamins or over-the-counter pills.

- The sticky-backed portion of a Post-it Note makes a great temporary label for travel bottles and jars.

- Carry fresh diapers in a gallon-size GLAD Food Storage Zipper Bag, which doubles as an emergency changing mat and can also store the dirty diapers until you get to a trash receptacle.

- Pack a child's suitcase using a gallon-size GLAD Food Storage Zipper Bag for each day of the trip. Put a complete outfit, including socks and underwear, into each bag. This makes dressing a snap and helps keep the suitcase tidy.

- A group of GLAD Food Storage Zipper Bags makes an excellent organizer for carrying cotton balls, pacifiers, medicines, and the like inside a baby bag. Store each group of items in a sandwich-size bag, then place the smaller bags in a quart- or gallon-size bag.

- After you return home and unpack your suitcases, place a Downy dryer sheet in each piece of luggage. They'll be sweet-smelling and ready for the next trip.

- You're checking into a hotel or motel late at night, the kitchen is closed (or nonexistent), and items from a vending machine or overpriced minibar won't cut it. The problem is solved if you've packed some cheese sandwiches wrapped in Reynolds Wrap Aluminum Foil. Use the innkeeper's iron to press both sides of the wrapped snack, and hot nutrition is yours in the form of a fresh grilled-cheese sandwich.

I Need a Vacation!

In ancient Rome, more than 100 days of the year were sacred feast days, when people rested from their usual routines. The remaining days were called *dies vacantes* ("vacant days"), on which people worked. In modern times, however, the resulting word *vacation* has come to mean the opposite—a time of rest or recreation. Often a vacation is associated with a sacred or secular *holiday* (a contraction of *holy day*); in fact, in Europe and other parts of the world, the phrase "on holiday" is synonymous with "on vacation."

- Write driving directions on a large Post-it Note. Stick it where you can see it easily and safely, such as on the dashboard or in the middle of the steering wheel.

THE GREAT OUTDOORS

Bicycles

- Clean the rust from bike handlebars or tire rims with a paste of 6 tablespoons Morton Salt and 2 tablespoons ReaLemon Lemon Juice. Apply the paste to rusted areas with a dry cloth, then rub, rinse, and dry thoroughly.

- To clean bike chains, chrome, and other fixtures, spray them with WD-40 and wipe off with a rag. This also lubricates and prevents rust.

- A quick spray of WD-40 may be all you need to stop squeaks on bicycles, in-line skates, swing sets, exercise machines, or any other outdoor equipment with moving parts.

- If you're out of lubricating oil, give your bicycle chain a light spritz of PAM cooking spray. The chain should not look wet, so remove any excess with a clean rag.

- Just a few drops of Suave conditioner can lubricate bicycle chains, in-line skates, and skateboard wheels.

- Remove old decals from a bicycle frame by spraying them with WD-40. Let sit for a few minutes, then peel or scrape off the decals.

- Attention, cyclists and bikers! Keep dust and dirt from sticking to your goggles by spraying the lenses with Static Guard before hitting the road.

Replacing the rubber grips on bicycle handlebars can be difficult. But if you spray the inside of each new grip with Suave hairspray, they'll slide into place easily. The hairspray first acts as a lubricant, then as an adhesive when it dries.

When you have to leave a bike in soft grass, soil, mud, or sand, a traditional kickstand is of no use. So cut a small opening in the seam of a Penn tennis ball and push it onto the end of the kickstand.

Keep your pant cuff away from your bicycle chain by wrapping a length of Scotch Duct Tape around it.

The Sporting Life

Attention soccer moms and dads and other fans: Bring a roll of GLAD Press'n Seal to cover a bench so you can stay dirt-free while watching a game or match.

Break in a new baseball glove with the help of Vaseline Petroleum Jelly. Rub some jelly into the leather, place a baseball in the palm, and close it with a large rubber band.

The Tennis Ball Racket

Tennis balls are made of a pressurized rubber core that's covered with high-quality cloth—most often wool mixed with up to 35 percent nylon. The outer surface must be uniform; if the ball has seams, they must be without stitches. According to the International Tennis Federation, the ball must be yellow or white, measure more than $2\frac{1}{2}$ inches but less than $2\frac{5}{8}$ inches in diameter, and weigh between 1.975 and 2.095 ounces. In 1922 the Penn company made the first pressurized can; in 1968 it made the first fluorescent yellow tennis ball.

Wait 1 or 2 days, then remove the band and ball. The glove is ready for action! Petroleum jelly can also restore an old glove—one in which the leather is very dry. Simply rub it in.

- Lubricate and soften old, dry leather on a baseball glove by rubbing Crisco Pure Vegetable Oil into it.

- To strengthen the wrist that powers your golf swing, open and close an extra-large binder clip repeatedly.

- Spiff up your golf balls with a bath in 1 cup water and ¼ cup Parsons' Ammonia.

- To clean golf balls, clubs, and carts, spray on WD-40 and wipe with a clean cloth.

- A dab of Alberto VO5 Conditioning Hairdressing on a clean cloth will make the shafts of your golf clubs sparkle.

- To prevent mud from sticking to your golf cleats on rainy days, spray them with WD-40 before you hit the links.

- A spray of WD-40 in the sockets of your golf cleats will also keep them from rusting.

- Help make your croquet wickets more visible on the lawn by running them through colorful flexible drinking straws.

- Meet your need for speed—at least over snow. Before you hit the slopes, coat the bottom of a snow saucer, snow tube, sled, or toboggan with PAM cooking spray.

- Another way to speed up your trip down the slopes is to rub some Simoniz Original Paste Wax on the runners of a sled or the bottom of a snow saucer. Hold on tight!

- Prevent rust on the blades of your ice skates with an application of WD-40.

- A smelly gym bag can give the nose quite a workout! Keep that stinky duffel fresh by storing a wrapper from a bar of soap inside.

- Protect your valuables when you're working out at the health club. Cut a 2-inch slit along the seam of a Penn tennis ball; put valuables inside, then keep the "safe" safe with the rest of your gear.

Watered Down

- Add a can of PAM cooking spray to your tackle box. Fishing line casts farther and more freely after you lightly coat it with the spray.

- Wrap a bit of Reynolds Wrap Aluminum Foil around a fishing hook, fringe the foil, cast, and then slowly reel it in. The wiggling action just might lure a fish.

- To attract fish, put a piece of an Alka-Seltzer tablet in a tube jig. Cast your line and reel them in!

- Add ARM & HAMMER Baking Soda to hollow fishing lures to give them spin in the water.

- Keep fish hooks from rusting by sticking them in a cork and submerging the cork in ARM & HAMMER Baking Soda.

- Don't throw out those old Folgers coffee grounds when leaving on a fishing trip—put the grounds back in an empty Folgers coffee can along with some soil and live worms.

- To bait your catfish hook with raw chicken liver, first contain the liver by putting it in a small piece of No nonsense pantyhose.

- Your child's waterslide will be slippery indeed when you give it 2 coats of Simoniz Original Paste Wax. Buff the surface with a soft cloth after each coat.

- The average basket-style pool skimmer misses lots of debris, hair, and other small particles that can clog your pool's filtration system. Cut a piece of No nonsense pantyhose and fit it over the skimmer. It will do a "fine" job of cleaning.

- Patch holes in a children's pool—whether molded plastic or vinyl blow-up style—with Scotch Duct Tape.

- Remove mildew odors from plastic and vinyl pool toys by soaking them in ¼ cup ARM & HAMMER Baking Soda and 1 quart warm water.

- Toss 2 or 3 Penn tennis balls into your pool to absorb swimmers' body oils. Replace every few weeks.

- Think ahead before you take a ride in a canoe, kayak, or other watercraft. Put your keys, cell phone, and other small valuables in a quart- or gallon-size GLAD Food Storage Zipper Bag. Blow air into it and seal. If the boat tips over, the bag—and your stuff—will float.

- Clean, empty Clorox Regular-Bleach bottles make great buoys for boating or swimming areas. Tighten the cap on one, tie a rope around the handle, and attach the other end of the rope to a second bottle filled with sand.

- Remove tree sap and bugs from your boat's windshield by rubbing with some WD-40 on a clean cloth.

- Clean stains on a fiberglass boat by scrubbing with ARM & HAMMER Baking Soda on a damp O-Cel-O sponge. For tough stains, leave wet baking soda on and wipe away when it dries.

- Brighten unlacquered brass on boats with a paste of ARM & HAMMER Baking Soda and ReaLemon Lemon Juice. Rub on; let dry. Rinse well with warm water.

- WD-40 is a great all-purpose cleaner for fittings, vinyl, mats, brass, and many other boat parts. It even removes tar and barnacles from the hull.

- Remove corrosion from stainless-steel fixtures on boats with Cascade automatic dishwashing detergent and a scrub brush dipped in water.

- To keep the spinnaker pole fittings on a sailboat from sticking or jamming, lubricate them with Alberto VO5 Conditioning Hairdressing.

- Goggles are great for skiing, scuba diving, woodworking, or whatever...but not when they fog up! Prevent this frustrating and potentially dangerous problem by coating the goggles with Crest toothpaste, then wiping them clean. Do this before you wear them!

- When it's lunchtime at the beach, every hand is covered in sand. Think ahead and bring a gallon-size GLAD Food Storage Zipper Bag filled with a generous amount of Johnson's Baby Powder. Put both hands in the bag; remove and rub them together. The sand will just slip off.

- Removing damp, head-to-toe sand—especially from a young child—after a day at the beach can be a real pain. Sprinkle on some Johnson's Baby Powder, then easily brush off the sand.

- Collecting shells at the beach is a relaxing adventure. Bring a pair of No nonsense pantyhose and use the legs to store the shells. When it's time to leave, dunk the whole pair in the water to rinse off excess sand and dirt.

- Putting tight-fitting water shoes on a squirming child can be quite a challenge. If you rub some Vaseline Total Moisture Lotion on the feet first, the shoes will slip on easily.

Picnics

- When buzzing bees keep you from drinking your beverage, cover the top of the can or cup with a small square of Reynolds Wrap Aluminum Foil. Poke a drinking straw through it, and enjoy.

- Repel mosquitoes, bees, and other bugs by tucking a few Downy dryer sheets in your picnic basket. You can also fight off pests by placing a Downy dryer sheet under lawn furniture, rubbing one on bare skin, or stashing one in your pocket.

- For a disposable platter to take on picnics or other outings, cover a piece of cardboard with Reynolds Wrap Heavy Strength Aluminum Foil.

- Is wind about to blow away your picnic tablecloth? Secure it to the underside of the table with Scotch Duct Tape.

- Picnic jugs and coolers often take on a musty or mildewy odor. Rinse smelly items

Analyze Acidic Reactions

Save a chicken bone from your chicken dinner and put it in a clear jar. Fill the jar with Heinz Vinegar, put lid on, and let it sit 1 week. Observe what happens. The bone should become flexible, because the vinegar has dissolved the calcium that makes bones hard.

Put an egg still in its shell into a jar of Heinz Vinegar. Check it the next day. What has happened to it? The eggshell, which is made of calcium, should become soft or disintegrate completely.

with undiluted Heinz Vinegar, then wash with soap and water to clean thoroughly. Rinse.

◆ An empty Scott Towel core or similar cardboard tube makes an ideal sheath in which to carry knives to a picnic or on a camping trip. Flatten an unused tube, then close one end with Scotch Duct Tape. For smaller utensils, cut the tube into shorter pieces.

◆ Store salt, pepper, and spices for a picnic or camp cookout in flexible drinking straws. Fold over the end of a straw to seal it; secure with a small rubber band or Scotch Duct Tape. Pour a spice into the straw, then fold over and secure the other end with another rubber band or more tape. Label each filled straw with a marking pen.

Camping Out

◆ Many people—including men—wear No nonsense pantyhose under their pants while hiking or hunting to repel wood ticks, chiggers, and the like.

◆ When camping season begins, deodorize your sleeping bag by sprinkling in ARM & HAMMER Baking Soda and letting it sit for half a day. Shake out and set the sleeping bag in the sun.

- If your tent develops mildew, clean the problem area by wiping it with Heinz Vinegar and letting it dry in the sun.

- To kill mold and mildew on a tent, scrub all surfaces with a mixture of 1 cup Clorox Regular-Bleach in 1 gallon water. Wear rubber gloves to protect your hands.

Camping Facts

According to the National Association of RV Parks and Campgrounds, there are 16,000 commercial and public campgrounds nationwide. Privately owned RV parks and campgrounds total 8,500. The average commercial campground has 133 sites. In recent years it has been estimated that 7.2 million RVs are on the road in the United States.

- Make it easier to pound tent stakes into the ground by first spraying the stakes with WD-40.

- Knots in tent ropes and other camping gear will untangle more easily if you sprinkle them with Argo Corn Starch.

- ARM & HAMMER Baking Soda can be your best friend on a camping trip. Bring it along to clean dishes, pots, hands, and teeth; to use as a deodorant or fire extinguisher; and to treat insect bites, sunburn, or poison ivy.

- An empty Folgers coffee can makes a great fire starter. Cut off both ends of the can and punch holes around the bottom. Stand the can in your fire pit or grill, fill with Kingsford Charcoal Briquettes, and soak with Kingsford Lighter Fluid.

When the coals are lit and burning well, slowly remove the can with oven mitts, leaving the hot coals behind.

- Keep your toilet paper dry when you're camping by storing it in a clean, empty coffee can or Folgers coffee canister with a plastic top.

Roll with It

Keep a roll of Scotch Duct Tape with your outdoor gear so you will have it when you need it. It is strong and waterproof, comes in various colors, adheres well, and tears easily into strips of any length.

- If you coat the bottoms of your pots with Dawn dishwashing liquid or Ivory Liquid Hand Cleanser before you start cooking, the soot will wash off more easily after your campfire meals.

- Consider packing a jumbo roll (or 2 or 3!) of Scotch Duct Tape for your next camping trip. It's just the fix for rips and leaks in tents, rain slickers, rubber boots, backpacks, kayaks, and more.

- To create an outdoor hand-washing station, cut off a leg from a pair of No nonsense pantyhose and drop in a bar of Ivory Soap all the way to the toe. Place a 5-gallon water jug on the end of a bench or picnic table, then tie the soap to the handle, making sure it doesn't drag on the ground.

The Art of Recycling

By age 3, Nathaniel Wyeth—son of American artist N. C. and brother of Andrew—showed his interest in gadgets and gizmos. As an engineer for DuPont in the late 1960s, he worked to produce a plastic beverage bottle that would withstand the pressure of carbonized beverages. He perfected the product when he jettisoned the polypropylene he had been working with and began using polyethylene terephthalate (PET), now the most commonly recycled plastic and designated with the number 1 in the recycling logo.

- Store miscellaneous camping items (food, medicine, batteries, and so on) in individual GLAD Food Storage Zipper Bags to keep them dry and organized.

- Make a propane or gasoline lantern mantle last longer. Soak it in undiluted Heinz Vinegar for several hours, then let dry. Reattach to lantern, then light.

- Zippers on outdoor equipment are prone to rusting. Spray the zipper with WD-40 and zip up and down to drive out moisture, remove rust, and lubricate.

- Deodorize and help remove mineral deposits in an RV water tank by flushing periodically with 1 cup ARM & HAMMER Baking Soda in 1 gallon warm water. Drain and flush the tank before refilling.

- To dissolve solids and control odor in toilets of recreational vehicles or boats, pour a small box of ARM & HAMMER Baking Soda into the tank after each cleaning.

- Keep your trailer hitch from getting scratched by cutting a slit in a Penn tennis ball and putting it over the ball of the hitch.

Index

on enamel and aluminum cookware, 296
on garage floors, 314
general, 100
on grout, 12
on nonstick surfaces, 299
on porcelain, 8, 35
pretreating laundry, 99
prevention, 37
on skin, 182
on tile floors, 52
on toilets, 12
on upholstery, 59
on vases and containers, 67
on wood, 25
Stale smells, 79
Starch, history of, 115
Static electricity
carpets and rugs, 46
clothes, 122
hair, 153
newly laundered items, 91, 93–94
potential for, 386
shower curtains, 18
Static Guard, about, 94
Stickers. See Decals/appliqués.
Stomach ulcers, 226
Stone floors, cleaning, 54
Stoneware, cleaning, 300
Stovetops, cleaning, 23, 30–31
Straws (drinking), history of, 259
Suede
grease stains, 106
ink stains, 106
spots, 118
Suitcases. See Luggage.
Sunburns, treating, 178, 193–95
Sweaters, fuzzballs on, 123
Sweat stains on washables, 110–11
Swimmer's ear, treating, 210–11
Swimming/swimming pools, 157, 158, 429, 431

T

Tablecloths and napkins, crease prevention, 73
Tar
on bare feet, 219
on carpets and rugs, 49
on cars, 304
on washables, 108
Tarnish
preventing on silver, 64, 72, 289
removing from brass and copper, 66
removing from jewelry, 71
removing from silver, 63, 288, 289
Tea
about, 291
on carpets and rugs, 49
history, 383
Teakettles, 290–91
Teeth
cleaning, 162–64
dentures, 165–66
gums, treating, 211, 212
history of brushing, 163, 213
history of dental floss, 164
history of toothpaste, 162, 163
mouth fresheners, 164–65
pets', 378–79
plaque buildup, 162
toothaches, treating, 211–12, 213
Telephones, cleaning, 69
Tennis balls, 426
Therapy aids, 236
Thermoses, deodorizing, 281
This Old House (television program), 371
3M Company history, 89, 99
Tick bites, 198, 382
Tile countertops, cleaning, 24, 26
Tile floors, cleaning, 51–53
Toasters, melted plastic on, 30
Toilets
cleaning, 12–13
condensation, 361
development of, 13
general cleaning, 12–14
odors in, 436
rust stains on, 16
stain prevention, 362
Tomatoes, 244
Tongue, burned, 214

Tools and accessories
duct tape and, 370
fireplace, 357
hobby and craft, 369, 401–3
household, 89
outdoor, 314–16, 332
workshop, 369
Toothbrushing, history of, 163, 213
Toothpaste, history of, 162, 163
Towel racks, 22
Toys, cleaning, 85–86
Travel and packing tips, 422–24
Trunks. See Luggage.
Tubs, 13, 14–20
TV screen cleaning, 40–41

U

Umbrellas, 133
Upholstery
bloodstains on, 104
cleaning, 58–60
cleaning car, 307
freshener, 83
grease stains on, 59
ink stains on, 60
lint on, 60
odors, 83, 85
oily stains on, 59
pet hair on, 60
Urinary tract infections, 230
Urine accidents
on carpets and rugs, 46
on mattresses, 85–86
odors from, 83

V

Vacuuming, 28, 43, 45, 183
Varnished woodwork, cleaning, 44
Vases, cleaning, 67
Vegetables, 239, 241–44, 255, 276–77
Velcro, 216
Venetian blinds, 39
Ventilation, importance of, 37
Vinegar, about, 291, 298
Vinegar "goo," 290
Vinyl car seats, 307
Vinyl floor, cleaning, 51–52
Vinyl furniture, cleaning, 61

Trademark Information

"3M" is a registered trademark of 3M.

"7-UP" is a registered trademark of Dr Pepper/Seven-Up, Inc.

"20 Mule Team" is a registered trademark of U.S. Borax Inc.

"Alberto VO5" is a registered trademark of Alberto-Culver USA, Inc.

"Alka-Seltzer" is a registered trademark of Bayer Healthcare LLC.

"All-Bran" is a registered trademark of Kellogg Company.

"Argo" is a registered trademark of ACH Food Companies, Inc.

"ARM & HAMMER" is a registered trademark of Church & Dwight Co., Inc.

"Blistex" is a registered trademark of Blistex Inc.

"Brer Rabbit" is a registered trademark of B&G Foods, Inc.

"Brillo" is a registered trademark of Church & Dwight Co., Inc.

"Budweiser" is a registered trademark of Anheuser-Busch, Inc.

"Campbell's" is a registered trademark of Campbell Soup Company.

"Canada Dry" is a registered trademark of Cadbury Beverages Inc.

"Carnation" is a registered trademark of Société des Produits Nestlé S.A., Vevey, Switzerland.

"Cascade" is a registered trademark of Procter & Gamble.

"Clabber Girl" is a registered trademark of Clabber Girl Corporation.

"Clorox" is a registered trademark of the Clorox Company.

"Colavita" is a registered trademark of Colavita.

"Contadina" is a registered trademark of Del Monte Corporation.

"Cool Whip" is a registered trademark of Kraft Foods.

"Country Time" is a registered trademark of Kraft Foods.

"Crayola" is a registered trademark of Binney & Smith Inc.

"Crest" is a registered trademark of Procter & Gamble.

"Crisco" is a registered trademark of The J. M. Smucker Company.

"Cutex" is a registered trademark of MedTech.

"Dannon" is a registered trademark of the Dannon Company, Inc.

"Dawn" is a registered trademark of Procter & Gamble.

"Dixie" is a registered trademark of James River Corporation.

"Dole" is a registered trademark of Dole Food Company, Inc.

"Domino" is a registered trademark of Domino Foods, Inc.

"Downy" is a registered trademark of Procter & Gamble.

"Elmer's" is a registered trademark of Borden, Inc.

"Febreze" is a registered trademark of Procter & Gamble.

"Final Touch" is a registered trademark of Phoenix Brands, LLC.

"Folgers" is a registered trademark of The J. M. Smucker Company.

"Fresh Step" is a registered trademark of the Clorox Company.

"Gillette" is a registered trademark of Procter & Gamble.

"Glad" is a registered trademark of The Glad Products Company.

"Gold Medal" is a registered trademark of General Mills, Inc.

"Grandma's" is a registered trademark of B&G Foods, Inc.

"Griffin" is a registered trademark of Hickory Brands, Inc.

"Hain" is a registered trademark of Hain Pure Food Company.

"Heinz" is a registered trademark of H. J. Heinz Company.

"Hershey's" is a registered trademark of Hershey Foods Corporation.

"Ivory" is a registered trademark of Procter & Gamble.

"Jell-O" is a registered trademark of Kraft Foods.

"Johnson's" is a registered trademark of Johnson & Johnson.

"Karo" is a registered trademark of CPC International, Inc.

"Kingsford" is a registered trademark of Kingsford Products Company.

"Kleenex" is a registered trademark of Kimberly-Clark Corporation.

"Knorr" is a registered trademark of Unilever.

"Knox" is a registered trademark of NBTY, Inc.

"Kraft" is a registered trademark of Kraft Foods.

"Krazy" is a registered trademark of Borden, Inc.

"Kretschmer" is a registered trademark of the Quaker Oats Company.

"Lipton" is a registered trademark of Unilever.

"Listerine" is a registered trademark of Warner-Lambert.

"McCormick" is a registered trademark of McCormick & Company, Incorporated.

"Melitta" is a registered trademark of the Melitta Group.

"Morton" is a registered trademark of Morton International, Inc.

"Mott's" is a registered trademark of Mott's Inc.

"Murphy" is a registered trademark of the Colgate-Palmolive Company.

"Niagara" is a registered trademark of Phoenix Brands, LLC.

"No nonsense" is a registered trademark of Kayser-Roth Corporation.

"Ocean Spray" is a registered trademark of Ocean Spray Cranberries, Inc.

"O-Cel-O" is a registered trademark of 3M.

"Orville Redenbacher's" is a registered trademark of ConAgra Foods Inc.

"PAM" is a registered trademark of American Home Foods.

"Pampers" is a registered trademark of Procter & Gamble.

"Parsons'" is a registered trademark of Church & Dwight Co., Inc.

"Penn" is a registered trademark of Penn Racquet Sports.

"Pepsi" is a registered trademark of PepsiCo, Inc.

"Phillips'" is a registered trademark of Bayer HealthCare LLC.

"Pine-Sol" is a registered trademark of the Clorox Company.

"Pledge" is a registered trademark of S. C. Johnson & Son, Inc.

"Polident" is a registered trademark of GlaxoSmithKline.

"Post-it" is a registered trademark of 3M.

"Q-tips" is a registered trademark of Chesebrough-Pond's USA Co.

"Quaker Oats" is a registered trademark of the Quaker Oats Company.

"Quilted Northern" is a registered trademark of Georgia-Pacific LLC.

"Reach" is a registered trademark of Johnson & Johnson.

"ReaLemon" and "ReaLime" are registered trademarks of Beverages Delaware, Inc.

"Revlon" is a registered trademark of Revlon Consumer Products Corporation.

"Reynolds Wrap" is a registered trademark of Reynolds Metals.

"Rite Aid" is a registered trademark of Rite Aid Corporation.

"Scotch" and "Scotchgard" are registered trademarks of 3M.

"Scott" is a registered trademark of Kimberly-Clark Worldwide, Inc.

"Simoniz" is a registered trademark of Simoniz USA, Inc.

"Skippy" is a registered trademark of Unilever.

"Static Guard" is a registered trademark of Alberto-Culver International, Inc.

"Suave" is a registered trademark of Unilever.

"SueBee" is a registered trademark of Sioux Honey Association.

"Swanson" is a registered trademark of Campbell Soup Company.

"Tide" is a registered trademark of Procter & Gamble.

"Tropicana" is a registered trademark of PepsiCo, Inc.

"Vaseline" is a registered trademark of Chesebrough-Pond's USA Co.

"WD-40" is a registered trademark of the WD-40 Company.